LIVING WITH HAZARDS
DEALING WITH DISASTERS

LIVING WITH HAZARDS DEALING WITH DISASTERS

AN INTRODUCTION TO EMERGENCY MANAGEMENT

WILLIAM L. WAUGH, JR.

M.E. Sharpe
Armonk, New York
London, England

Library of Congress Cataloging-in-Publication Data

Waugh, William L.
    Living with hazards, dealing with disasters : an introduction to
emergency management / by William L. Waugh, Jr.
        p. cm.
    Includes bibliographical reference and index.
    ISBN 0-7656-0195-8 (cloth : alk. paper)
    ISBN 0-7656-0196-6 (pbk : alk. paper)
    1. Emergency management—United States.   2. Disaster relief-
-United States.   I. Title.
    HV551.3.W38 1999
    363.34'8—dc21   99-41194
                                                                            CIP

Printed in the United States of America

The paper used in this publication meets the minimum requirements of
American National Standard for Information Sciences—
Permanence of Paper for Printed Library Materials,
ANSI Z 39.48-1984.

BM (c)   10   9   8   7   6   5   4   3
BM (p)   10   9   8   7   6   5

CONTENTS

LIST OF TABLES, FIGURES, APPENDIXES, AND CASES

TABLES

FIGURE

APPENDIXES

CASES

PREFACE

Emergency management is one of those fields that grows the more one gets to know it. Drawing the boundaries of the field is getting to be very difficult. The temptation is to include everything from radon gas contamination to alien invasion. Emergency management is also one of those fields that provides a fascinating array of issues. How people deal with risk says a lot about human nature. How communities deal with risk says a lot about social values and structures. How government deals with risk says a lot about our institutions and political culture. In many respects, emergency management provides testament to the utility of the current public policy models. Crisis disrupts the complacency that normally pervades the public agenda.

Hazards and disasters are the reasons we have government. The multitude of natural and technological hazards that exist in modern society provide more than enough risk to justify government intervention and to enlist the aid of public, private, and nonprofit organizations and of individuals. Disasters also bring out the best and the worst in human beings. Greed and selfishness are balanced by compassion and altruism.

Some choices were made in putting this book together. There is a growing social science literature on hazards and disasters and a wealth of information on specific disasters and how to deal with them. This book is intended to tie that literature together and to provide a sense of the culture of the field. Put another way, it is intended to link social science research with the war stories that permeate the practice of emergency management. There have been catastrophic disasters that have shaped our emergency management policies and programs and many have been included in short case studies. There are also processes that follow each major disaster in the United States and most are described or illustrated through the Federal Emergency Management Agency (FEMA) and the Office of Foreign Disaster Assistance (OFDA) announcements and situation reports. There is an incredible amount of information available via the Internet, and Web sites are noted whenever practicable. Web addresses change so frequently, however, that it is better to provide home page addresses rather than very specific document or program addresses. For instance, students can easily track information through the FEMA web page and its library.

In works such as this, it is always difficult to thank all those who contributed. In the references, some names appear frequently and many of those people are my friends. Also, a number of the references cited are from former students who found emergency management interesting enough to warrant thorough research. I would like to say that the analysis is based on rigorous scientific research, but, while there is some of that, there is also information from conversations with emergency managers, disaster researchers, and others with more interest than expertise. I thank them for their insights and observations. I would also like to thank the retired general overheard in a bar discussing relations between two nonprofit organizations during a disaster relief operation, the local emergency manager who made a conference presentation on his difficulties in dealing with state officials, the official who made a public speech on "weapons of mass destruction" without betraying any real knowledge of what he was talking about, and many others who contributed without knowing it. I hope that their experiences have been accurately interpreted here.

Statistics on human and property losses vary from source to source, and I have had to guess which were the more credible numbers more than once. However, all errors of fact and omission are my own.

William L. Waugh, Jr.

LIVING WITH HAZARDS
DEALING WITH DISASTERS

1

THE EMERGENCY MANAGEMENT PROFESSION AND FIELD OF STUDY

In an era in which the role of government is being reduced and programs are being cut, the scope and practice of emergency management are expanding rapidly and the field is becoming professional in response to the demand for technically and politically skilled emergency managers. The principal reasons for the increased interest in and support for emergency management policies and programs are an increase in the number of major disasters in recent years, the increased exposure of people and property to natural and technological hazards, and, perhaps most important, the critical nature of the function. Emergency management is the quintessential governmental role. It is the role for which communities were formed and governments were constituted in the first place—to provide support and assistance when the resources of individuals and families are overwhelmed.

In the simplest terms, emergency management is the management of risk so that societies can live with environmental and technical hazards and deal with the disasters that they cause. Emergency management is not solely a governmental responsibility. Individuals are responsible for protecting their own lives and property, as well as the safety of family members and neighbors. When they do not have the wherewithal to protect themselves as individuals and families, they can rely on the resources and capabilities of the community. In some cases, the support of a few neighbors or a single community is sufficient. In other cases, the support of a broad network of public, nonprofit, and private organizations is necessary to respond to and recover from major disasters. When the economic and social costs of disaster become unacceptable, a broader approach to hazard management and risk reduction is needed. As other values, such as protecting the environment and the quality of life, become important issues, the approach needs to be even broader. When the interests and needs of the community become more important than those of the individual, trade-offs are necessary. All this is to say that the politics of emergency management can become intense as individuals and organizations weigh the costs of potential disasters against their own economic and social interests. Policy choices have shaped the current national emergency management system and have had profound impact on its effectiveness.

The national emergency management system is a complex network of public, private, and nonprofit organizations and individuals. It includes federal, state, and local government agencies, as well as special districts and quasi-governmental bodies. It includes nonprofit service and charitable organizations, as well as *ad hoc* volunteer groups and individuals. It includes private sector firms that provide governmental services by contract; services and products not available from government; and/or services and products not needed by enough victims, responders, or other participants to justify their provision by government agencies. And it includes the media, as well as individuals. However, because catastrophic disasters can overwhelm even the largest communities and private organizations, the ultimate guarantor of aid is the government. For all practical purposes, this means the federal government is the last resort when the resources of all other responsible governments and all other private and nonprofit organizations are insufficient.

The governmental actors in the national system include emergency management agencies, scientific agencies with expertise in areas such as meteorology and geology, public safety and emergency response agencies, public health agencies, and regulatory agencies. There are some agencies with very specific emergency management responsibilities and expertise, such as the Federal Emergency Management Agency (FEMA) and its state and local counterparts, and others for which disaster operations are only a peripheral mission, such as military, public works, land-use planning, and natural resources agencies. There are some agencies that are full-time, well staffed, highly professional, and very capable, and others that have part-time, unpaid personnel and very little technical or administrative capacity. As is the case in American government in general, capabilities are very uneven. Some local, state, and federal agencies have little or no capacity to handle their emergency management roles, and others have considerable disaster experience and remarkable capabilities.

The nonprofit sector participants range from the American Red Cross to local community groups. There are organizations that specialize in providing emergency medical care, temporary food and shelter, pet rescue and care, urban search and rescue, disaster communications, and other needed skills and services. There are also organizations that provide manpower to staff shelters, assist in filling sandbags, hand out water, assist in debris clearance, counsel victims, and so on. Like their governmental counterparts, some of the nonprofit organizations are highly professional and very capable, while others are equipped with little more than good intentions.

The private sector participants range from national and international insurance and reinsurance companies to small firms selling sandbags and emergency rations. Some sell products and services critical to the emergency management system and the victims of disaster, while others have less useful wares. The news media also fulfills a critical public information role, educating the public about hazards and how to prepare for disasters, and communicating information concerning appropriate preparedness measures, disaster warnings, and evacuation information. In short, the national emergency management system includes a large cast of actors with a broad range of capabilities and a variety of intentions. As a result, coordinating the efforts of such an intergovernmental, multiorganizational, public–nonprofit–private sector network in a large disaster can be a monumental task. It is a task that requires considerable technical, administrative, political, social, and interpersonal skill.

The responsibilities of the actors in the national system are as different as their capabilities. Government emergency management agencies generally deal with life- and property-threatening situations that are beyond the resources and capabilities of individuals, community groups, and private organizations and often beyond the resources and capabilities of individual communities and even regional or state governments. But, as the discussion to follow will suggest, those roles may be expanded or contracted for a variety of practical and political reasons. It is also important to note that individuals have a responsibility for their own safety and the safety of their families and neighbors, and thus are an integral part of the emergency management system. Defining individual, governmental, community, and private responsibilities and integrating them into an effective, cooperative network is the challenge and the focus of this text. In many cases, the public, nonprofit, and private sector participants have common purpose and ample reason to cooperate. In other cases, there is conflict over ends and means. Good intentions are found at all levels and bad intentions are all too common. Disasters bring out the best and the worst in individuals and organizations.

While there is a tendency to view emergency management primarily as disaster planning and response, it involves much more. In general terms, it is a process of managing risk so that we can live with known and unknown natural and man-made hazards and can deal with the disasters that do occur. While disasters often occur with little warning, in many cases they can be anticipated and measures can be taken beforehand to prevent them entirely or to minimize their effects. For some natural hazards, there are known cycles of destruction. For example, floodplains typically have histories of major and minor flooding, and experts can determine probable flood levels and prescribe appropriate measures to reduce the level of risk. The 100– and 500–year flood levels are familiar benchmarks in many communities, although residents may not be aware that several 100– or even 500–year floods may occur within matters of days or weeks. The uncertain risk certainly complicates the process and the politics of emergency management. Indeed, the process is intensely political, with potentially high costs for failure or perceived failure, great rewards for success or perceived success, and a confusing array of competing needs and interests. Political and media careers have been made and broken during times of crisis, and disaster provides a dramatic backdrop that attracts politicians, news reporters, trained emergency responders, good Samaritans, and curious bystanders, as well as looters, scam artists, dishonest and incompetent home repair people, and others hoping to take advantage of the situation for private gain.

Serious environmental and technological hazards and the disasters they cause may also test the limits of scientific knowledge, requiring very sophisticated means to prevent or limit damage. In other cases, there may be very simple solutions. The range of capabilities necessary to address the variety of hazards and disasters that may face a community is uncertain, and that, in itself, poses political and administrative problems. The necessary technical capabilities and logistical requirements for regional and state governments to support local efforts and the mechanisms to deliver needed assistance in a timely fashion are uncertain. The kinds of support that federal officials may provide, given the complex intergovernmental legal environment and the practical problems involved in designing programs to fit state and local needs, also create uncertainty. What is certain, however, is the need for effective disaster management policies and programs at all levels of government. That need is most evident in the aftermath of catastrophe when lives and property have been lost and more may hang in the balance.

While the need for effective policies and programs is manifest, the fundamental issue is how much capacity is necessary. To what extent can individuals, families, communities, and states rely upon their own resources and expertise when disasters strike? How prepared need communities be? How much help can and should state and national governments provide? These questions are central to the determination of political responsibility, including responsibility for providing funding and technical expertise, and to the design and administration of disaster management policies and programs. The issue is made more complicated by the uncertainty of disasters in terms of their intensity, timing, and locations. Indeed, experience may not encompass the kinds and scale of disasters that may occur.

We are only beginning to understand some of the natural forces that have shaped our world and are still rearranging our living space. Earthquakes and volcanoes, hurricanes and tsunamis, and floods of monumental scope have moved the earth, creating mountain ranges, shifting coastlines, and redirecting rivers. Those processes continue, although we seldom notice their work and only occasionally find ourselves in their paths. When we do find ourselves in danger, we are forced to live with the risk or find safer ground for homes and livelihoods. Many natural and man-made hazards are well known through experience and historical record. In most communities, floodplains, seismic fault lines, hazardous waste storage areas, and a variety of other hazards are reasonably well known, although there are frequent surprises still. Science, too, is helping define the less frequent threats.

For example, Amos Nur, a Stanford geophysicist, argues that many ancient civilizations in the eastern Mediterranean were buried in the rubble of their cities, or made vulnerable to invaders, at the end of the Bronze Age by "earthquake storms." The destruction of cities, such as Mycenae, Troy, and Knossos, may be explained by a 50–year "storm" along major fault lines in the area. Nur warns that the increased seismic activity may follow a roughly 400–year cycle and cites historical accounts of intense earthquake activity in the fourth, eighth, and fifteenth centuries. Similar activity in the Americas may account for the destruction of the Mayan and other civilizations (Cowen 1988). If the pattern continues, one might expect the next period of strong seismic activity in the eastern Mediterranean to begin soon and, in fact, recent major earthquakes in Turkey, Greece, and Iran might signal such a "storm." In fact, the 7.4 earthquake in Turkey in August 1999 showed unusual activity along the fault line.

Closer to home, there is new evidence that powerful earthquakes have occurred along the Sierra Madre Fault, 12 miles from what is now downtown Los Angeles. Earthquakes with estimated magnitudes of 7.2 and 7.6 shook the region some 10,000 years ago. Similar earthquakes today would be much more devastating than the magnitude 6.7 Northridge earthquake (Allen 1998). There is also new evidence of a cycle of "megadroughts" in western North America that would make the "Dust Bowl" of the 1930s seem like "little more than a bad dry spell" (Nesmith 1998). Severe droughts lasting 25 years or more in the 1300s and 1500s are evident in the growth rings of ancient trees in Arkansas, Texas, and California. Lake sediment also indicates long periods of drought in which waters became more saline and affected surrounding vegetation and wildlife. Serious water shortages in Pennsylvania, New Jersey, Delaware, Maryland, and Virginia in 1998 and 1999 have drawn attention to unusual rainfall patterns across North America that may signal drastic climatic changes. Recent droughts and resultant wildfires in the southeastern United States have raised more concerns about climate change.

In fact, in 1998, storms caused by El Niño uncovered ancient forests buried along the Oregon coastline. The evidence suggests that tsunamis caused by a cycle of major undersea earthquakes have altered the coastline significantly and that, if the cycle continues, heavily populated areas on or near the coast, including Portland, may be in danger. Historical evidence and computer modeling are also leading to a better understanding of the El Niño and La Niña phenomena, and are helping scientists and officials anticipate the cycles of flooding, drought, hurricanes and cyclones, and other weather-related problems associated with the heating and cooling of the Pacific waters. Similarly, U.S. Geological Survey (USGS) and state geological scientists are warning that Mt. Rainier in Washington State, as well as other Cascades volcanoes, may be about to enter a period of higher activity. It has been about 5,600 years since the Osceola Mudflow filled part of Puget Sound with mud and rock, but lesser debris flows have reached the Puget Sound lowland much more recently (USGS 1995). Now, Olympia, Tacoma, and even Seattle lie in zones affected by past lahars (debris flows). Scientists at the Cascades Volcano Observatory in Vancouver, Washington, are monitoring all the major volcanic hazards in the Pacific Northwest and participate in a working group of federal, state, and local scientists and officials developing emergency plans for communities that might be in the path of debris flows, should Mt. Rainier or other volcanoes erupt. Evacuation routes, safe ground, and particularly hazardous areas are being identified, warning systems are being installed, and the public is being prepared for a variety of scenarios.

The 1998 prediction by a Harvard University astronomer of a near miss of earth by a mile-wide asteroid in 2028 has raised awareness of the risk of such cosmic disasters. The evidence of earth-shaking asteroid strikes every 100,000 years or so is compelling. Humans may meet the same end as the dinosaurs, and that possibility is profoundly disturbing to many. Hollywood has taken advantage of the situation by translating the scientific evidence into fictional threats of asteroid impacts and suggesting efforts to intercept and deflect threatening cosmic bodies. The films may well encourage the development of mitigation measures, such as the development of technologies and plans to intercept or destroy near-earth objects (NEOs) if a strike appears imminent. In fact, the National Aeronautics and Space Administration's (NASA's) Office of Space Science has announced the creation of an office to support NEO observations and analysis and to coordinate public information on the issue (Friedman 1998).

The damage caused by the Exxon Valdez oil spill to the wildlife, fishing industry, and scenic beauty of Prince William Sound in Alaska; the tragic loss of life caused by a chemical release at the Union Carbide plant in Bhopal, India; and the long-term human and economic costs of the Chernobyl nuclear plant disaster have all sensitized us to the risk of technology. Following the bombings of the World Trade Center in New York City and the Murrah Federal Office Building in Oklahoma City, officials are warning that the threat of terrorism, particularly nuclear, biological, and chemical terrorism or "weapons of mass destruction," necessitates significant investments of time and money in national security and intelligence, law enforcement, and disaster management programs. Cyberterrorism and workplace violence are also being touted as growing hazards that need to be addressed by emergency managers. There are even concerns about "millennium madness" if the new millennium opens with the same kinds of mass hysteria and violence that have characterized the beginnings of past millennia (Waugh 1996). Certainly, if warnings about the year 2000 (Y2K) problem are correct, the new millennium may be celebrated with a crashing of computer systems, resulting in catastrophic events ranging from financial crises to aircraft crashes.

The list of environmental hazards of man's making and of nature's is very long and growing. The purpose here is not to argue that the "sky is falling," but the list does serve to illustrate the diversity of hazards and the nature of risk. Earth has a history of catastrophe and that history will continue. Indeed, a large asteroid, a microbe, a nuclear war, or any number of other phenomena could bring an end to human life on earth. Life is fragile, as the demise of the dinosaurs demonstrated. The practical problems are how to live with the lesser hazards while minimizing their effects and how to develop capacities to deal with the major disasters so that they will not overwhelm us. Those are the tasks of policymakers and emergency managers. In some measure, dealing with disasters is a process of determining how much risk specific hazards pose and how much risk society is willing to accept, and reconciling the two values. Disasters occur when hazards have not been adequately managed, but they may also occur with little or no warning and without apparent reason. Simply put, stuff happens and communities are forced to respond as best they can.

DISASTER MANAGEMENT IN BRIEF

Disaster management involves actions and demands resources beyond the means of individuals and family groups. Indeed, threats to life and property from nature and from humankind encouraged the development of communities to pool resources and to find common solutions. Communities charged leaders with responsibility to assess risk and devise strategies to minimize their exposure. As societies became more complex, community action, through voluntary associations and government agencies, addressed known hazards. Fire brigades, militias, law enforcement agencies, military units, and volunteer groups were mobilized in response to disaster, and churches and charitable organizations were relied upon for disaster recovery. But, as the exposure of society to risks increased, it became more difficult to rely solely upon well-meaning but ill-prepared volunteers and inadequately trained public agencies. There was increasing need for full-time, technically trained, professional emergency response and recovery agencies. Although some communities still have volunteer fire departments and most still rely upon the American Red Cross, the Salvation Army, and other volunteer organizations to assist victims of fire, flood, and other more common disasters, the resources of nongovernmental organizations are often inadequate to support effective response and recovery efforts. Much the same can be said of municipal, county, state, and federal capacities to manage hazards and to provide support for the victims of catastrophic events. But that is changing. Communities can be made disaster-resistant, more resilient, and better able to respond effectively and to recover from disasters with minimal assistance.

The national emergency management system is still evolving. The first modern local government emergency management efforts focused on fire hazards. They were often reactive, relying on *ad hoc* fire brigades to respond to fires, but occasionally proactive in terms of encouraging the use of nonflammable building materials and provisions for escape in the event of a major fire. The Great Chicago Fire of 1871 and major conflagrations in other cities, including a fire in Boston in 1872 that destroyed 800 buildings, encouraged greater attention to building standards and materials and encouraged insurance companies to insist on fire escapes and, later, smoke detectors, fire alarms, and sprinkler systems.

With the exception of disaster responses such as firefighting in urban areas and forests, programs to address hazards and respond to disasters were almost unknown in the United States prior to World War I. Disaster relief or recovery was largely the province of charitable and religious institutions. Just as communities relied on church and nonprofit organizations to provide social services for the poor, infirm, and homeless, they relied on those same organizations to respond to minor and major disasters and to assist disaster victims. In fact, American communities still rely very heavily on organizations such as the American Red Cross and the Salvation Army. The Red Cross remains the principal source of aid to families left homeless by fires and floods, for example. Large-scale disasters, however, have increasingly required concerted regional and national government action. Also, as science and technology have expanded our abilities to understand hazards and to anticipate catastrophic disasters, the responsibility to reduce the potential for massive losses of human lives and property has increasingly been assumed by local, state, and federal governments.

Prior to World War II, government programs to reduce environmental hazards were very limited. Regulation of construction through enforcement of building standards, land-use regulation, and other programs to reduce hazards were rare in rural areas and only sporadically enforced in most urban areas. The exceptions to this generalization were the seismic building standards set in California after the 1906 San Francisco earthquake, flood-plain management programs designed and managed by the U.S. Army Corps of Engineers along the nation's major waterways to address severe and frequent flooding problems, and civil defense programs designed and managed by the U.S. Department of Defense. The Tennessee Valley Authority (TVA) was created in 1933 to help reduce flooding along the Tennessee River and its tributaries, as well. Nonetheless, few state and local governments developed hazard reduction programs beyond discouraging residents from building homes or businesses in known danger areas. Communities still maintained fire departments, but the role of the fire service was limited to responding to fires. Fire departments have only recently focused on prevention efforts.

In the 1970s, the National Governors' Association developed a four-phase emergency management model to describe the process and to categorize policies and programs. That model is now the basis of the so-called all-hazards model, and the terminology has now become the language of contemporary emergency management in the United States and, increasingly, in other nations. The four phases are mitigation, preparedness, response, and recovery. *Mitigation* is predisaster activities involving the assessment of risk and lessening the potential effects of disasters and, increasingly, postdisaster activities to reduce the potential damage of future disasters. Mitigation programs include land-use regulations, building codes, structural barriers to prevent or control hazards, and insurance programs to lessen the economic impact of disaster. Increasingly, mitigation efforts are focusing on government buyouts of property in hazardous areas with the land used for public parks and other recreational purposes that do not expose people to risk. *Preparedness* is predisaster activities involved in readying for expected threats, including contingency planning, resource management, mutual aid and cooperative agreements with other jurisdictions and response agencies, public information, and the training of response personnel. *Response* is activities during the disaster, including search and rescue, evacuation, emergency medical services, and firefighting. Response efforts also include reducing the likelihood of secondary damage, such as putting plastic over damaged roofs to preserve the contents of buildings, and preparing for recovery. *Recovery* is postdisaster activities designed to restore basic services, including repairing lifelines such as power and water. It includes temporary housing, food and clothing, debris clearance, psychological counseling, job assistance, and loans to restart small businesses. Increasingly, the recovery process is focusing on long-term reconstruction of the community and its economy (more detailed descriptions of the functions are in the next chapter).

The all-hazards emergency management concept is based on the idea that there are generic processes for addressing most kinds of hazards and disasters. While the model's four "phases" may be a bit simplistic, given that mitigation, preparedness, response, and recovery processes often overlap, it does provide functional categories that facilitate administration. A question raised in some communities concerns the need to invest in hazard and disaster management programs that are not immediately relevant to the dangers faced by the communities. Building emergency management capacities in the abstract may be difficult to sell to voters and officials who are only interested in the last disaster. Nonetheless, all-hazards programs can provide considerable flexibility and be far more cost-effective than stand-alone, disaster-specific programs. Emergency response almost always involves adaptation and that is a guiding principle of all-hazards programs. Evacuation programs, for example, are adaptable to needs during floods, hazardous materials spills, hurricanes, and other kinds of disasters. Warning systems, communications systems, intergovernmental networks, mutual aid agreements, and other components of an emergency management system can also be used in a variety of scenarios.

One of the original intents in the adoption of the all-hazards model was to use the civil defense programs designed for nuclear war for natural and other technological disasters, and vice versa. However, some communities refused to have mass evacuation plans for fear of encouraging risk taking by nuclear strategists. Fear and distrust of national priorities also made some communities reluctant to invest their resources in programs that might not address local needs. While the end of the Cold War has helped assuage those fears, there is still considerable distrust of federal programs related to national security. The distrust is evident in the implementation of programs related to terrorism and "weapons of mass destruction." It is uncertain how those programs will be received by the public in general and how well they might be integrated into the largely civilian state and local emergency management capabilities. The "civilianization" of the profession of emergency management may also make it more difficult to implement military-type programs. Differences in organizational culture and decision-making processes, particularly between command-and-control–oriented military organizations and more collaborative and informal nongovernmental organizations (NGOs), will certainly complicate the coordination of response and recovery efforts (see Waugh 1993). Nonetheless, cooperation and coordination is essential if a major terrorist-sponsored disaster causes enough damage to necessitate utilization of the diverse resources of the current national emergency management system. Dealing with the consequences of such a disaster may be much more critical than the speedy apprehension of the terrorists (Waugh 2000).

FROM AIR RAID WARDENS TO CERTIFIED EMERGENCY MANAGERS: THE PROFESSIONALIZATION OF EMERGENCY MANAGEMENT

Emergency management is one of the most challenging professions to be found in any sector. It is a field demanding expertise and experience in a wide variety of technical skills, ranging from land-use planning to engineering and from financial management to public relations, and considerable skill in political negotiation, conflict resolution, and logistics. Disaster management may involve multiorganizational and intergovernmental efforts, often with organizations as culturally divergent as military units and volunteer groups, and complex administrative arrangements that require considerable political acumen. Increasingly, too, disaster management involves dealing with non–English-speaking populations, groups that may not trust government officials or be knowledgeable about bureaucratic processes, and special populations that may have extraordinary needs. The effectiveness of emergency managers may depend more upon interpersonal skills, trust and trustworthiness, flexibility and adaptability, intuition, and confidence than technical skill and legal authority.

While emergency management agencies at the local, state, and federal levels are responsible for flood mitigation and other natural hazard programs, they typically have their origins in the national civil defense system. Some agencies are still called offices or departments of civil defense. In some cases, the offices are staffed by individuals experienced in national security programs, but often inexperienced in many natural and technological hazard programs. Veterans preference in governmental hiring increases the likelihood that personnel will have military experience and the nature of the job may attract veterans. And, as a practical matter, local and state agencies have limited funds for personnel and retired military personnel are often willing to accept lower salaries in exchange for increased retirement benefits. As a result, agencies can hire personnel with far more experience than they might otherwise be able to afford. Over time, personnel gain administrative and disaster experience, but management styles, programmatic preferences, and other values may be slower to change. Agencies, however, are also attracting employees experienced in managing hazards and responding to disasters from environmental groups, nonprofit disaster relief organizations, and other occupations, including firefighting and emergency medical services. In that regard, emergency management agencies, like other public organizations, are becoming more diverse.

The profession has largely shaken off its image as the domain of 1950s-style "air raid wardens." The stereotype of the warden armed with whistle, armband, helmet, and officious manner has taken decades to overcome and may account for the credibility problems of some emergency management agencies. The activities of the early agencies simply were not taken seriously by some local officials or the public. The broadening of responsibilities to include more natural and technological hazards and disasters, as well as concerns about the political and legal costs of failure, have encouraged local governments to hire professionally trained and experienced emergency managers. The capabilities of state and local agencies, however, are still very uneven. Some are highly professional and very capable, and others clearly are not. Capacities are largely determined by the level of experience with hazards and disasters and by funding levels.

Professionalization is also changing the practice of emergency management. Although former military personnel still dominate many emergency management agencies, as well as some nonprofit and private sector disaster management organizations, the command-and-control leadership style and military-style organizational culture are increasingly giving way to more cooperative and collaborative approaches to administration (Waugh 1993). Strict hierarchical, command-and-control approaches are more appropriate to smaller disaster operations that involve only one or two jurisdictions when intergovernmental and organizational relationships are relatively clear and operational concerns are relatively narrow. The Incident Command System (ICS) common to firefighting is such a case.

As the field professionalizes, emergency managers are finding some commonality of interest with other public sector professionals. Many are affiliated with the Section on Emergency and Crisis Management of the American Society for Public Administration, the Council on Emergency Management of the American Public Works Association, the American Planning Association, and/or the International City/County Management Association. Increasingly, however, emergency managers are finding support in organizations specifically focused on emergency management, such as the International Association of Emergency Managers (IAEM) (formerly the National Coordinating Committee on Emergency Management), whose members are primarily from local agencies; the National Emergency Management Association (NEMA), whose members are largely senior officials from state agencies; and The International Emergency Management Society (TIEMS), whose members are drawn from all areas of the profession. The members of IAEM and NEMA are primarily from the United States, although international membership is increasing. The members of TIEMS are from all over the world and include social science researchers, as well as emergency managers and others with related administrative responsibilities.

With the assistance of FEMA, a professional certification program was developed by representatives of the several professional associations. Administered by IAEM, the Certified Emergency Manager (CEM) program permits individuals to achieve professional certification by demonstrating a minimum level of education, specific training in emergency management, and experience in the field. To maintain certification, individuals must continue their training and education. As in most professional certification programs, the process permits the "grandfathering in" of those experienced in the field, but lacking the desired formal education or training. IAEM currently offers a certification program for emergency managers without four-year college degrees, but it may be expected that a bachelor's degree will become a minimum requirement in the future, and that other educational and experiential requirements will increase.

FROM NATURAL SCIENTISTS TO SOCIAL SCIENTISTS: THE STUDY OF DISASTER MANAGEMENT

The study of emergency management has expanded tremendously with the increased public and government interest in the field. The literature is diverse, ranging from technical reports in architecture, engineering, construction sciences, and floodplain management to studies in community psychology, sociology, and political science. The earliest literature focused on technical issues, mostly dealing with building construction and seismic safety concerns. As the perspective on hazard reduction has broadened, the research has expanded. The current literature is a mixture of technical reports and social science analyses. There are more syntheses of the research and more translations of scientific and engineering studies into plain English, so that emergency managers, policymakers, and other researchers can understand their policy implications.

Social science research, particularly on the sociology of disasters, was centered in the Disaster Research Center at Ohio State University and, after its move, at the University of Delaware. The International Research Committee on Disasters of the International Sociological Association also provided a focus for disaster-related social science research through its journal, the *International Journal of Mass Emergencies and Disasters,* and its conference panels and other activities. To improve communication within the fragmented scientific community and between researchers and practitioners in the field, the Natural Hazards Information and Applications Center was created at the University of Colorado in Boulder in 1975. The center grew out of a social science project funded by the National Science Foundation. The initial concern was with disseminating information from a variety of public and private sources. Now the center is funded by the National Science Foundation, Federal Emergency Management Agency, National Oceanic and Atmospheric Administration, U.S. Geological Survey, Tennessee Valley Authority, U.S. Army Corps of Engineers, U.S. Environmental Protection Agency, and National Institute of Mental Health (Myers, 1993). In recent years, similar centers have been created in England, Australia, Canada, the Netherlands, the Caribbean, Southeast Asia, the South Pacific, and other nations and regions. In the United States, research and education expanded through the development of educational programs specifically designed for emergency managers, such as the degree and/or certificate programs at the University of North Texas, University of Wisconsin, University of Louisville, New York University, George Washington University, and University of California–Berkeley, as well as at FEMA's Emergency Management Institute.

FEMA itself encouraged greater attention to emergency management issues among policy analysts and public administrationists in 1984 when the agency and the National Association of Schools of Public Affairs and Administration (NASPAA) co-sponsored a two-week workshop at the National Emergency Training Center's Emergency Management Institute in Emmitsburg, Maryland, for approximately twenty public administration faculty members. Many of the participants in that workshop helped found the American Society for Public Administration's Section on Emergency Management (now the Section on Emergency and Crisis Management) and have been active researchers in the field.

A major problem in defining emergency management today is finding the boundaries of the field. In addition to dealing with natural and technological disasters, there are compelling reasons to include public health threats that may affect millions of people, such as acquired immune deficiency syndrome (AIDS); environmental issues that may result in tremendous economic loss, such as acid rain and global warming and deforestation; and even astronomical issues as seemingly farfetched as the possibility of large meteor strikes on earth. It is a challenge to find common ground for discussions of sinkholes in Florida, avalanches in the Alps, killer bees in Mexico and Texas, and tsunamis on Pacific shores, as well as to accommodate professional interests in everything from structural engineering to psychological counseling for disaster workers and victims. While research interests expand and contract with the available funding, and public interest follows the latest disasters or predictions of disaster, the field is as broad as the risks that society faces. As the academic field expands, there is also increased interest in the application of theoretical frameworks and more attention to the philosophical implications of disaster management. Certainly, there is something to be gained from a better understanding of the reasons disaster policies succeed or fail, some individuals and communities are more resilient in the aftermath of disaster than others, and some individuals are more risk taking than their neighbors (to mention but a few of the questions that might be examined). On a practical level, there is a need to find patterns in the "lessons learned" so that general principles can be identified to guide future action. Anecdotal evidence is of limited practical value, not easily communicated, and too frequently misapplied.

THE FUTURE OF EMERGENCY MANAGEMENT

The field of emergency management is undergoing great change on many levels. As a political issue, emergency management is finding greater public support. The principal reason for the increased public and government interest is the unusual number of recent catastrophes. Major earthquakes, volcanic eruptions, hurricanes, droughts, nuclear accidents, wars, floods, and other disasters are frequent occurrences and television coverage is compelling. The international media provided graphic accounts of the devastating hundred-year floods in northern Europe and the Kobe earthquake in Japan. Less dramatic, but no less devastating, disasters such as the persistent droughts in Africa and Australia, may be less familiar to people outside those geographic regions, but their effects are broadly felt. The wars that have caused famine, displacement and homelessness, disease, and devastation of populations have become all too familiar to the international community. Millions have died, and many more have been physically and psychologically injured. The economic impact of the disasters has been staggering and some impacts have yet to be fully realized. The health costs of the nuclear disaster at Chernobyl, for example, will likely be paid by generations of Ukrainians. While the negative effects of the 1989 Exxon Valdez oil spill on Prince William Sound are touted as resolved by the oil companies, the long-term impact on that fragile environment will not be known for decades and there are still serious problems in the fishing industry in the Sound and with the wildlife.

The human and economic costs of disaster are addressed internationally through the activities of the United Nations (UN), the Organization of American States (OAS), and other organizations. The UN's International Decade for Natural Disaster Reduction (IDNDR) (1990–2000) has focused world attention on the need to reduce exposure to hazards and lessen the impact of disaster, and its efforts have expanded the capacities of developing nations to identify and manage hazards, but concerns have been raised about the slow adoption of adequate mitigation programs even in the developed nations like the United States (National Research Council, 1994). At the World Conference for Natural Disaster Reduction in Yokohama, Japan, in 1994, the conference adopted the Yokohama Strategy and Plan of Action for a Safer World, which reaffirmed the need to develop national capacities to mitigate the effects of natural disasters, particularly in terms of establishing early warning systems and disaster-resistant structures in developing nations; bringing scientific and technical knowledge to bear; focusing scientific and engineering efforts on critical questions; disseminating information; and developing and evaluating the effectiveness of programs of technical assistance, technology transfer, and education and training. The expectation is that all nations will have comprehensive assessments of risks and appropriate mitigation and preparedness strategies integrated into their development plans (IDNDR n.d). Final assessment of the IDNDR efforts and the development of plans beyond the year 2000 are scheduled for late 1999.

While scientists improve their capabilities to predict earthquakes, the frequency and intensities of cyclones (hurricanes and typhoons), and the development of droughts and floods, other natural phenomenon increase the risks to society. Terrorist attacks, including bombings of aircraft in flight and of the World Trade Center in New York City, have the potential to be as destructive as natural and technological disasters. Bombings of oil and gas pipelines, mines, oil rigs, gas storage facilities, dams, and transportation facilities can be catastrophic in terms of property damage and the loss of human life. Natural hazards, too, are becoming more dangerous as people build homes and businesses along flood-prone rivers and on storm-prone coastlines, with too little regard for seismic, fire, and wind hazards. Society continues to create new hazards, from super-toxic biological materials to high-speed trains.

The challenge may be to develop a flexible strategy for managing a variety of environmental hazards and preparing for a variety of potential disasters. That would require a commitment to address known hazards; identify potential hazards; and cultivate public awareness of hazards to assure appropriate responses by individuals, families, communities, and states. Increased professionalization of emergency management personnel and agencies and increased scientific expertise that can be brought to bear in the assessment of environmental risks and the prediction of disasters are positive developments in that regard. At issue, however, is how to reduce the levels of risk to minimize costs without seeming to overregulate individual behaviors. For example, it is often suggested that private insurance can take the place of government programs. But can government officials refuse to provide aid to those who chose not to purchase insurance when those victims of disaster may number in the thousands? Private insurance, too, does not replace public facilities, and simply relying on a system of private insurance will not address the broader public issues involved, for example, in the reinvigoration of business districts devastated by flood waters. More stringent construction standards and land-use regulations, too, may keep people out of harm's way if officials and voters can be persuaded to support the regulations The fundamental questions are: How much risk is there? How much are citizens willing to spend to reduce the risk?

In recent decades, the news media have drawn attention to the function of emergency management, although they have not always educated the public about the role of emergency managers in preparing for and preventing or mitigating the effects of disaster. More often than not, the focus has been on the roles of officials in responding to disasters and in assisting communities during recovery efforts in the aftermath of disaster. The recognition that catastrophic disasters might be averted or at least lessened through broader government programs and that environmental hazards can be managed has been a recent development. For example, government regulation of building standards, most notably requirements that houses and other structures be built of stone or brick rather than flammable wood and be situated away from flood-prone areas, is only a few centuries old.

Epidemics, wars, floods, hurricanes, earthquakes, and other major disasters present government leaders with challenges and opportunities. There can be high political costs if officials fail or appear to fail; conversely, there can be enhanced prestige and power if they appear successful and effective. Government leaders also cannot afford to appear insensitive to the plight of the victims of disaster. The "CNN effect" is powerful. News coverage often makes events seem more important than they actually are. The international coverage provided by Cable News Network (CNN) often imbues the events with global importance. Even minor disasters can become the focus of international public attention during a slow news week. Pictures of crying children and interviews with pleading property owners can create a compelling case for assistance. Public administrators, whether elected officials or career civil servants, may be held accountable, even if the disaster is so catastrophic as to be beyond the capabilities of even the best-prepared governments or so minor as not to justify government action.

In some sense, we all learn to live with hazards and manage disasters. Those are skills we develop as we mature. The same holds true for maturing societies. The risks that are acceptable when resources are scarce and opportunities are few are not acceptable when social and economic investments are too dear to lose. The risks that communities and the national government could accept early in the nation's history when our society was largely agrarian are not as acceptable today. Population growth and migration to relatively hazardous regions of the United States, increased risks from old and new technologies, and a variety of other factors make it more difficult to ignore hazards and risk-taking behaviors.

ORGANIZATION OF THIS BOOK

This book is designed as an introduction to the field of emergency management in the United States, focusing primarily on the politics, policies, and programs relating to how we manage environmental and technological hazards and the disasters they cause. Chapter 1 provides an overview of the history, the profession, and the study of emergency management, with some suggestions concerning topics that might be discussed in class. Chapter 2 focuses on the national emergency management system from the local "first responders" to the Federal Emergency Management Agency and other federal agencies, including nonprofit and private participants in the system and the connections between the American system and international agencies. Whether communities, states, the federal government, or private individuals should be financially responsible for managing hazards and dealing with disasters is a fundamental question that will be raised more than once in the discussion. Chapters 3 and 4 focus on the management of natural and manmade disasters, respectively. The chapters provide overviews of major disaster types and the complex of policies and programs designed to reduce the risk they pose and to manage their consequences. Chapter 5 focuses on some of the major policy issues in disaster management, ranging from the notion of "acceptable risk" and how communities may be more willing than others to live with hazards to the issues of disaster insurance and "taking" private property to reduce the likelihood of property losses. Chapter 6 summarizes the discussion and offers a view of the field as it enters the twenty-first century. Particular attention is paid to the impacts of technological innovation and political reform.

Each chapter also contains a short list of questions to generate class discussion. There is a wealth of information available via the Internet and some of the more useful Web sites are identified. There is also a wealth of information available on videotape through public and commercial television (e.g., *NOVA* programs and the *Raging Planet* series), slides (e.g., the National Geophysical Data Center's slide sets on recent disasters), and other media. Students and instructors can follow U.S. disaster responses and other developments on the Emergency Information Media Affairs listserve <eipa@fema.gov>, get status reports on international disaster responses via the Office of Foreign Disaster Assistance listserve <*ofda-l@info.usaid.gov*>, and keep up with disaster-related research and training efforts through the publications of the Natural Hazards Center at the University of Colorado <*http://www.colorado.edu/hazards*>, as well as keep up with everything from earthquakes over a 5.0 magnitude to the annual hurricane prediction by Dr. William Gray at Colorado State University <*http://typhoon.atmos.colostate.edu/forecasts*>. A selected bibliography, including Internet resources, completes the text.

DISCUSSION QUESTIONS

1. What should be the responsibilities of local, state, and federal governments when major disasters strike?
2. Why can't individuals, families, and communities be forced to rely on their own resources when disasters strike? Won't they be less risk taking and more willing to invest in measures to reduce their exposure to disasters, if they have to rely on their own resources?
3. Should the United States prepare for disasters that occur on average every 10,000 to 100,000 years, such as major asteroid strikes?

REFERENCES

Allen, Jane E. 1998. "Quake Danger: Scientists Upgrade L.A.'s Peril." *Atlanta Journal/Constitution* (July 17): B1.

Cowen, Robert C. 1998. "The Trojan Horse Just Might Have Been an Earthquake." *Christian Science Monitor* (January 6, 1998) http://csmonitor.com/durable/1988/01/06/feat/scitech.2.html.

Drabek, Thomas E. 1987. *The Professional Emergency Manager.* Monograph 44. Boulder: University of Colorado, Institute of Behavioral Science.

Friedman, Louis D. 1998. "World Watch." *Planetary Report* XVIII (July–August): 19.

IDNDR Secretariat, UN Office for the Coordination of Humanitarian Affairs. n.d. "The International Decade for Natural Disaster Reduction 1990–2000: Background and Primary Themes" (pamphlet). Geneva, Switzerland: United Nations.

May, Peter J., and Walter Williams. 1986. *Disaster Policy Implementation: Managing Programs Under Shared Governance.* New York: Plenum.

McLoughlin, David. 1985. "A Framework for Integrated Emergency Management." *Public Administration Review* 45, Special Issue (January): 165–172.

Myers, Mary Fran. 1993. "Bridging the Gap Between Research and Practice: The Natural Hazards Research and Applications Information Center." *International Journal of Mass Emergencies and Disasters* 11 (March): 41–54.

National Academy of Public Administration. 1993. *Coping with Catastrophe: Building an Emergency Management System to Meet People's Needs in Natural and Manmade Disasters.* Washington, DC: NAPA, February.

National Research Council. 1994. *Facing the Challenge: The U.S. National Report to the IDNDR World Conference on Natural Disaster Reduction, Yokohama, Japan, May 23–27, 1994.* Washington, DC: National Academy Press.

Nesmith, Jeff. 1998. "Scientists Predict Massive Droughts." *Atlanta Constitution* (December 16): A1.

U.S. Geological Survey. 1995. *Report: Volcano Hazards from Mount Rainier, Washington.* Open-File Report 95–273, http://vulcan.wr.usgs.gov/Volcanoes/Rainier/ Hazards/ OFR95–273/OFR-273.html.

Waugh, William L., Jr. 2000. *Terrorism and Weapons of Mass Destruction: From Crisis to Consequence Management.* New York: Marcel Dekker, forthcoming.

———. 1996. "Disaster Management for the New Millennium." In *Disaster Manage-*

ment in the U.S. and Canada: The Politics, Policymaking, Administration, and Analysis of Emergency Management, 2d ed., eds. Richard T. Sylves and William L. Waugh, Jr., 344–359. Springfield, IL: Charles C. Thomas.

———. 1993. "Co-Ordination or Control: Organizational Design and the Emergency Management Function." *International Journal of Disaster Prevention and Management* 2 (December): 17–31.

———. 1990. *Terrorism and Emergency Management: Policy and Administration.* New York: Marcel Dekker.

Waugh, William L., Jr., and Ronald John Hy. 1990. "Introduction to Emergency Management." In *Handbook of Emergency Management: Policies and Programs Dealing with Major Hazards and Disasters,* eds. William L. Waugh, Jr., and Ronald John Hy, 1–10. Westport, CT: Greenwood.

2

EMERGENCY MANAGEMENT IN THE UNITED STATES

The U.S. emergency management system has largely developed in response to specific major disasters. Policies and programs have been instituted in the aftermath of disaster, based almost solely on that disaster experience, and with little investment in capacity building to deal with the next disaster. There are increasing political and economic pressures to reduce disaster loses, but there are still political, economic, and sociocultural obstacles to the development of an effective national emergency management system. While there has been more investment in emergency management during the last decade and capabilities are expanding, much needs to be done to improve the national system.

Fire and flood have been the most common disasters in the United States and they were the focus of the earliest emergency management efforts. Farms, ranches, and other structures were often built in woodlands, on high grass prairies, and in other locations prone to wildfire. Fires were also common because early communities were largely built of wood with fireplaces or pits for heat and cooking. Structures often were so close together that a faulty chimney, an ill-managed rubbish fire, or a lightning strike could burn down an entire town. Communities initially did little to reduce the risk and they responded to fires on an *ad hoc* basis. Firefighting was done by the residents living or working close enough to the fire to respond to the alarm. The firefighters were often armed only with buckets and shovels. There was little or no formal organization. The effectiveness of the effort was largely dependent upon the experience and leadership of those on the scene, their proximity to a river or lake or stream, the size of the fire, and how early the fire was discovered.

As populations and the risk of major fires grew, communities organized volunteer fire brigades. Quick response was the key to limiting damage. By the late 1800s and early 1900s, firefighting equipment, particularly pumps to carry water to the scene and to increase water pressure so that it could be sprayed some distance, improved and the profession demanded more technical skill. Formal training became more important, although employment by many cities and towns was still based on social and political criteria rather than on the firefighters' training and work experience. Most communities still rely upon volunteer fire departments, although some employ a few full-time firefighters as well. Fire insurance rates and public pressure for more effective government have encouraged more professional and technical training departments, but the capabilities of many local fire departments are still uneven. Some fire departments are extremely capable and others are not.

State governments generally provide training for local firefighters and many attend courses offered at the U.S. Fire Academy in Emmitsburg, Maryland. While volunteer fire departments may be well trained and very capable, the trend is toward full-time, paid, professional fire services with broader technical skills. That trend is consistent with developments in the public service and it reflects changes in American society as a whole. It is also getting more difficult to recruit and retain volunteer firefighters because more and more people work far from where they live and thus may lack the strong community commitment that volunteer departments require, many have spouses who work and thus have no one to take care of children during fire calls, and congested urban areas simply make it difficult for scattered volunteers to gather quickly when called. Liability issues, too, are encouraging communities to support full-time, paid staffs in their fire departments and other offices.

Community responses to flood hazards have been similar. Cities and towns were established near water because the locations afforded convenient water supplies and opportunities for fishing and hunting, as well as offering easy access to the water for wagons and other vehicles fording riverways or for loading boats and ferries. Farm communities were located in fertile bottom land with easy access to water. Shorelines attracted residents because of the views and cooler temperatures. While the oral histories and legends of Native American groups often noted ancient disasters and offered warnings of future events, the records were not accurate or specific enough to communicate the danger posed to modern communities. As a consequence, when European settlers began building homes and communities, they were generally unaware of the dangers posed by 100– and 500–year floods. The early lessons were often fatal. One has only to read an account of a hurricane approaching Florida or Texas prior to the twentieth century to get a feel for how important an understanding of such natural phenomena is. By the time that the storms approached land, residents had few escape options. Rising seas and winds were the only warning and, by then, it was too late to seek high ground and protection from the wind.

In essence, early settlers often had little understanding of the hazards they faced, and there were a lot of reasons people settled in floodplains even when the risk of flooding was known to be very high. As cities and towns grew, the social and economic costs of periodic disasters encouraged community efforts to control flooding though the building of levees and dams. Such flood control projects protected small towns to some extent, but major floods often exceeded their capacities. Frequent, severe flooding tended to discourage the building of homes and businesses in the worst areas, but the lower property values also tended to attract poor residents who either had little choice but to live with the risk or simply did not fully understand the hazard. Some, too, felt that they had little control over such "acts of God" and could do little to protect themselves. Little has changed. The poor still often have little choice but to live and work in hazardous areas and the more affluent could choose to live close to hazards because of the view or water access or because they can afford property losses.

THE EVOLUTION OF EMERGENCY MANAGEMENT IN THE UNITED STATES

At the federal level, the first emergency management programs dealt with floods and civil defense. The *Disaster Relief Act of 1950* gave the president authority to issue disaster declarations authorizing federal agencies to provide direct assistance to state and local governments. The *Flood Control Act of 1936* and the *Disaster Relief Act of 1950* were passed because of the long history of flooding along the Mississippi River and its major tributaries. These acts created the National Flood Program and established a federal responsibility to assist in flood mitigation programs along the Mississippi and other major rivers. The effort was led by the U.S. Army Corps of Engineers. The Tennessee Valley Authority (TVA) also created a system of dams to control flooding along the Tennessee River, as well as to generate electricity and to encourage economic development along the river.

Civil defense programs, such as air raid warning and emergency shelter systems, were established during World War II to protect the civilian population from attack. Following the war, the *Federal Civil Defense Act of 1950* created a nationwide system of civil defense agencies. After the Soviet Union exploded its first atomic bomb, the principal focus of the civil defense program became protection of the civilian population from nuclear attack. As the Cold War heated up in the early 1950s, offices had been established in hundreds of towns and cities and civil defense drills became a routine in schools, government agencies, and other organizations. "Duck and cover" drills were part of growing up in the 1950s. At least initially, the federal role was to support state and local government preparedness programs. In 1957, the act was amended to assign joint responsibility for civil defense to both the federal and state governments. Communities drafted emergency plans and designated local shelters, individual families built their own fallout shelters, and the Cold War became a stalemate based on the U.S. and Soviet capacities for "mutually assured destruction." As the saying went, once both sides had more warheads and delivery systems than necessary for an initial strike and counterstrike, the effect of using nuclear weapons would simply be "to make the rubble bounce." Concerns about causing a "nuclear winter" were raised in the 1980s as arguments against continued buildups in nuclear weaponry and to counter statements by Reagan Administration officials that a nuclear war would be winnable.

Despite occasional threats that the Cold War might be heating up, such as the Cuban Missile Crisis in October 1962, public attention was being drawn to other hazards in the 1960s and 1970s. Earthquakes, particularly the 1964 Alaskan quake that killed 131; hurricanes, particularly Hurricane Camille in 1969 that killed 256 in Louisiana and Mississippi; and several major tornado outbreaks drew public attention to the need to address the risks posed by catastrophic natural and technological disasters. The postwar migrations of Americans to southern coastal areas vulnerable to hurricanes and to California and the Pacific Northwest with their seismic hazards increased public concern about such hazards, as well. The political climate was also supportive of federal action to assist state and local governments in addressing such problems. Following Camille, the *Disaster Relief Act of 1969* was passed to create a federal coordinating officer to represent the president in disaster relief efforts. The *Disaster Relief Act of 1974,* following the damage wrought by Hurricane Agnes from Florida to New York, authorized individual and family assistance. This act extended federal responsibilities to provide assistance to state and local governments to include individuals and families.

By the mid- to late 1970s, federal responsibilities included civil defense, disaster assistance to state and local governments, disaster assistance to individuals and families, training of firefighters though the U.S. Fire Academy, flood mitigation programs through the U.S. Army Corps of Engineers, and flood insurance. But federal responsibility for disaster management was still scattered among the Department of Defense (DOD), the Department of Commerce (DOC), the Department of Housing and Urban Development (HUD), and the General Services Administration (GSA). The fragmented disaster preparedness and recovery system was viewed as a serious administrative problem, particularly when responsibility for emergency preparedness under the *Federal Civil Defense Act of 1950* was moved from the Executive Office of the President to GSA.

As federal disaster programs expanded, the fragmented responsibility for the programs was also viewed as a serious political problem. It was very difficult to coordinate the federal response, and, increasingly, victims and their elected representatives blamed the president for slow and ineffective efforts. To some extent, as well, antimilitary sentiment during the 1960s and 1970s caused some people to question the reliance on programs administered by DOD. Those conflicts were exacerbated when conflicts arose between DOD officials and civilian state and local officials over policy and program priorities.

THE FEDERAL EMERGENCY MANAGEMENT AGENCY

Upon assuming office in 1976, President Jimmy Carter began a series of efforts to clarify agency responsibilities and to assure executive control over administrative processes. The Civil Service Reform Act of 1978 was one such effort. The reorganization of federal emergency management programs was another. In 1978, at the request of the National Governors' Association, President Carter initiated the reorganization of federal preparedness programs through *Reorganization Plan No. 3*. The Federal Emergency Management Agency (FEMA) was thus created. Through a series of executive orders, FEMA was charged with coordinating federal efforts with state and local efforts and designated the lead agency for the national emergency management system. The responsibilities of the new agency included:

- Civil preparedness programs from the Department of Defense;
- The National Flood Insurance Program from the Department of Housing and Urban Development;
- The National Fire Prevention and Control Administration and the National Fire Academy from the U.S. Department of Commerce;
- The Community Preparedness Program from the National Weather Service and the U.S. Department of Commerce; and

- Programs in dam safety, earthquake hazard reduction, and terrorism and the national emergency warning systems from the Executive Office of the President.

There were fundamental organizational and political problems within FEMA from the beginning. The first directors, including John Macy, who served on the Civil Service Commission, were civilians, but the agency was criticized for giving priority to civil defense–related programs at the expense of the flood insurance and natural disaster programs. During the Reagan Administration, the agency was further damaged by scandal, organizational turmoil, and political conflict. Senior agency officials were investigated by a subcommittee of the House Committee on Science and Technology, the U.S. Department of Justice, and a grand jury. Faced with a variety of charges ranging from an inappropriate relationship with a private contractor to the misuse of federal monies, the director and his top aides were forced to resign. High turnover among top agency personnel indicated serious morale and administrative problems, and frequent conflicts with state and local emergency management officials over priorities raised questions about the ability of the agency to coordinate the national emergency management system effectively. Politically appointed officials, in particular, often had little experience in emergency management and the agency became known as a "dumping ground" for the president's political cronies.

FEMA's troubles continued into the 1990s. The agency had always had its critics, but the criticism became sharper and the number of critics grew when FEMA was very slow to respond to the devastation of Hurricane Hugo in 1989. State officials and members of Congress, in particular, were looking for a scapegoat for the poor initial disaster response, and FEMA was the obvious candidate. FEMA was not the major culprit, however. The emergency communication system in South Carolina had broken down. Responsibility for the state effort resided in the Adjutant General's Office, which lacked effective communication with local emergency management officials. When the governor could not get the necessary damage assessments from National Guard officials to document his request for federal aid, he had to use the state highway patrol radio network to contact local officials directly. Rather than being proactive, prompting state officials to ask for power generators and other equipment commonly needed in hurricane disasters and staging supplies close to the disaster area, FEMA officials waited for the governor's formal request before acting. As a result, federal assistance arrived days later than it might have. FEMA's effectiveness was also questioned during subsequent smaller disaster operations.

The agency's image reached a second low point when administrative responsibility for the Hurricane Andrew response in 1992 was assigned to the secretary of transportation, rather than to the director of FEMA. In fact, FEMA and other federal agencies were so slow to respond to Hurricane Andrew that President George Bush's political support in Florida was in jeopardy and it nearly cost him the state's critical electoral votes later that year. More criticism followed with the slow federal responses to Hurricane Iniki in Hawaii and to the Loma Prieta earthquake both later in 1992. In many respects, FEMA was blamed for problems over which it had little or no control. The responses to devastating disasters in the late 1980s and early 1990s demonstrated that there were serious problems in state disaster planning generally and poor communication linkages between state and local emergency management offices and governors' offices, as well. Notwithstanding evident problems in state and local disaster preparedness and response capabilities, FEMA was a convenient target for media commentators and for elected officials trying to appear responsive to their constituents' complaints.

The criticism of FEMA prompted the U.S. Congress to commission a review by the U.S. Government Accounting Office (GAO), and broader criticism prompted it to ask for a review of the national emergency management system by the National Academy of Public Administration (NAPA). Hearings were also held by the U.S. Senate's Committee on Governmental Affairs when funding for the agency was reauthorized. The GAO reports largely focused on the administrative problems within the agency, including the high rates of turnover among agency personnel, and FEMA's problems dealing with state and local agencies. The NAPA report, *Coping with Disaster: Building an Emergency Management System to Meet People's Needs in Natural and Manmade Disasters* (1993), pointed out the political problems inherent in the agency's mandate and suggested reforms beginning with a reduction in the number of political appointees. The director of FEMA is appointed by the president and subject to confirmation by the U.S. Senate, as are seven other FEMA officials. In total, there are over thirty political appointees in FEMA positions, which is a very high number for such a small agency (Wamsley et al., 1996; 271). The large number of appointees reflects the agency's origin as a collection of smaller agencies, offices, and programs.

Well aware of FEMA's problems under the Bush Administration, President Bill Clinton appointed James Lee Witt, the former head of the Arkansas emergency management agency and a former local government official, as director of FEMA in 1993. The potential political costs of appointing an ineffective director were apparent from the Hurricane Andrew debacle. Clinton, too, had been a state governor and likely appreciated the problems that state and local officials had had with previous FEMA directors. Witt has been able to build stronger working relationships with FEMA's state and local counterparts. His orientation toward natural and technological disasters has likely served to defuse some of the political opposition that FEMA experienced in its dealings with other agencies, as well. While the agency has not been without its critics, its reputation has benefited tremendously from the change in focus from national security programs to natural and technological disaster programs in the 1990s. In fact, FEMA has been one of the biggest success stories of the Clinton Administration. The agency's effectiveness in supporting state and local disaster efforts, building partnerships with state and local agencies and the private sector, and increasing public awareness of hazards and appropriate self-help measures has given it a high profile and a positive image. Problems still remain, but the agency has proved itself in recent disasters. The new emphasis on mitigation or prevention programs has given the agency greater public visibility, as well.

Director Witt also initiated reorganizations and reforms suggested in the agency's National Performance Review studies and many of the problems identified by GAO and NAPA have been addressed. He began with a new mission statement emphasizing mitigation and partnership with state and local governments and the private sector. He administratively integrated the civil defense program with the other disaster programs to make better use of the agency's resources and to reduce conflict between the "military" and natural and technological disaster components of the agency.

The changes have not simply been cosmetic; rather, they seem to reflect fundamental changes in the values of the organization. The organizational culture of the agency has undergone a transformation since the early 1990s, which has likely helped improve relationships with state and local emergency management agencies, public officials, and, in particular, private and nonprofit sector disaster response and relief organizations. The change can be attributed in part to Director Witt and the appointment of officials with appropriate experience and expertise, but it can also be attributed to the National Performance Review encouraging pragmatic, rather than ideological, adjustments in agency processes and procedures and to the Government Performance and Results Act of 1993 with its emphasis on broad policy goals that can only be achieved in partnership with state and local agencies and with private and nonprofit sector organizations. The agency's approach is much more collaborative and cooperative than it was in the 1980s, and it is much more consistent with the legal and political realities of the American federal system of government. The agency's approach acknowledges the authority and the responsibilities of its state and local counterparts.

FEMA is a small agency with roughly 2,400 full-time employees, but it can mobilize nearly 7,000 temporary disaster assistance employees (DAEs) to respond to a disaster. The agency is organized around the four functions of (1) mitigation, (2) preparedness, (3) response, and (4) recovery and has ten regional offices to coordinate with its state and local government counterparts and with nonprofit and for-profit organizations. FEMA also operates the *National Emergency Training Center* in Emmitsburg, Maryland, which includes the *National Fire Academy* and the *Emergency Management Institute.*

The mission of FEMA is to:

Reduce the loss of life and property and protect our institutions from all hazards by leading and supporting the Nation in a comprehensive, risk-based emergency management program of mitigation, preparedness, response, and recovery (FEMA Strategic Plan, September 30, 1997)

FEMA's strategic goals are to:

1. Protect lives and prevent the loss of property from all hazards.

   Reduce by 10 percent the risk of loss of life and injury from hazards and reduce by 15 percent the risk of property loss and economic disruption from hazards by the end of FY 2007.

   With 5-year strategies for mitigation and preparedness, and provisions to evaluate progress toward these goals.

2. Reduce human suffering and enhance the recovery of committees after disaster strikes.

   Reduce human suffering from the impact of disasters by 25 percent and increase, by facilitated restoration of eligible public services, by 20 percent the speed with which individuals, businesses, and public entities are enabled to recover from disasters by the end of FY 2007.

   With 5-year strategies for response and recovery, and provisions to evaluate progress toward these goals.

3. Ensure that the public is served in a timely and efficient manner.

Improve the efficiency by which FEMA delivers its services by 20 percent and achieve and maintain 90 percent overall internal and external customer satisfaction with FEMA services.

With 5-year strategies to improve efficiency and customer service, and provisions to evaluate progress toward these goals.

The strategic plan outlines FEMA's responsibility to work "in close consultation with partners in State and local governments, business and industry, the American Red Cross and other volunteer and non-profit organizations."

State and Local Emergency Management Agencies

The national emergency management system is designed to provide state assistance to communities when local capabilities and resources are overwhelmed, and federal assistance to states and localities when state capabilities and resources are overwhelmed or seriously taxed. The determination of these threshholds is a technical process of damage assessment, but it is also a political process in terms of the need for state and federal officials to appear responsive.

Local agencies are generally the "first responders" to disaster, responsible for the initial disaster response and protecting lives and property until state and federal resources can be brought to bear. As a practical matter, local officials have primary responsibility for disaster response because few state governments have strong response capabilities, aside from assigning National Guard units and providing technical assistance. FEMA is not a response agency as such, although it has some response capabilities.

State emergency management agencies are responsible for coordinating state disaster response and recovery efforts, but the amount of involvement in local operations varies widely. The state of California has adopted a "standardized emergency management system" (SEMS). The SEMS framework provides for a common approach based on the all-hazards model, comprehensive planning processes, communication networks, and state-local and local-local coordination. Emergency management is an assigned "functional area" for county governments and the state has regional coordinating bodies to assure effective delivery of resources to local agencies. Perhaps most importantly, SEMS assures that emergency agencies have a common technical language (see Winslow 1996).

The state of Florida's Division of Emergency Management is located in the Department of Community Affairs and provides a number of services to local and regional emergency management organizations, including providing geographic information system (GIS) databases to facilitate local disaster operations and training for local officials. In other states, the arrangements are less well developed. The size of the state, the tax base and other resources, the level of professionalization within state government, the form of government (i.e., strong or weak executive), state-local politics, and the orientation of officials and the public to proactive government programs are factors that influence the organization and function of the state emergency management system and its ultimate effectiveness.

To request federal disaster assistance, the governor must file a formal request and document the extent of damage and the level of need. The request must include a damage assessment and must specify the kinds of aid that are needed. Federal officials, however, may prompt state officials to ask for particular kinds of aid that are commonly needed and may accept damage assessments that are less than complete. When the speed of response is critical, there are strong political and humanitarian incentives to act as quickly as possible. Under normal circumstances, the state emergency management office or agency has to collect data from local offices to document the need for federal assistance. The process requires significant administrative capability and technical expertise, and requires an effective communications link to assure that information is conveyed from the local level to the state emergency management agency or governor's office. In recent years, some state agencies have run training exercises focused solely on how to complete the necessary paperwork for the presidential disaster declaration request.

After the damage assessment is complete and state officials agree to commit state resources to recovery, FEMA evaluates the request for aid and makes a recommendation to the president. The president may approve the request or not. If the request is not approved, the disaster has to be handled by state and local agencies. If the request is approved, an array of federal resources are made available and victims, public and private, are eligible for federal disaster assistance loans and/or grants.

PRESIDENTIAL DISASTER DECLARATIONS

The granting of federal disaster aid is a political decision, as well as an administrative one. The president may weigh the documented need for assistance, the political costs associated with not providing aid, the political advantage associated with giving aid, and a variety of other political and economic factors before issuing a *presidential disaster declaration.* A disaster declaration may be awarded in a matter of hours or it may take weeks. There is little question about the need for assistance after a major disaster, such as Hurricane Hugo or Andrew, although the formal request is still necessary. A slow-developing disaster, such as a flood, may take days or weeks to overwhelm local and state resources, and the extent of damage may not be known for some time. In those cases, the declaration may be issued long after the disaster and even after the recovery process has largely been completed. However, emergency declarations were issued before the expected landfall of Hurricane Floyd in October 1999 in anticipation of catastrophic damage and as residents were being evacuated from coastal communities. The decision to issue the disaster declaration may also be speeded up when the president and the governor or mayors are of the same political party or have close personal connections and when the disaster occurs in an election year or in a state with a large number of electoral votes.

Once awarded, the presidential disaster declaration makes available individual and public assistance. *Individual assistance* is for damage to private residences and businesses and for the loss of personal property, and *public assistance* is for the repair of infrastructure (such as highways and bridges), public facilities, and the removal of debris. FEMA is responsible for coordinating the federal aid and for setting up the *disaster assistance hotline* to deliver the aid. The choice of locations for disaster assistance centers can also be a political decision. The handling of requests for assistance is now done largely by telephone through FEMA's teleregistration system. Individual assistance generally includes:

- Temporary housing;
- Low-interest disaster loans for property losses;
- Disaster grants to cover expenses for those who cannot repay loans;
- Other programs ranging from crisis counseling and unemployment assistance, to legal aid and assistance with Social Security benefits.

Emergency housing may be available for as long as eighteen months and may also include moneys for repairing damaged homes. Hotels and motels may be used as emergency housing, and FEMA may also bring in mobile homes to provide temporary shelter for those without local housing. Zoning regulations in some communities do not permit mobile homes. As a consequence, such housing can become a very controversial issue, particularly when the recovery process is long, and little or low-income housing is built.

TABLE 2–1   President Declares Major Disaster for Oklahoma: Eleven Counties Designated for Aid to Tornado Victims

Washington May 4, 1999—Eleven Oklahoma counties ripped by a swarm of tornadoes reports Federal Emergency Management Agency (FEMA) under a major disaster declaration issued for the state today by President Clinton.

FEMA Director James Lee Witt said the President authorized the assistance immediately following a review of the agency's analysis of the state's expedited request submitted this morning for federal relief. The declaration covers damage from severe storms and tornadoes that hit the state May 3–4.

"The President is deeply concerned about the tragic loss of life and destruction caused by these devastating storms," Witt said. "He has acted quickly in committing all necessary federal resources, and we will work as fast as humanly possible in aiding all those in need."

Witt, who arrived in Oklahoma City today, reported that two advanced teams of FEMA disaster specialists and seven Civil Air Patrol ground assessment units were deployed to assist state and local emergency operations. U.S. military aircraft, as well as federal public works and health and medical resources, also have been activated to support immediate response efforts.

The 11 counties designated by Witt for federal aid to tornado-stricken residents and business owners include Caddo, Cleveland, Creek, Grady, McClain, Oklahoma, Kingfisher, Lincoln, Logan, Pottawatomie, and Tulsa.

The assistance, to be coordinated by FEMA, can include grants to help pay for temporary housing, minor home repairs, and other serious disaster-related expenses. Low-interest loans from the U.S. Small Business Administration also will be available to cover residential and business losses not fully compensated by insurance.

Additionally, Witt said federal funds will be provided for the state and affected local governments in the eleven designated counties to pay 75 percent of the eligible cost for debris removal and emergency services related to the disaster. The declaration also makes cost-shared funding available to the state for approved projects that reduce future disaster risks.

Witt indicated that more counties and additional forms of assistance for state and local government agencies may be designated later based on the results of further damage assessments. He named Robert Hendrix of FEMA's regional office in Denton, Texas, to coordinate the federal relief effort.

Hendrix said residents and business owners who sustained losses in the designated counties can begin the disaster application process by calling 1-800-462-9029, or 1-800-462-7585 (TDD) for the hearing and speech impaired. The toll-free telephone numbers will be available starting Wednesday, May 5, from 8 A.M. to 6 P.M. (CT) seven days a week until further notice.

Source: Federal Emergency Management Agency (FEMA), Office of Emergency Information and Public Affairs, Washington, DC.

TABLE 2–2   Plains States Tornado Disaster Update

Washington May 6, 1999—Following are selected highlights of current federal response activities related to the Oklahoma/Kansas tornadoes.

The situation in brief as of 5:00 P.M. Thursday, May 6, 1999:

The Federal Emergency Management Agency (FEMA) is working closely with state and local officials in Oklahoma, Kansas, Texas and Tennessee following the deadly tornadoes and storms that moved through the south and southwest this week.

President Clinton Tuesday issued major disaster declarations for 11 Oklahoma counties (Caddo, Cleveland, Creek, Grady, McClain, Oklahoma, Kingfisher, Lincoln, Logan, Pottawatomie, Tulsa) and one Kansas county (Sedwick). The President's disaster declaration makes available a variety of programs to help people and communities recover and rebuild more safely for the future.

FEMA Director James Lee Witt continues his visits to the affected areas. He was in Kansas today with Vice President Gore. He was in Oklahoma Tuesday and Wednesday.

Thousands of homes in Oklahoma, Kansas and Texas are damaged or destroyed. Many people remain in shelters as the cleanup begins.

Highlights of the Federal Response:

- The National Teleregistration Center in Denton, Texas is taking registration information from tornado victims from 7 A.M. to 10 P.M. (CDT) daily. The toll-free number is 1–800–462–9029.
- Nearly 3,000 have registered so far.
- FEMA and state personnel are working to establish Disaster Field Offices.
- More than 300 federal employees are deployed to the affected areas.
- A FEMA Mobile Emergency Response System (MERS) with 19 vehicles is in Oklahoma City. A second MERs detachment is deployed to Kansas.
- FEMA community relations teams in the field will meet with victims to help them understand the disaster recovery process. Disaster programs include temporary housing or minimal repairs assistance; low-interest loans for major repairs or rebuilding; individual and family grants for disaster needs, and public assistance.
- FEMA is providing eight trained Disaster Search Canines and handlers, plus one Search Team Manager. The state of Texas is providing two additional canines and handlers.
- Removal of debris and damaged automobiles will require a major effort. The U.S. Army Corps of Engineers is ready to assist.

(continued)

TABLE 2–2 *(continued)*

- A U.S. Public Health Service Disaster Mortuary Team and a Management Support Team are deployed to Oklahoma City.
- Tinker Air Force Base in southeast Oklahoma City has been designated as the base support installation in support of federal disaster operations.
- The Army 249th Engineering Battalion has deployed two platoons to Oklahoma City.

Source: Federal Emergency Management Agency (FEMA), Office of Emergency Information and Public Affairs—Washington, DC.

Some more affluent communities also may object to moving low-income disaster victims into their areas, even on a temporary basis. Following the Loma Prieta earthquake in 1989, "temporary" shelters operated for over a year because property owners chose to replace damaged and destroyed low-income housing with more profitable structures. Some low-income residents found themselves without affordable housing.

The low-interest loans are made available by the U.S. Small Business Administration (SBA) to cover uninsured personal and business losses. The loans can be for homes, automobiles, and/or other property. There have been cases in which property owners have complained about the effectiveness of disaster mitigation efforts because losses were kept so low that they did not qualify for SBA loans.

Disaster grants have ranged from a few hundred dollars to just over $13,000 (in 1998) and are made when victims are not able to repay loans. The payments can be used to replace clothing, automobiles, and other essentials and to pay medical expenses. Other disaster aid programs provide for psychological counseling, unemployment assistance, legal aid, and assistance with other government programs, such as Social Security and veterans' benefits.

Public assistance is given to state and local governments to cover part of the costs of replacing or repairing infrastructure. The federal share is usually 75 percent, with the state and local governments paying the remaining 25 percent. The assistance is generally used to remove debris, repair government buildings, and rebuild public schools.

How much the federal government can help varies according to the nature and severity of the disaster. Authority and responsibility for responding to natural and technological disasters resides in the states, but the federal government may assume authority and responsibility for disasters that threaten national security or the very existence of the government. Consequently, federal agencies can act directly and assume leadership in crisis situations related to war, terrorism, and certain types of criminal activity, such as bombings, kidnappings, bank robberies, and attacks on civil aviation. In emergencies in which the civil defense system is activated, federal officials assume extraordinary authority. However, the *Posse Comitatus* law and other laws restrict the use of U.S. military forces and intelligence services in domestic crises and disasters.

For example, the *Posse Comitatus* Act prohibits the use of federal troops to enforce civilian laws, but military personnel can support civilian officials exercising their authority and local commanders can provide assistance under the Immediate Response Authority when there is not enough time to seek approval from higher authorities and the action is necessary in order to "save lives, prevent human suffering, or mitigate great property damage." Military resources may also be called upon under the Stafford Act. While Immediate Response Authority has been used in many cases, such as the Great San Francisco Earthquake of 1906 and the Murrah Federal Building bombing in Oklahoma City in 1995, there is no support for such actions in the Constitution or in statute. Consequently, commanders have to be very careful about their involvement in disaster response and recovery operations without a presidential disaster declaration.

Military resources can be used after a presidential disaster declaration and, since passage of the 1988 amendments to the Disaster Relief Act of 1974, for up to ten days in lesser emergencies. Under the Stafford Act, FEMA can call upon appropriate federal agencies (as defined by the Federal Response Plan), including the Department of Defense, to save lives, property, and public health during a disaster. Such was the case during the Oklahoma City bombing disaster (Winthrop, 1997).

Federal authority was less ambiguous during the Oklahoma City tragedy than it has been in other disasters. The principal target of the bombing was a federal facility and many of the victims were federal employees. The Federal Bureau of Investigation (FBI) and the Bureau of Alcohol, Tobacco, and Firearms (ATF) had jurisdiction because the disaster involved a bomb and because federal agents were killed. President Clinton declared the event an "emergency" under the Disaster Relief Act of 1974 as amended, and more federal assets were made available (Winthrop, 1997).

Since passage of the Nunn-Lugar-Domenici or Defense Against Weapons of Mass Destruction Act of 1996, there has been an attempt to integrate federal, state, and local emergency response mechanisms. DOD was designated the lead federal agency initially, but responsibility for "crisis management" during events involving "weapons of mass destruction" (WMD) was transferred to the FBI in the fall of 1998 with responsibility for coordinating the counterterrorism effort vested in the National Domestic Preparedness Office. Lead responsibility for "consequence management" was assigned to FEMA and a major role was assigned to the Department of Health and Human Services (HHS) to assure ready access to Public Health Service and other medical resources. DOD has responsibility for providing technical support, including decontamination training, and for the transfer of surplus equipment to state and local authorities, as well as for supporting the efforts of other federal agencies until October 2000. At that time, DOD's training and support responsibilities will be transferred to the Department of Justice (*Emergency Preparedness News*, 1999, 80).

Although the antiterrorism program involves training state and local emergency responders and officials, the network being developed is far less inclusive than the network that is involved in natural and technological disasters. In part the antiterrorism effort is a closed system, rather than an open system like the national emergency management network that deals with natural disasters. The antiterrorism system reflects the cultures of the lead agencies. DOD and the FBI are not collaborative agencies as a rule. Interacting effectively with civilian organizations, particularly volunteer groups and other nonprofit organizations, is not a strength of DOD. The FBI is concerned about securing disaster sites and preserving evidence, as well as apprehending the terrorists, and does not want civilians trampling the crime scene. In a large WMD event, however, the full complement of disaster response and relief organizations will be needed, and preserving evidence may be far less important than rescuing victims and containing the responsible nuclear, biological, or chemical agent (see Waugh 2000).

THE ORGANIZATION OF STATE AND LOCAL EMERGENCY MANAGEMENT OFFICES

State emergency management agencies take many forms, although there is a growing tendency to mimic FEMA in name and function. Given that most state agencies were originally created as part of the civil defense system, many are still housed in the state adjutant general's office and are called civil defense offices or agencies. However, in keeping with the trend toward greater executive control over administrative functions in government at all levels, more and more state emergency management agencies are being located in or very near the office of the governor. The administrative problems evident in South Carolina's response to Hurricane Hugo in 1989 have raised questions about the structure of state offices. In that case, responsibility for emergency management was vested in the adjutant general of the National Guard, who is a separately elected state official.

Communication with local officials was limited. Because emergency management was a secondary mission of the Guard, few resources were devoted to building and maintaining an effective communication network among state and local agencies. Communication between the National Guard and the Governor's Office was also poor.

There is also a slow transition of emergency management agencies from civil defense–oriented organizations to more civilian natural disaster–oriented organizations. Transition reflects a number of fundamental changes in state and local government. First, the economic costs of disasters are encouraging more attention to the effective management of natural and technological hazards. While there is some evidence that disaster relief can provide an economic boost to a community, there are also serious economic costs to property owners, particularly if they are uninsured. Small businesses, too, often fare poorly because they tend to be underinsured and overvalued. As a result, the insurance payments are inadequate to repair facilities and restock shelves, and loans are too small to compensate for the losses. Communities have benefited from redevelopment following disasters, largely because old structures are destroyed and new structures built, but there are social and economic costs realized by the community despite the good fortune of some property owners. Local elected officials may find themselves with significant personal legal exposure if they fail to respond reasonably to a known hazard. In large measure, state officials enjoy legal immunity because they are agents of a sovereign government.

A continuing problem at the city and county levels is that local agencies have drastically different capabilities (see Waugh 1988a). That is no less true of other government functions, but it is particularly troublesome when a disaster occurs or there is a hazard that poses a serious threat to public safety and residents cannot depend upon local agencies. A slow or ineffective initial disaster response can increase property loss and endanger lives. Some local emergency management agencies are little more than one-person operations with volunteer, part-time coordinators, no staff, no technical resources, and little authority vis-à-vis other agencies and the public at large. By contrast, some local agencies are highly professional organizations with state-of-the-art information technology and large staffs with extensive training and experience. Indeed, in some cases, local agencies have more experience with particular kinds of hazards and disasters than their federal and state counterparts and, thus, need little more than financial assistance. In other cases, local agencies need all the assistance that they can get and then some. Forging such disparate capabilities together into an effective emergency management system is a challenge. It can also be a political challenge when some local authorities cannot be entrusted with critical tasks in a disaster response or when they fail to address a serious hazard adequately and leave people and property at risk.

To some extent, the more capable agencies are where one might expect them, in larger cities and counties with histories of disaster and recent experience in disaster response, in more affluent communities where tax revenues permit greater attention to such needs, and in states and municipalities where public employment tends to be more professional and accountable to the public. Like other government agencies, the personality and expertise of the chief administrative officer, the emergency manager, also determines the capabilities of the local agency. A single, highly motivated professional emergency manager can have a significant impact on a community's capacities to address hazards and respond to disasters effectively. Interpersonal skill and political acumen can be more important than technical expertise and experience (Drabek 1987; Waugh 1996).

The common wisdom is that emergency management offices operate best when they are located within or very close to the office of the chief executive officer, be that the governor, the mayor, the city or county manager, or the chairperson of the city or county commission. Proximity facilitates communication, gives more status to the emergency management function, generally gives greater access to resources, and gives emergency management officials more political and administrative visibility. Proximity to power is not enough, however. The emergency management office needs public support in order to be effective. Nonethess, many local offices are still attached to departments of public safety or public works, and their mission is secondary to that of the parent or host agency.

Local elected officials also need an effective emergency management agency because they may be held legally liable for failing to prepare for and respond to disasters effectively. That threat of liability, as well as concern for public health and safety, has also encouraged attention to the capabilities of local officials and offices. However, reform has been slow. Many city and county officials still do not understand the need to hire professionally trained and experienced administrators for emergency management offices, although there is a growing awareness of the need for effective administrators in finance and other critical day-to-day operations. Again, the professionalization of local government has progressed much faster in some states, like California and North Carolina, than in others. Low salaries and little attention to the need for technical training and education make it difficult for many communities to recruit and retain highly qualified, full-time personnel.

State emergency management agencies are responsible for all phases of disaster mitigation, preparedness, response, and recovery, calling upon federal support only when damage exceeds local and state capacities and/or when technical assistance and other kinds of support are needed. The authority of the governor and the responsibilities of state and local agencies are usually spelled out in state law. Governors are responsible for declaring and ending states of emergency during which agencies are granted extraordinary powers to assure public health and safety.

State emergency management agencies are typically responsible for coordinating the activities of other state and local agencies during disasters and for assisting the governor in the exercise of his or her emergency powers. The need for close collaboration with the governor and his or her staff has encouraged the location of the state emergency management agency in or near the office of the governor. The need for effective and fast communication is manifest. There can be serious repercussions when a governor appears ineffective or indecisive in dealing with a major disaster. The political costs associated with a poor response during an emergency are too high for officials to ignore the need for effective policies and programs.

In terms of specific functions, state emergency management agencies are responsible for maintaining state disaster plans that define responsibilities during emergencies and generally are responsible for maintaining the state emergency operations centers (EOCs) from which state and local disaster operations can be directed. Federal requirements for documentation of damages caused by disasters, in order to qualify for a presidential disaster declaration and other aid, and for the development of a mitigation strategy to lessen the likelihood of future losses are encouraging more attention to the qualifications of state and local emergency management personnel. Local emergency management offices or agencies may be located in or near the office of the mayor, city or county manager, city or county commission, or other elected official or appointed administrator. Local emergency managers are often part-time officials and may also be responsible for law enforcement, fire services, emergency medical services, public works, and/or other administrative functions. In larger jurisdictions, local emergency managers are increasingly professionally trained, full-time, paid officials with broad responsibilities for hazard management and disaster operations.

Local government officials, as the "first responders," have to handle disasters for hours or even days before state and federal resources arrive on the scene. Unless the disaster occurs close to a city or a staging area for disaster resources (where material resources and personnel are gathered until they can be distributed where they are needed, e.g., tents and mobile emergency hospitals), it may take considerable time for needed resources and personnel to be brought in. The first hours of a disaster can determine the overall success (or failure) of a disaster response. Treatment of casualties, search and rescue operations, and restoration of lifelines, such as power and water, have to be done quickly. Quick action can also reduce property losses and the likelihood of additional casualties. The mayor, city or county manager, or commission chairperson is the chief executive of the local government and can assure that other local agencies make resources available for disaster response, such as public works department equipment, overtime for firefighters and emergency medical personnel, and communication with state officials. Close proximity to the office of the chief executive officer has great symbolic value in that it suggests that the function of emergency management is considered important and has high-level support. Close proximity to the office of the chief executive officer may also increase the likelihood that that official will understand the emergency management function and provide the resources necessary for it to be effective. Unfortunately, state and local elected officials often do not see the need for large, professional emergency management offices or agencies. State and local governments have other pressing needs that take precedence over emergency management, so it is not a high priority and the responsibility is often assigned to an office or department that may not have a strong interest. If emergency management is a secondary mission, it does not have a priority and does not get the resources it needs.

Given that FEMA's mission includes capacity building at the state and local levels, the agency is concerned about defining minimum and desired capabilities. The actual measurement of performance will be impossible in many cases and the agency will have to rely on assumed performance based on measurements of capabilities. In fact, FEMA has the State Capability Assessment for Readiness (CAR) program, which is designed to measure capabilities [see *State Capability Assessment for Readiness (CAR)* 1997].

THE INVOLVEMENT OF NONPROFIT AND FOR-PROFIT ORGANIZATIONS IN EMERGENCY MANAGEMENT

There are literally thousands of organizations, large and small, in the United States that are engaged in monitoring environmental hazards, encouraging hazard reduction efforts, providing disaster assistance to victims, counseling victims and their families, lobbying for public health and safety regulations for everything from foodstuffs to civil aviation, and promoting the professionalization of the field of emergency management. A disaster relief effort may involve religious organizations, civic organizations, environmental groups, university research and training centers, associations of businesses, associations of professional planners and other technical personnel, chambers of commerce, private firms with particular disaster expertise, private firms with applicable nondisaster expertise (e.g., construction firms), firms and individuals intent upon cheating disaster victims and/or the agencies involved in disaster relief, *ad hoc* groups of "good samaritans," and altruistic individuals drawn to the tragedy. They converge on the disaster scene to offer help and/or to find opportunities for personal gain.

For the most part, disasters attract well-meaning groups and individuals. However, competition among groups, differences in approaches and philosophies, conflicts in ideology, and a variety of other factors complicate the politics and the economics of hazard management and disaster response and recovery. The real challenge for emergency managers may be blending these disparate elements into a working, effective system. In most cases, the key is providing mechanisms for communication and coordination, that is, helping them work together. In some cases, it may be deciding which organizations should or should not be permitted to participate based on their skills and competencies, and on their intentions.

Professional organizations active in promoting the professionalization of the field and the development of effective federal, state, and local programs can be useful in assuring the competency of officials and offices. They include:

- The National Emergency Management Association, which largely represents state emergency management agencies and managers;
- The International Association of Emergency Managers, which largely represents local emergency managers in the United States and increasingly in other nations;
- The American Society for Public Administration's Section on Emergency and Crisis Management, which brings together emergency management practitioners, researchers, consultants, faculty, and students preparing for careers in the field;
- The American Psychological Association's (APA's) Disaster Response Network, which provides a mechanism for psychologists involved with disasters or their effects to interact; and
- The American Public Works Association's Council on Emergency Management, which represents public works professionals with emergency management responsibilities.

The interests and concerns of planners, engineers, architects, airline pilots, floodplain managers, dam safety officials, local government officials, insurance companies, fire chiefs and firefighters, risk managers, and experts on hazards ranging from sinkholes to avalanches to earthquakes are represented through a variety of professional organizations. Such organizations have been very active in promoting safety regulations, land-use regulations, building standards, codes of professional conduct, and the development of comprehensive emergency management programs. The organizations encourage their own members to promote more effective policies and programs, and they may actively lobby public officials for changes.

Private sector organizations involved in emergency management range from firms that provide technical assistance to government agencies to associations of firms from particular industries, such as the Association of Chemical Manufacturers, that have common concerns related to hazard management. In California, in particular, there is an industry associated with hazard reduction and disaster preparedness, response, and recovery which provides critical services in the statewide emergency management system. Private firms or consultants may be hired to develop, evaluate, and even operate disaster programs.

Voluntary organizations, such as the American Red Cross and the Salvation Army, are primary response and recovery agencies. Government agencies often contract with such organizations to provide disaster services. For smaller fire and flood disasters, many communities rely entirely on the relief and recovery programs provided by local Red Cross offices. The American Red Cross has a national network of offices, a broadly focused training program for volunteers with their own organization and with other disaster-related organizations, an extensive list of volunteers and supporters, and very well-developed capabilities to respond to many kinds of disaster. When disasters occur, the agency mobilizes emergency medical teams, activates food and shelter programs, and responds to other community and victim needs.

Smaller organizations, including religious groups and local charities, also provide critical services, but their resources tend to be limited. *Ad hoc* or "emergent" groups of volunteers also form in the aftermath of a disaster. Some groups can be highly organized and very effective in response and recovery efforts and others may be more amorphous groupings of volunteers that are only minimally integrated into the regular emergency management system.

There is a phenomenon of "convergence behavior" as people are attracted to disasters for a variety of reasons. Such volunteers can provide needed manpower for disaster operations if integrated into the existing emergency management system, but may interfere with the operations of response agencies if they are not organized and used effectively.

Coordinating the activities of volunteer and other nonprofit groups (i.e., nongovernmental organizations or NGOs), for-profit organizations and individuals, and government agencies is a complex and difficult task. Public officials are frequently reluctant to rely heavily upon volunteers and non-governmental groups during disasters because they distrust the intentions of the volunteers, lack confidence in the volunteers' skills and resources, fear that volunteers may endanger themselves or others, are concerned that volunteers may get in the way of professional responders, and fear that there may be legal liability for volunteers' actions.

To be sure, some volunteers may have less than honorable intentions. It is increasingly common for militia groups and other extremist organizations to volunteer their services during disasters. Some groups have caches of emergency food supplies, military tents and other shelters, and all-terrain vehicles, to mention only a few possibilities. They may volunteer because they wish to demonstrate their civic mindedness and recruit new members. They may volunteer because they want access to the disaster area for other purposes. They may volunteer because they see the experience as good training for a future war or natural disaster. Whatever their intentions, it may not be certain that they will act in accordance with official policies and the public interest. Their participation may also embarrass political leaders and suggest official sanction of their purposes.

Many volunteers come armed with good intentions, but little else. They lack skills and capacities useful in a disaster relief operation and may become a burden to their own group or other response and relief agencies. A disaster operation is usually physically demanding and stressful for responders as well as victims, consequently physical stamina and psychological strength are minimal requirements. Integrating the NGOs into the disaster operation can reduce the likelihood that they will interfere with the professionals in the field. In fact, some NGOs have much more disaster experience than the government agencies with which they will be working, so integrating them into the operation can significantly increase capacities to respond.

"Good Samaritan" laws are making it possible for bystanders and volunteers to respond to disasters with minimal risk of legal liability. There have been cases in which medical personnel, doctors and nurses, have chosen not to help disaster victims because they might be sued. State laws are providing more protection for those who do help, including emergency response personnel who might suffer legal liability while working in jurisdictions other than their own. Without such protection, communities cannot easily loan public safety and medical personnel to other communities. State laws can also provide coverage for emergency responders who may be injured working outside the jurisdictions where they do have personal medical insurance coverage.

ALL-HAZARDS EMERGENCY MANAGEMENT

An all-hazards or comprehensive emergency management model was developed by the National Governors' Association in the early 1970s and adopted by FEMA soon after the agency's creation. The all-hazards model divides emergency management activities, policies, and programs into four functional areas: mitigation, preparedness, response, and recovery. The underlying principle is that local, state, and federal governments can develop generic disaster programs that can be used in a variety of circumstances. Mass evacuation programs can be used to move populations away from flood waters, wildfires, hazardous materials spills, and even nuclear attacks. Temporary shelter programs can be used in any circumstances in which people are evacuated from their communities or their homes are severely damaged. And so on. The expectation was that programs developed for national security-related disasters, such as nuclear wars, would be adaptable to natural and technological disasters and vice versa. Given that many of the emergency management programs transferred to FEMA when it was created were from DOD, that expectation was logical and far more cost effective than developing dedicated programs for every kind of possible disaster. The problem, however, was that the utility of such programs was viewed by some citizens as a potential precipitant of nuclear war. As a consequence, many communities refused to have mass evacuation programs because they might encourage reckless action by nuclear strategists. Those fears were fed by Reagan Administration officials who talked about the "survivability" of nuclear war and the utility of crude fallout shelters for personal protection. While the end of the Cold War has reduced the level of international tension, there is still considerable suspicion concerning the intentions of national security decision makers.

Initially, the four all-hazards functions were described as "phases," with mitigation and preparedness being predisaster activities, response being disaster activities, and recovery being postdisaster activities. To some extent, the notion of phases is still assumed, but there is increasing recognition that the activities can and should overlap considerably. Disaster responders, for example, should be taking measures to facilitate recovery, as well as to encourage preparedness for the next disaster and mitigation to reduce its impact. Indeed, an interagency disaster mitigation team assesses the causes of each presidentially declared disaster and issues recommendations to reduce losses from subsequent disasters.

The all-hazards model includes the following activities:

- *Mitigation* is those activities designed to prevent or reduce losses from disaster. It is usually considered the initial phase of emergency management, although it may be a component in the other phases. Examples include land-use planning to limit or prevent development in floodplains, building codes to reduce losses from earthquakes and hurricanes and fires, dams and levees to prevent flooding, and designing buildings to facilitate surveillance to lessen the likelihood that terrorists can plant bombs.
- *Preparedness* is planning how to respond in an emergency or a disaster, and developing capabilities for a more effective response. Examples include training programs for emergency responders and the public, warning systems, disaster communications systems, and contingency planning.
- *Response* is the immediate reaction to disaster. It may occur as the disaster is anticipated, as well as soon after it begins. Examples include mass evacuation, sandbagging buildings and other structures, securing emergency food and water, covering windows, providing emergency medical services, search and rescue, firefighting, and restoring public order to prevent looting.
- *Recovery* is those activities that continue beyond the emergency period to restore lifelines. Examples include providing temporary shelter, restoring power, critical stress debriefing for emergency responders and victims, job assistance, small business loans, and debris clearance.

The process normally stops short of reconstructing the community, although there is growing interest in developing disaster resistant, resilient, and sustainable communities. FEMA's Project Impact focuses on encouraging communities to become disaster resistant. In exchange for training and technical assistance, communities agree to reduce the likelihood of disaster through land-use regulations, building codes, and other mitigation programs. Developing more resilient communities is a relatively new idea. The extent to which communities develop the necessary medical, social service, public education, and other capabilities useful in disasters and other crises, such as plant closings, has been associated with more effective disaster recoveries (see, e.g., Comfort et al. 1998). Sustainable development is a more familiar concept, although it is also somewhat ambiguous. In essence, sustainable communities will integrate hazard mitigation into their economic, environmental, and social programs and live "more lightly and sensibly on the earth" (Beatley 1998, 233). The ideal is concentrated development with ample "green space," public transportation, energy-efficient construction, low pollution levels, and effective hazard mitigation programs.

The major reorganization of FEMA that took place in 1993 under Director James Lee Witt was based on the all-hazards model. The model also provides the basic framework for FEMA's *Integrated Emergency Management System* (IEMS), which has helped shape FEMA's policy development since the early 1980s. IEMS is a process model that focuses on the following functions:

- *Hazard analysis*—including the identification of hazards; assessment of the probability of a disaster and the probable intensity and location; assessment of its potential impact on a community; the property, persons, and geographic areas that may be at risk; and the determination of agency priorities based on the probability level of a disaster and the potential losses.
- *Capability assessment*—including assessing the current organization and plan; the warning system; the communications system; available shelter facilities; evacuation plans; emergency medical services; and, the training and education of emergency personnel. Capability assessment includes identification of shortfalls and long- and short-term plans to build capacity. FEMA suggests that programs and agencies have a 5-year plan and an annual development plan that addresses the shortfalls in capabilities.
- *Emergency planning*—including coordinating planning efforts of all responsible officials, not just emergency managers; planning for the unique aspects of a particular kind of hazard; setting standards with which to assess current readiness; and planning for capacity building.
- *Capability maintenance*—including the testing and updating of plans; testing equipment; and training and educating emergency personnel, other officials, and the public.
- *Emergency response*—including operationalizing the emergency plans; adjusting for unanticipated consequences; and evaluating the response. Based on the experience, adjustments can be made in the emergency plan and/or the organization. The evaluation should also help improve the hazard analysis and the capability assessment.
- *Recovery efforts*—including returning vital life support systems to minimum levels as soon as possible; using the experience to improve mitigation and hazard analysis; and using the experience to improve the disaster response.

The underlying assumption is not that all disasters are alike and that generic functions will fit all contingencies. It is that there are enough similarities in the responses to justify some commonalities in the program.

OBSTACLES TO EFFECTIVE EMERGENCY MANAGEMENT

Historically, emergency management agencies and programs have not received the level of political and fiscal support that they should have, although that is changing as the costs of disaster increase and officials face personal legal liability, as well as political liability, for failing to prepare and respond adequately. In most respects, emergency management programs have not competed well for public dollars or for political support. Tax-cutting state legislatures, budget-cutting state and local governments, and a public often seemingly unwilling to support even basic public services created intense competition for scarce public resources. During the 1980s and 1990s, many government agencies at all levels shifted their focus from "getting a bigger bang for their buck" through more efficient operations to "doing less with less" by cutting all but the most critical services. The first casualties of budget cuts tended to be training programs, insurance, and facility maintenance. Indeed, there is a growing hazard resulting from deferred maintenance to bridges, piers, dams, buildings, and other structures because of the extreme budget cutting in some communities and states. Reductions in force and hiring freezes also meant less flexibility to accommodate secondary missions and too few personnel to add or expand programs.

Effective emergency management programs are also very difficult to design, implement, and coordinate. The reasons for those difficulties are numerous:

- Emergency management is a low-salience political issue, only getting on the public agenda during or immediately after a disaster. Officials and the public are also quick to forget the lessons learned from disaster and, thus, are fated to repeat mistakes.
- Emergency management programs generally do not have strong political constituencies to support effective action and to encourage larger budget allocations. Residents seldom lobby for stronger building codes and more restrictive land-use regulations or vote for funding of flood control projects.
- Regulatory efforts to reduce the impact of disasters and to manage known hazards better often meet strong opposition. Without data to substantiate the need for regulatory programs, with the benefits expressed in dollar terms, there is little to offset the economic costs of regulation.
- Emergency management programs generally do not have politically influential administrative constituencies. Relatively few elected officials

and career public administrators understand and appreciate the importance of emergency management programs. Emergency managers are often out of the administrative mainstream, in small, ill-funded offices. They may be viewed as "ambulance chasers" and "air raid warden-type" characters when they do not have recognized technical expertise and administrative skill, and/or the level of education of other officials.

- The effectiveness of emergency management policies and programs is difficult to measure unless there has been a disaster.
- The technical complexity of emergency management programs frequently makes them difficult to explain to the public and to officials who control budgets, as well as making it difficult to design effective programs.
- The horizontal and vertical fragmentation of the federal system creates jurisdictional confusion and leads to coordination problems.
- It is often difficult to create good working relationships among federal, state, and local agencies because fiscal, administrative, and policymaking capacities differ greatly.
- The current political climate is more hospitable to programs that are decentralized.
- The current political milieu is also more supportive of state and local self-reliance, particularly in fiscal matters;
- There is little money available at any level for new programs and initiatives, unless it can be documented that they will save money or a "policy window" is created by a major disaster so that there is public support for action.
- The diversity of hazards complicates the assessment of risk and the design of emergency management programs (Petak 1985; Waugh 1990; Waugh and Sylves 1996).

To be effective, emergency management programs must be in place prior to the occurrence of disasters, but such programs seldom have high salience as an issue until after a disaster strikes. Low-probability events do not carry great weight in policymaking unless the consequences are so great that they cannot be ignored. Current concerns about legal liability arising out of failure to prepare for known hazards, however, may force public officials to pay greater attention to risks to public health and safety.

Low issue salience is difficult to overcome because of the lack of a strong political constituency supporting emergency management efforts. Indeed, there may be very strong political forces resisting attempts to regulate land use, enforce strict building codes, restrict access to potentially dangerous areas, and divert funds from more popular programs. As in any regulatory activity, there usually is very strong opposition to programs that may affect the prerogatives and profits of the business community. To the extent that state and local government emergency management programs are perceived as complementary to federal civil defense efforts, there is support for increased federal funding and technical assistance. But, that perception can also mean strong community opposition to civil defense–related or even civil defense–applicable programs. The refusal of dozens of communities to have crisis relocation or evacuation plans because of their utility for civil defense authorities, thus potentially affecting decisions regarding nuclear war, is a case in point (May 1985). Communities have also refused to have mass evacuation and other emergency management plans in order to stop the licensing of nuclear power facilities. Such was the case with the controversy over the Seabrook Nuclear Facility in New Hampshire that was prevented from coming on line by the refusal of a number of communities and the State of Massachusetts to develop the necessary emergency plans. Nonetheless, the connection of emergency management and civil defense has likely increased the attention and resources given to non–defense-related programs. Indeed, the principal reason for the creation of the Federal Emergency Management Agency in 1979 was to increase the effectiveness of civil defense (GAO 1980, 1984a).

There is also tremendous resistance to centralized planning efforts of all sorts because such activities may impinge upon the prerogatives of local authorities, business interests, and property owners. The resistance may be a manifestation of a general distrust of central authority, be it state or national, or it may be a product of a more specific political or economic concern, such as a concern that regulations might affect economic development. There may also be ideological reasons for opposing government planning. When the governor of Georgia proposed that communities be required to do at least some land-use planning in order to participate in the state economic development program, outraged citizens called state officials to complain that to require planning was "communism." That may have been the most extreme reaction, but citizens are often unwilling to engage in the regulation of land use and construction even when it is in their own best interests to do so. Regardless of the reason, the American aversion to planning can have a profound impact on the effectiveness of policies and programs.

Also, there is no strong administrative constituency for emergency management, although the trend is toward greater involvement by elected officials and chief administrative officers in emergency management because of increased concern over liability for failure to respond to emergencies effectively, as well as to facilitate coordination. Nonetheless, there is no single, strong professional organization supporting the development of emergency management standards. The National Fire Protection Association (NFPA), the International Association of Emergency Managers, the National Emergency Management Association, and FEMA are developing a standard for disaster or emergency management programs, NFPA 1600, which demonstrates that collaborative efforts can affect the field. There are also organizations of architects, public works managers, public health professionals, applied geographers, and other professionals who do some standard setting in very specific program areas and/or limited geographic areas. But the field is still very fragmented.

That situation may change in time due to the efforts by the Federal Emergency Management Agency and the National Association of Schools of Public Affairs and Administration to stimulate academic interest in emergency management as a field of study and as a field for professional training and education, and due also to the increased focus on emergency management by organizations such as the American Society for Public Administration and the American Public Works Association, which have special sections on emergency management to bring together practitioners and academics. Notwithstanding those efforts, the development of a professional orientation has been slow. Indeed, the reluctance to provide adequate funding for and to invest personnel resources in emergency management programs may be traced in part to the perception that emergency managers are less professional than their counterparts in other agencies. However, this is changing as the field attracts more young people with broad training and education in emergency management (see Waugh 1996).

Due to the low probability and relative infrequency of most disasters, it is difficult to measure the benefits of a strong emergency management program. The ultimate measure of the benefit cannot be made until a disaster occurs, and even the best efforts may prove inadequate when the magnitude of catastrophies exceeds expectations. Costs, however, are much more visible to policymakers and the public.

The technical sophistication demanded of emergency management programs can also be problematic. Mitigating the effects of and responding to volcanic hazards, for example, are relatively simple processes and very similar to the programs designed for other kinds of hazards. Strict regulation of land use and restricted access to threatened areas are the most effective responses to volcanic hazards. Preparedness, however, is somewhat complicated by the gaps in knowledge concerning volcanic processes and the potential effect on public health. Those gaps have been filled somewhat since the eruption of Mount St. Helens in 1980, but basic research is needed if scientists are to be able to inform policymakers adequately (Waugh 1988a). Similarly, acts of terrorism using biological, chemical, or radiological agents will present complex technical issues for emergency managers, quite apart from the issues that the police will have to address. There is a race to develop effective diagnostic kits, biohazard monitors, protective suits, and other specialized equipment before a catastrophic WMD event occurs.

Horizontal and vertical fragmentation characterizes the governmental response to disasters of all sorts (Mushkatel and Weschler 1985; May 1985; Waugh 1988b). The federal structure of U.S. government results in jurisdictional ambiguities with overlapping responsibilities in some cases, sharply defined but uncoordinated responsibilities in other cases, and no clear governmental responsibilities in still other cases. This is a particularly important aspect of the management of emergencies as it is not always clear which government will have principal responsibility for overseeing the disaster operation and which agency will have lead responsibility for managing the disaster response. Federal authority wins out in terrorist events and national security emergencies, and state authority wins out in most other disasters. Multistate disaster operations are unusual enough that the issue of which state would take the lead has seldom been raised. It is far more common for there to be conflicts among local agencies, sometimes within the same government, concerning authority and responsibility.

Fundamental changes have taken place in the intergovernmental system in the past decade in terms of the expectations concerning the roles of federal, state, and local officials. The trend has ostensibly been toward greater decentralization based on local self-reliance, but there are questions about whether authority is in fact recentralizing at the state level because few states are increasing the capacities of local governments to respond to local needs (Waugh 1988b). What is important for emergency managers is that there is less likelihood of federal dollars to support programs and more likelihood of changing programmatic emphases for the few dollars that they do receive from Washington. From the states they can expect little expansion of taxing or borrowing authority to finance local programs, but more responsibility for administering programs. Because of those limitations, local officials are hungry for any money that FEMA can provide directly to them for training and equipment. Transfers of equipment under the Defense Against Weapons of Mass Destruction Act of 1996 are popular, although local officials do not always know what they need and are often frustrated by the lack of information on choices. Good "consumer" information is needed.

The current economic situation also mitigates against increased fiscal resources to support new emergency management programs. While some communities have enjoyed fiscal surpluses that could be used to address natural and man-made hazards, those are the exceptions rather than the rule. Budget cuts are the more likely prospect for emergency management programs, even when economies are thriving, and there should be more investment in essential programs.

The variety of types of disasters that may occur also suggests that it is difficult to design effective programs to address the problems raised by each. To the extent that multihazard and multidisaster emergency management programs can be developed, jurisdictions can try to adapt programs to particular circumstances. This is no less true of terrorism-related disasters, but the forms that terrorism can take may be a real test of the applicability of multihazard programs.

Having outlined those obstacles, it must be mentioned that recovery or relief efforts fare somewhat better in the policy process. Recovery in the aftermath of a disaster does in fact have high issue salience. Administrative and political constituencies do respond with special legislation and the clarification of related policies. Peter J. May has noted that about two-thirds of the twenty-five key disaster relief laws enacted in the United States since 1950 have come as a result of specific disasters (1988, 244). Despite this attention to relief efforts, however, the capacities of state and local governments to respond to major disasters are still questionable.

DISCUSSION QUESTIONS

1. Why do people choose to live and work in hazardous areas, despite the risk?
2. Why can't communities simply rely upon local churches and community groups for disaster relief?
3. Why was FEMA created?
4. Why don't state and local emergency management agencies compete better for public monies and political support?

REFERENCES

Beatley, Timothy. 1998. "The Vision of Sustainable Communities." In *Cooperating with Nature: Confronting Natural Hazards with Land-Use Planning for Sustainable Communities,* ed. Raymond J. Burby, 233–262. Washington, DC: Joseph Henry Press.

Comfort, Louise K., ed. 1988. *Managing Disaster: Strategies and Policy Perspectives.* Durham, NC: Duke University Press.

Comfort, Louise K.; Ali Tekin; Ernesto Pretto; Bulent Kirimli; Derek Angus; and others. 1998. "Time, Knowledge, and Action: The Effect of Trauma upon Community Capacity for Action." *International Journal of Mass Emergencies and Disasters* 16 (March): 73–91.

Drabek, Thomas E. 1987. *The Professional Emergency Manager.* Monograph #44, Boulder: University of Colorado, Institute of Behavioral Science.

Emergency Preparedness News. 1999. "Special Report: Counterterrorism." 23 (April 27): 77–82.

Federal Emergency Management Agency and National Emergency Management Association. 1997. *State Capability Assessment for Readiness (CAR).* Emmitsburg, MD: FEMA, June 6.

Federal Emergency Management Agency. 1997. Strategic Plan: Partnership for a Safer Future, September 30 http://www.fema.gov/library/splan_1.htm.

May, Peter J. 1985. "FEMA's Role in Emergency Management: Examining Recent Experience." *Public Administration Review.* Special Issue: 40–48.

———. 1988. "Disaster Recovery and Reconstruction." In *Managing Disaster: Strategies and Policy Perspectives*, ed. Louise K. Comfort. Durham, NC: Duke University Press, pp. 236–251.

May, Peter J., and Walter Williams. 1986. *Disaster Policy Implementation: Managing Programs Under Shared Governance.* New York: Plenum.

Mushkatel, Alvin H., and Louis F. Weschler. 1985. "Emergency Management and the Intergovernmental System." *Public Administration Review.* Special Issue: 49–56.

National Academy of Public Administration. 1993. *Coping with Catastrophe: Building an Emergency Management System to Meet People's Needs in Natural and Man-made Disasters.* Washington, DC: NAPA, February.

Perry, Ronald W. 1985. *Comprehensive Emergency Management: Evacuating Threatened Populations.* Greenwich, CT: JAI.

Petak, William J. 1985. "Emergency Management: A Challenge to Public Administration." *Public Administration Review* 45 (January): 3–8.

U.S. General Accounting Office. 1980. *States Can Be Better Prepared to Respond to Disasters.* Washington, DC: GAO, CED-80-60, March 31.

———. *The Federal Emergency Management Agency's Plan for Revitalizing U.S. Civil Defense: A Review of Three Major Plan Components.* 1984. Washington, DC: GAO, NSIAD-84-11, April 16.

Wamsley, Gary L.; Aaron D. Schroeder; Larry M. Lane. 1996. "To Politicize Is Not to Control: The Pathologies of Control in Federal Emergency Management." *American Review of Public Administration* 26 (September): 263–285.

Waugh, William L., Jr. 1988a. "States, Counties, and the Question of Trust and Capacity." *Publius: The Journal of Federalism* (Winter): 189–198.

———. 1988b. "Current Policy and Implementation Issues in Disaster Preparedness." In Louise K. Comford, ed. *Managing Disaster: Strategies and Policy Perspectives.* Durham, NC: Duke University Press, pp. 111–125.

———. 1990. "Emergency Management and State and Local Government Capacity." In *Cities and Disaster: North American Studies in Emergency Management,* eds. Richard T. Sylves and William L. Waugh, Jr., 221–237. Springfield, IL: Charles C. Thomas Publishers.

————. 1994. "Regionalizing Emergency Management: Counties as State and Local Government." *Public Administration Review* 54 (May–June): 253–258.

————. 1996. "Disaster Management for the New Millennium." In *Disaster Management in the U.S. and Canada,* eds. Richard T. Sylves and William L. Waugh, Jr., 344–359. Springfield, IL: Charles C. Thomas.

Waugh, William L., Jr., and Richard T. Sylves. 1996. "The Intergovernmental Relations of Emergency Management." In *Disaster Management in the U.S. and Canada,* eds. Richard T. Sylves and William L. Waugh, Jr., 46–68. Springfield, IL: Charles C. Thomas.

————. 2000. *Terrorism and Weapons of Mass Destruction.* New York: Marcel Dekker.

Winslow, Frances E. 1996. "Intergovernmental Challenges and California's Approach to Emergency Management." In *Disaster Management in the U.S. and Canada,* eds. Richard T. Sylves and William L. Waugh, Jr., 101–125. Springfield, IL: Charles C. Thomas.

Winthrop, Jim. 1997. "The Oklahoma City Bombing: Immediate Response Authority and Other Military Assistance to Civil Authority." *Army Lawyer* 3 (July): 3–16.

Wright, Deil. 1983. *Understanding Intergovernmental Relations.* 2d ed. Monterey, CA: Brooks-Cole.

3

MANAGING
NATURAL HAZARDS AND
DISASTERS

While floods, earthquakes, wildfires, hurricanes, volcanoes, and other natural disasters may cause serious damage to the environment, they are also natural processes that shape and reshape our world. Wildfires clear underbrush and dead trees to permit new growth, hurricanes move heat from one part of the hemisphere to another and carry water to regions like Florida, and floods deposit sand and soil along waterways to support plant and animal life. Mountains are created, soils are enriched, and so on. To be sure, the natural processes can be stopped, changed, or even encouraged in some cases. Volcanic debris flows have been channeled, rivers have been dammed, floods have been contained, wildfires have been deprived of fuel, and other mitigation efforts have lessened and even prevented damage. But seldom can the disasters be averted completely.

Indeed, although natural disasters may permanently and severely alter the environment, there are often compelling reasons not to intervene even when it is possible. Preventing some disasters, such as wildfires and floods, may well alter the ecological system and cause long-term environmental damage. A logical response to environmental hazards may well be to remove people and their property from harm's way, rather than attempting to control nature. We might simply live with hazards and the disasters they cause were it not for the damage that they do to human lives and property.

When lives and property are lost during natural disasters, the victims often are aware of the risks beforehand and simply have underestimated the possible harm to life, limb, and property or have chosen to ignore it. People living on farms on Mississippi River bottomland, in homes along California or Utah fault lines, in homes perched on unstable California hillsides, in beach houses on barrier islands along the Georgia coast, and in ranch houses in Wyoming amid woodland prone to wildfire have to assume some responsibility for the risks they take. They may also have to assume some responsibility for the damage they cause by their very presence in sensitive areas. Building on barrier islands, in floodplains, and in other hazardous areas often increases the environmental damage caused by disasters. The pathways created by residents and/or nonresidents taking shortcuts to the beach can damage the dunes that serve as barriers to tidal surges from hurricanes and lesser storms, and, thus, may exacerbate problems of coastal flooding. Removing or cutting sea grasses that hold dunes in place can also reduce the natural barriers to storm surges and, thereby, cost lives and property. Building in floodplains can increase the severity of flooding by raising the level of the water and speeding its flow. Poorly anchored buildings can literally float into other structures, damaging more secure buildings, bridges, levees, and dams. Landscaping around homes and businesses without appropriate attention to wildfire risks can increase the likelihood of fire damage. In short, people too often put themselves in the path of known hazards and fail to take even the most rudimentary precautions. As the following discussion of natural disasters suggests, hazard reduction has to begin with the commonsensical approach of separating people and their property from hazards, even if they do not want to move.

FLOODS

There is little wonder that floods are the most common of disasters. The history of settlement along waterways and coastlines has left thousands of communities under threat of periodic flooding. Where flooding has been a frequent event measures often have been taken to minimize property damage and loss of life. The bigger problem is the less frequent major floods (i.e., the 100– and 500–year floods) that exceed expectations and overwhelm a community's mitigation measures. While several such events may occur within a short span of time and may provide ample evidence of their destructive potential, there may be few residents who remember the last occurrence and little public recognition of the danger and willingness to invest in mitigation efforts. Such momentous floods are not the whole story, however. There is also a serious threat of flash flooding in desert and mountains, along otherwise dry riverbeds and streambeds, and in other low-lying areas. Strong, localized rainfall can saturate the ground, and the runoff can become a raging torrent as it follows riverbeds, ravines, ditches, and canyons to lower ground. Rains brought by hurricanes and other major storms can make the problem even more serious with their high winds and dangerous lightning, as Tropical Storm Dennis and Hurricane Floyd demonstrated in 1999. As a result of flooding, there has been an average of 101.4 deaths in the United States annually between 1916 and 1985. While the number of deaths per capita does not appear to be changing significantly, property losses are increasing. Given that there are almost 22,000 communities that are prone to flooding, the increasing property losses are understandable. In fact, flooding accounts for most U.S. expenditures for disaster aid (Federal Interagency Floodplain Management Task Force 1991).

While flooding has caused billions of dollars in property damage and killed many in the United States, there are certainly locales elsewhere in the world that have suffered far greater losses. Periodic, severe flooding along the world's major rivers, such as the Nile, Yangtze, Mekong, Zambezi, Amazon, Ganges, Danube, Lena, Rhine, and Volga, have shaped the social, political, and economic history of entire continents. After thousands of years of severe flooding, including a 1954 flood that killed 30,000 people, the government of the People's Republic of China is building a dam to control the flow of water on the Yangtze River. The dam will flood the picturesque Three Gorges area of the river when it is completed in 2003. Severe flooding in 1998 caused 3,656 deaths and left fourteen million homeless, according to official Chinese government reports, and served to reaffirm the need to proceed with the flood control and hydroelectric power project. Programs to address the flooding problem also have to be sensitive to the demand for water in China as agricultural areas and cities compete for increasingly scarce supplies.

In contrast to China's experience, the infamous Johnstown flood of 1889 that killed 2,202 people seems relatively minor. The Johnstown flood was a man-made catastrophe. Heavy rainfall in a mountainous area of Pennsylvania broke through a badly designed and poorly maintained earthen dam at a lake resort for a group of wealthy families. When a wall of water hit Johnstown miles downstream, the town's residents were decimated. Entire families were drowned. Flooding was a common problem in that region, but the disaster resulted from the negligence of the private dam owners. Since that time, major floods have killed 189 in western Virginia in 1969, 118 in Buffalo Creek, West Virginia, in 1972, and 236 in Rapid City, South Dakota, in 1972.

The history of flooding in the central United States has been considerably less lethal than that in China because of the relatively sparse population along American rivers. However, frequent property losses provided impetus for the establishment of the Tennessee Valley Authority in the 1930s to reduce flooding and produce hydroelectric power along the Tennessee River and its tributaries, and encouraged a very proactive role by the U.S. Army Corps of Engineers to reduce flooding along the Mississippi, Missouri, Ohio, and other major U.S. rivers. Prior to 1965, the risk of flooding was largely addressed through structural mitigation programs, which essentially meant building levees and dams. U.S. policy broadened in the 1960s with a focus on nonstructural approaches. Land-use planning; zoning; improvements in prediction, warning, storm-water management; and relocation of properties on floodplains became the principal tools of floodplain management. The Unified Program for Floodplain Management established national goals and strategies to reduce losses and protect natural resources. The strategies involved:

- Modifying susceptibility to flood damage and disruption by avoiding land uses that might increase property losses and damage natural resources, and by improving preparedness systems.
- Modifying the flooding itself by using structural mitigation programs to contain and channel potential floodwaters.
- Modifying the impacts of flooding on individuals and communities by increasing public awareness of the hazards, providing flood insurance to cover losses, and encouraging risk reduction through tax incentives and other means.
- Restoring and preserving the natural and cultural resources of floodplains by avoiding development that might damage flora and fauna and the scenic beauty, as well as reduce the value of floodplains as reservoirs for groundwater. Recreation areas, greenways, and other low-density development are the preferred land uses (Federal Interagency Floodplain Management Task Force 1991).

The effort to reduce flood losses was given even more impetus in the 1990s when they rose from $6.6 billion between 1988 and 1992 to $40.3 billion between 1993 and 1997. Although the 1988–1992 losses were unusually low, the tremendous jump in public and private outlays encouraged far greater attention to mitigation measures. Repeated flooding of structures, in particular, has been a focus of the disaster reduction program. A National Wildlife Federation study in 1998 concluded that 40 percent of all the money paid by FEMA for flood losses have gone to 2 percent of the properties insured under the National Flood Insurance Program (NFIP), and

---

CASE 3–1   Big Thompson Canyon Flood of July 31, 1976

U.S. Highway 34 runs from Interstate 25 to the Rocky Mountain National Park through Big Thompson Canyon. The canyon narrows between Estes Park and Loveland, and the river flows over and around large boulders. Approximately 600 people lived in the canyon in 1976, and many more vacationed in and around it, especially during the summer months. On July 31, 1976, the canyon had a large number of late summer visitors when heavy rainfall caused the river to rise rapidly that night. As the flash flood moved down the canyon in the dark, homes, automobiles, trucks, trailers, and people were washed downstream. The flood killed 139 people (Gruntfest 1996).

The Big Thompson Canyon flood reminded Colorado officials and residents of the dangers to other cities, such as Boulder, and the need to let the public know how to avoid getting caught in flash floods. The Big Thompson Canyon hazard is not unique and the problem is increasing as canyon areas are developed. Signs concerning the risk of flash flooding are now posted in Colorado's canyons and other states are adopting signage policies. Automated stream and rain gauge networks offer early warning of rising waters and residents can monitor water levels through Web sites now (Gruntfest 1996, Gruntfest and Weber 1998).

---

all those properties have been flooded more than once. In fact, many have been flooded sixteen to thirty-four times and, in many cases, the NFIP payments exceed the value of the property. Although the low cost NFIP insurance may have speeded recovery for many victims, it also may have encouraged rebuilding in very hazardous areas. The solution has been increased buyouts of properties in the most hazardous areas. FEMA director James Lee Witt has estimated that the buyouts result in $2 in savings for each $1 spent. However, while President Clinton has proposed an expansion of the buyout program, Congress has been slow to provide the money (National Wildlife Federation 1998). Nonetheless, there is growing support for buyouts and restrictions on coastal building, despite the opposition of developers and landowners.

EARTHQUAKES AND TSUNAMIS

Seismic hazards are very familiar in many parts of North America. There have been major earthquakes in Alaska and Mexico City, as well as along

---

CASE 3–2   Midwest Floods of 1993

Unusually heavy rainfall in the upper Midwest in the fall of 1992, followed by heavy snowfall that winter, caused severe flooding from Minnesota to Louisiana. The flooding began in Minnesota in May, spread to Wisconsin in June, and proceeded southward along the Mississippi, Missouri, and Kansas rivers. The Missouri River was 17.5 feet above flood stage at Kansas City. "Some sections of the Mississippi River were above flood stage from late March through most of August" (Lott 1993). Highways, farms, and residential areas were flooded. Some communities, like Des Moines, were without drinking water. People were stranded as floods surrounded roadways and homes. Twenty of 275 federal levees and 767 of 1,091 state, local, and private levees were overtopped or breached. Cattle and crops were lost. Travel was difficult as floodwaters covered roads and destroyed bridges. The Missouri River was 5 to 6 miles wide at St. Joseph, Missouri, rather than its usual 1/2 mile wide. Property damage has been estimated to be about $21 billion. Forty-eight people died as a result of the floods (Lott 1993). The scope of the disaster was difficult to grasp because of the number of states and communities affected, but the frustration and anguish of victims was symbolized in the plight of the residents of Grand Forks, North Dakota. The town was flooded by rising river water and the waters caused electrical fires that burned a large part of the business district while a national television audience watched.

---

the San Andreas and other faults in California, in recent memory. As with flood disasters, the United States has not experienced seismic catastrophes comparable to the 1976 earthquake in Tangshan, China (magnitude 8.2), that killed almost a quarter of a million people, or the 1988 quake in Armenia (magnitude 6.8) that killed over 55,000. But there is ample reason for concern, given the history of major quakes in North America and the increasing populations in seismically active areas of the country. The Great San Francisco Earthquake (magnitude 7.7) in 1906 left 503 dead and a city devastated by the quake and the firestorm that followed. The Anchorage earthquake of 1964 (magnitude 9.2) left 131 dead and rearranged the terrain in and around the city. It is still the largest earthquake in U.S. history. The Mexico City earthquake in 1985 (magnitude 8.1) left over 4,200 dead and raised questions about the safety of buildings previously considered disaster resistant.

The Loma Prieta earthquake in 1989 (magnitude 6.9) left 62 dead and again raised questions concerning the adequacy of land-use regulations and building codes. Most of the 42 deaths were the result of the collapse of a 1.25–mile-long section of the double-decker freeway, the Cypress Viaduct, on Interstate Route 880 in Oakland which was built before current earthquake standards were in place. Given that the California Department of Transportation (CalTrans) had identified about 9,700 similar structures in the state and had only begun a three-stage retrofitting program to make them less vulnerable, the loss of life could have been far greater. The Bay Bridge, which was also damaged (killing one), was not on CalTrans's list of vulnerable structures (GAO 1990). Of particular concern, as well, was the damage to a section of San Francisco built upon landfill at least partly comprised of debris from the Great Earthquake of 1906. The quake induced liquefaction causing water and gas lines to break and buildings to collapse. The Loma Prieta earthquake, along with the Mexico City quake in 1985, focused attention on the types of soils on which major structures were being built. The Northridge and Kobe (Japan) earthquakes that followed, in 1994 and 1995, respectively, provided further evidence that too little was known about the seismic risk in major urban areas and that soils could be critical variables. Scientists have now determined that there is historical evidence of major earthquakes close to what is now downtown Los Angeles, and this risk is being assessed.

The Kobe, Japan, earthquake in 1995 occurred along a previously unknown fault line and caused liquefaction along the waterfront area, destroying docks and buildings. Thousands were killed and the central government has been criticized severely for its slow response to the disaster. The devices used to measure the strength of earthquakes and to alert emergency response agencies were knocked out by the shaking. As a result, disaster assistance was delayed. Collapsed freeways and debris-filled streets made it extremely difficult to move stockpiled emergency supplies from Tokyo to Kobe. The effects of the quake are still being felt. The destruction of the docks on which Japan depended for much of its international shipping has had an economic impact calculated to be in the tens of billions of dollars, as Asian competitors capitalized on Japan's reduced shipping capacity.

As well as the San Andreas and other major fault lines in California, there is significant seismic risk along the Cascadia zone in the Pacific Northwest, east through Nevada, Idaho, Montana, and Utah and Colorado. There is also significant risk in the central United States; in the Northeast; and even in the Southeast around Charleston, South Carolina. There is also a significant risk of major earthquakes in Ontario, Quebec, and the Maritime Provinces of Canada.

Major earthquakes, ranging from 7.8 to 8.1, along the New Madrid Fault

TABLE 3–1   Largest Earthquakes in the United States

No.	Location	Date	Magnitude
1.	Prince William Sound Great Alaska Earthquake	3/28/1964	9.2
2.	Andreanof Islands	3/9/1957	8.8
3.	Rat Islands	2/4/1965	8.7
4.	Shumagin Islands	11/10/1938	8.3
5.	Lituya Bay, Alaska	7/10/1958	8.3
6.	Yakuta Bay	9/10/1899	8.2
7.	Cape Yakataga, Alaska	9/4/1899	8.2
8.	Andreanof Islands, Alaska	5/7/1986	8.0
9.	New Madrid	1811–1812	
10.	Fort Tejon	1/9/1857	7.9
11.	Ka'u District, Island of Hawaii	4/3/1868	7.9
12.	Kodiak Island	10/9/1900	7.9
13.	Gulf of Alaska	11/30/1987	7.9
14.	Owens Valley	3/26/1872	7.8
15.	Imperial Valley, California	2/24/1892	7.8
16.	San Francisco, California	4/18/1906	7.7
17.	Pleasant Valley	10/3/1915	7.7
18.	Kern Valley	7/21/1952	7.5
19.	Lompoc, California	11/4/1927	7.3
20.	Dixie Valley, Nevada	12/16/1954	7.3
21.	Hebgen Lake, Montana	8/18/1959	7.3
22.	Borah Peak, Idaho	10/28/1983	7.3

Source: FEMA, http://www.fema.gov.

caused extensive damage in Missouri and surrounding states in 1811–1812 and there is some expectation that another earthquake will occur in the near future. The prediction of a major earthquake along the New Madrid fault by Browning in the late 1980s prompted local governments to cancel vacations for public safety and other emergency personnel and to spend public monies to prepare for the expected catastrophe. T-shirt vendors and other entrepreneurs benefited from the prediction, but there are concerns that residents will be less willing to respond to warnings in the future.

Earthquakes, as well as landslides and volcanic eruptions, also can cause

---

CASE 3-3 The New Madrid Earthquakes of 1811–1812

Over a period of almost a year in 1811–1812, there were as many as 2,000 tremors in the central Mississippi Valley. Three major series of tremors caused considerable damage. The first series, on December 16, 1811, had an estimated magnitude ranging from 8.6 to 8.0 (on the Richter scale) and destroyed the small communities of Big Prairie and Little Prairie. On January 23, 1812, an 8.4 quake occurred, and on February 7, 1812, a quake of 8.8 magnitude destroyed the town of New Madrid, Missouri (Street and Nuttli 1984). River navigation was interrupted as the major quake caused two temporary falls to form on the Mississippi River, banks to crumble, and other hazards. It was also reported that the flow of the river was reversed temporarily. The population along the river was relatively small during that time, and it is uncertain how many people were killed or injured, but there were reports of extensive damage. Fortunately, log cabins were remarkably resilient and suffered little from the tremors. The shaking was felt as far away as Hartford, Connecticut; Charleston, South Carolina; and New Orleans, Louisiana (Street and Nuttli 1984). Major shocks were felt in the same area in 1776 and again in 1791 or 1792; in the Illinois Territory in 1795; at Niagara Falls, New York, in 1796; and south of Lake Michigan in 1804 (Fuller [1912] 1988).

---

tsunami. Hawaii and other Pacific islands, including Japan, have had destructive tsunamis in recent history. *Tsunami* is a Japanese word meaning "harbor wave." A tsunami is actually a series of waves and not a "tidal wave" as it is commonly called. The crests of the waves may not extend far above the level of the water, but may extend far below. The wavelength (distance between wave crests) may stretch for a hundred or more miles, making the tsunami difficult to detect until it is in shallow water. As the wave approaches the coastline, it increases in height, pulling water from the shore. The first warning that a tsunami is about to hit is usually the receding water. The *run-up* is the maximum height the wave reaches and the *inundation* is the maximum distance it travels once it reaches shore. Because there may be considerable time between waves, even though they can travel 500 miles an hour, people have been killed returning to their homes after the initial wave (Pacific Tsunami Museum, 1998).

After a major tsunami destroyed communities along the Hawaiian coast in 1946, the Seismic Sea Wave Warning System (now the Pacific Tsunami Warning System) was created to monitor seismic activity that might cause tsunamis, measure water level changes at stations located throughout the

CASE 3–4   The Charleston Earthquake of 1886

On August 31, 1886, an earthquake in Charleston, South Carolina, killed sixty. The quake destroyed 102 buildings, damaged 90 percent of the buildings in the city, and damaged nearly all the city's 14,000 chimneys. Forty-five seconds later, the ground shook in Savannah, Georgia, 90 miles to the south. Atlanta, 250 miles away, felt the tremors within minutes. Structural damage occurred within a 125–mile radius of the epicenter and moderate damage within about a 300–mile radius (Nuttli 1983). Lesser damage was caused in Louisville, Pittsburgh, Cleveland, Chicago, New York, and Boston, and the shaking was felt in Bermuda and Cuba. The earthquake had an estimated magnitude of 7.7 (on the Richter scale) and it was not the first major earthquake to occur around Charleston. U.S. Geological Survey (USGS) scientists have estimated that a similar quake today would cause thousands of deaths and property losses in the billions of dollars in South Carolina and the neighboring states of North Carolina and Georgia, as well as serious damage in other eastern and southern states. Indeed, earthquakes in the eastern United States may be more damaging than those in the West and Midwest because of the instability of sandy and clay soils, the nature of the surface waves, the kinds of buildings in eastern cities, and the lack of attention to seismic hazards in local building codes in cities like Atlanta (Toner 1986).

Pacific, and estimate arrival times to assure sufficient notice for evacuation. Tsunami "warnings" are issued and emergency management agencies are notified for any 7.5 (Richter scale) earthquake and any 7.0 earthquake in the Aleutian Islands where the lead time for evacuation of coastal communities may be much shorter. If the monitoring stations indicate that a tsunami has been created, a "watch" is issued and the public is notified (Pacific Tsunami Museum 1998; National Geophysical Data Center 1998).

Hawaii has borne the brunt of recent Pacific tsunami. On April 1, 1946, an earthquake in the Aleutian Islands generated a large tsunami. As the tsunami approached Hilo, Hawaii, and the water receded, a group of schoolchildren ventured onto the reef to see the stranded sea life. When the wave hit, they were pulled out to sea and drowned. Damage was suffered all along the Hawaiian coastline with run-ups up to 55 feet and inundation as much as a half mile inland. In all, 165 people died in Hawaii and the Aleutians. In November 1952, an earthquake off the coast of Kamchatka Peninsula, Russia, caused a Pacific-wide tsunami that caused extensive damage in Hawaii, as well as elsewhere. In 1957, a similar event, generated

CASE 3–5   The Northridge Earthquake of 1994

On September 17, 1994, at 4:31 in the morning, an earthquake (magnitude 6.7) struck the San Fernando Valley just north of the city of Los Angeles. The quake caused the collapse of freeway overpasses, damaged homes, severed lifelines, and killed 57 people. Freeways up to 20 miles from the epicenter suffered major damage. Roads were closed. Homes were without electricity. Dramatic television coverage of rescues, including the freeing of residents trapped in a collapsed apartment building near the California State University campus in Northridge, focused national attention on the catastrophe (Bolin and Stanford 1998).

Because of the early hour and the fact that it was a national holiday, there were relatively few people on the highways and in office buildings and stores. Consequently, the death toll was relatively low. Nonetheless, the property losses of over $20 billion were higher than those of any other earthquake in U.S. history. The effectiveness of newer building codes was evident. Older buildings suffered more damage than those built after building codes were strengthened in 1976. Over 112,000 older buildings were damaged. However, while newer buildings fared better, some were damaged more than expected because of the nature of the shaking (Godschalk et al. 1999, 234–236). Freeway overpasses that had been retrofitted after the Loma Prieta earthquake also fared better than those that had not yet been retrofitted by CalTrans.

The Northridge earthquake also demonstrated the vulnerability of nonstructural elements in buildings. While many structures were not severely damaged, water and gas pipes broke, suspended ceilings fell, heavy appliances and furniture were moved and overturned, lighting fixtures fell, and air conditioning systems broke loose. California's Office of Emergency Services (OES) and FEMA signed a memorandum of understanding in May 1995 to fund nonstructural retrofits under the Hazard Mitigation Grant program, and the agreement was amended two months later to include suspended ceilings and lighting in schools (Godschalk et al. 1999, 244). Many injuries were caused by falling furniture and appliances, and residents have since been encouraged to secure them to walls so that they will not tip over easily. The damage to lifelines, that is, water and utility lines, also raised concerns and mitigating such damage has been made a priority. OES's mitigation staff was also expanded from two part-time positions to seven full-time positions following the earthquake (Godschalk et al. 1999, 251).

by an earthquake in the Aleutian Islands, again caused millions of dollars of damage in Hawaii. In 1960, Hawaii was again hit by a major tsunami that originated off the coast of Chile. While there was considerable property damage in Hawaii and even along the California coast, especially Crescent City, the devastation was greatest in Chile, where 330 to 2,000 were killed.

Smaller tsunami disasters have resulted from seismic activity in the Hawaiian Islands themselves. In 1975, two campers were killed by a tsunami in Volcanoes National Park. To reduce the hazard, Hawaiian authorities have identified "inundation zones" so that residents will know how far inland water may be expected to reach. Evacuation out of the zone is expected once a "tsunami watch" has been issued. Typically, a hill, a road, or some other geographic feature or structure is identified as the boundary of the inundation zone so that residents will know how far they have to evacuate. Impetus has been provided to develop similar programs along the Oregon coast. The evidence of a 200– to 600–year cycle of catastrophic earthquakes in the Cascadia subduction zone, with tsunamis inundating coastlines in the Pacific Northwest, is encouraging serious preparedness efforts. The state of Oregon has followed the Hawaiian lead and has developed inundation maps for its coastlines (Center for Coastal and Land-Margin Research 1998).

The tsunamis that resulted from the Great Alaskan Earthquake of 1964 prompted the creation of the West Coast and Alaska Tsunami Warning Center in Palmer, Alaska, which monitors potentially dangerous seismic activity and water levels and issues warnings and watches for Alaska, British Columbia, Washington, Oregon, and California. The necessity for close monitoring of tsunami was further underscored by the disaster that occurred in Papua, New Guinea, on July 17, 1998. Thousands (over 3,000 at last count) died as coastal communities were inundated with little or no warning. The magnitude of the tragedy is a reminder of the potential loss of life from tsunamis in Hawaii, along the west coast of North and South America, and elsewhere in the Pacific. There have been tsunamis along the Atlantic Coast, but the risk is considered much lower than that of the Pacific Coast, because of the smaller threat of earthquakes and volcanoes and the configuration of the coastline itself. Nonetheless, an undersea earthquake or landslide or (as the 1998 movie *Deep Impact* suggested) an asteroid strike could trigger a catastrophic Atlantic tsunami.

VOLCANIC HAZARDS

When one thinks of volcanic eruptions and the damage that they can cause, the image that most readily comes to mind is the people and homes of

---

CASE 3–6   The Great Alaskan Earthquake and Tsunamis of 1964

The Great Alaskan Earthquake of 1964 was the strongest earthquake measured in North America and second only to the Chilean earthquake of 1960 in the Americas. It occurred at 5:36 P.M. on March 27, measured 8.4 to 8.6 on the Richter scale and 9.2 on the moment magnitude (Mw) scale, and was centered in the northern Prince William Sound. Anchorage experienced ground motion for 4–5 minutes. Avalanches and landslides followed. Areas east of Kodiak island rose 30 feet, and areas around Portage fell 8 feet (Sokolowski, 1998). Pictures of Anchorage just after the earthquake show tremendous fracturing of the earth, with fissures swallowing automobiles and downtown buildings collapsing. The landscape along the waterfront was rearranged, and tour guides still like to show visitors the areas near Earthquake Park that slid into the water.

Earthquake-induced landslides caused at least five tsunamis around the Prince William Sound, and other tsunami were created by landslides elsewhere in the Pacific. In Seward, for example, 11–13 people were killed by tsunamis. In Alaska, 106 people were killed and there was $84 million in damage to boats, homes, businesses, and other facilities. In Oregon, 4 campers were drowned on a beach. In California, 13 were killed. There was property damage in British Columbia, Washington, and elsewhere in the Pacific, including Hawaii where the tsunami reached a height of almost 5 feet on parts of Oahu and 3 feet on the Big Island. Tsunamis resulting from the Alaskan quake were measured as far away as Chile and Japan. Ninety percent of the fatalities in Alaska were from the tsunamis rather than directly from the earthquake (Sokolowski, 1998).

Pompeii that were buried in the eruption of Mount Vesuvius in 79 A.D. Until the dramatic eruption of Mount St. Helens in 1980, volcanic hazards did not draw much public or governmental attention in the United States, beyond the rather spectacular but relatively nonthreatening activity in Hawaii. The common perception of the risk from volcanic hazards in North America was that they were essentially like Kilauea and the other Hawaiian volcanoes. The expectation was that eruptions would take the form of lava flows with minimal property damage and few or no injuries and deaths. Since 1980, we have been reminded of the dangers posed by volcanic hazards in other parts of the United States. In 1982, El Chichón in Mexico killed 1,800. In 1989, the eruption of Mount Redoubt in Alaska produced dangerous ash, although the area around the volcano was not heavily populated and few lives were threatened. In 1991, Mount Pinatubo forced the evacuation of military personnel and their families from Clark Air Force Base in the Philippines,

TABLE 3–2   The Decade Volcanoes

1. Colima (Mexico)
2. Etna (Sicily, Italy)—now erupting
3. Galera (Colombia)
4. Mauna Loa (Hawaii)
5. Merapi (Indonesia)
6. Mount Rainier (Washington State)
7. Nyiragongo (Zaire)
8. Sakura-jima (Japan)
9. Santa Maria (Guatemala)
10. Santorini (Greece, island)
11. Taal (Philippines)
12. Teide (Spain)
13. Ulawun (New Guinea)
14. Unzen (Japan)
15. Vesuvius (Italy)

Source: International Association of Volcanology and Chemistry of the Earth's Interior, in cooperation with the United Nation's International Decade for Natural Disaster Reduction.

Note: The Decade Volcanoes have been selected by IAVCEI for intensive research because of their potential impact.

as well as civilian residents in the surrounding area. For the most part, however, volcanic eruptions were relatively uncommon in the United States and the rest of North America, and potentially active volcanoes were monitored by the U.S. Geological Survey's volcano observatories in Hawaii and Vancouver, Washington.

Increased volcanic activity around the world, greater understanding of the geolophysics of volcanoes, and increased knowledge about past volcanic eruptions in North America are encouraging more attention to the risk that volcanic hazards pose. The International Association of Volcanology and Chemistry of the Earth's Interior has identified fifteen decade volcanoes that bear watching. All fifteen are located near areas that are heavily populated. There are identifiable cycles of activity, often measured in millennia but sometimes much more frequent, and disturbing evidence that there may be increased seismic and volcanic activity in several parts of the world in the near future.

In recent years, warm ground, gas releases, and increased seismic activity

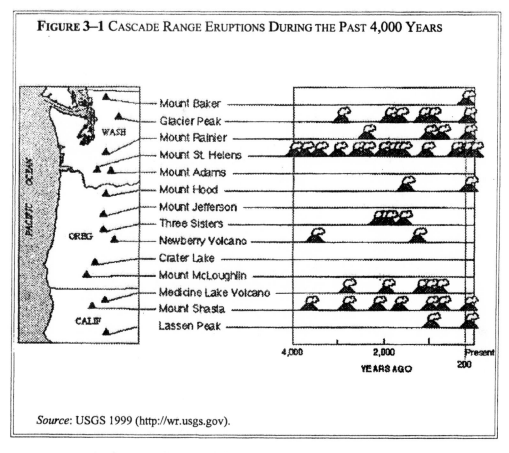

FIGURE 3–1 CASCADE RANGE ERUPTIONS DURING THE PAST 4,000 YEARS

Source: USGS 1999 (http://wr.usgs.gov).

in the Long Valley and Mammoth Lakes area of eastern California have raised concerns about a possible eruption or a lesser, but potentially dangerous, volcanic event. Fortunately, the area is not heavily populated, and most of the damage would be to the tourism industry in the area. However, there are volcanic hazards near major population centers in the United States and scientists are warning of possible disaster in the Pacific Northwest. The U.S. Geological Survey's Volcano Observatory in Vancouver, Washington, is analyzing the evidence of past eruptions to predict the nature and extent of future eruptions. Geologic evidence, such as remnants of past lahars (debris flows) and ashfalls, is being mapped to help identify potentially dangerous areas and possible routes to safety for communities near volcanoes. In fact, studies of Mount Rainier's past eruptions suggest that there may be another in the foreseeable future. The risk is considered high enough for the formation of intergovernmental working groups to develop mitigation and response plans (Wolfe 1998). The state of Washington has drafted the "All-Volcano" Plan to define roles and responsibilities for potential events at any of the four volcanic peaks in the state. The Emergency Management Division of the Washington Military Department is addressing the problems experienced prior to, during, and following the Mount St. Helens eruption in 1980. The efforts include increasing communications capabilities, improving comprehensive planning, assuring that there are personnel on duty around the clock at state and most local emergency management agencies, and increasing capacities to mobilize resources quickly (Uphaus 1998). Local agencies near Mount Rainier and other Washington volcanoes are developing evacuation plans and identifying areas that might provide safe haven for communities located within or near past lahars. Past eruptions, too, have resulted in floods as glaciers have melted causing rivers and streams to overflow their banks. Early warning, identified escape routes, and greater attention to the risk of flooding and lahars in local development plans are some of the topics being addressed (Reed 1998).

Elsewhere around the world, volcanic hazards are being recognized and, to the extent possible, are being addressed. The "decade volcanoes" identified above are only part of the list of active or potentially active volcanoes. The threat of an eruption of Mount Vesuvius in the crowded Naples metropolitan area is causing increasing concern. Spectacular lava flows at Mount Etna on the island of Sicily may be a precursor of increased volcanic activity in the region. In North America, Popocatépetl near Mexico City threatens a population of twenty-two million. The U.S. Geological Survey, through the Volcano Disaster Assistance Program, a cooperative effort with the Office of Foreign Disaster Assistance of the U.S. Agency for International Development, dispatches teams of scientists to assist officials in other nations when a volcano is expected to erupt. The team collects data and helps authorities reduce fatalities and property losses. The team then integrates the "lessons learned" into U.S. volcano programs (Ewert et al. 1997).

HURRICANES

There have been remarkably few deaths from hurricanes in the United States over the past several decades. The Great Galveston Hurricane of 1900 killed over 8,000, but there have been few disasters of such magnitude in recent American history. Hurricane Camille, a Category 5 storm in 1969, killed 256 in Louisiana and Mississippi. Hurricane Agnes, a Category 1 storm in 1972, caused 122 deaths. Hurricane David in 1979 killed 1,100 in the United States and the Caribbean. Those storms were devastating, but, after a few years, public concern waned, and there was little interest in investing public

CASE 3–7   Mount St. Helens Eruption in 1980

Scientists were monitoring seismic activity around Mount St. Helens. As the likelihood of an eruption at Mount St. Helens grew, media attention focused on efforts to evacuate the residents on and around the volcano. Frequent interviews with an elderly resident, Harry Truman, on the steps of his lodge near Spirit Lake punctuated the coverage. His refusal to leave as others were packing up and moving to safety epitomized the public's lack of understanding of the magnitude of the events that were to follow. While millions followed the broadcast and print media coverage, a side of the mountain collapsed, sending lahars over Spirit Lake and up the valley to the west. A cloud of ash and gases rose in the sky. Fifty-seven people were killed in the initial explosion and in the lahars that followed. Much of Washington State and surrounding states was covered in ash. Trees were blown down for miles by the blast (Waugh 1990b). The sight of trees lying flat and pointing away from the direction of the blast still provides a memorable image of the power of volcanoes. The slow rebirth of the area around Mount St. Helens is also providing a lesson in nature's processes.

or private money in mitigation efforts. Attitudes about hurricanes changed radically with Hurricane Hugo in 1989 and even more with Hurricane Andrew in 1992. Hurricane Hugo killed over 400 people in the United States and the Caribbean and left $7 billion in damage. The destruction was graphically detailed in the media coverage, and the American public saw state and federal disaster responses develop much too slowly. Criticism of FEMA and other disaster agencies was severe, but there was enough blame to go around and the stories of survival and recovery slowly won out in the media.

Hurricane Andrew in 1992 killed 61 in the United States and caused an estimated $26.5 billion in damage. During Andrew, 160,000 were left homeless as sustained winds of 175 mph and fierce updrafts or microbursts destroyed homes and businesses. Some communities were literally leveled. Again, the emergency responses were much slower than they should have been. Criticism of state and federal officials continued during the response to Hurricane Iniki two weeks later. Congress commissioned a study of FEMA by the National Academy of Public Administration, asked the General Accounting Office to examine the national emergency management system, and held hearings to determine whether FEMA's responsibilities should be transferred to other federal agencies. The 1992

Category	Winds (Mph)	Storm (Feet)	Surge Damage Potential
TABLE 3–3	Saffir-Simpson Damage Potential Scale		
1	74–95	4–5	Minimal
2	96–110	6–8	Moderate
3	111–130	9–12	Extensive
4	131–155	13–18	Extreme
5	Over 155	Over 18	Catastrophic

Source: Adapted from Simpson and Riehl 1981, 368.

election brought in a new administration and a new set of FEMA officials who have changed the organizational culture of the agency and greatly improved its performance and its public image (see Chapter 2).

The United States has been fortunate thus far. We have experienced nothing to compare with the cyclone that hit Bangladesh in 1970, killing over 300,000 people in the coastal lowlands. There are concerns, however, about our exposure in the Florida Keys and in beach communities in south Florida; along the western coast, particularly around Tampa Bay; and on the barrier islands stretching from Florida to New England and along the Texas coast. There are some low-lying areas, such as the islands and marshlands on the coast of Louisiana, as well as the city of New Orleans itself, that would be inundated by the tidal surge of a major storm. In the Tampa Bay area, experts have expressed fears that a storm hitting south of the bay might push so much water into the bay that there would be flooding from the inland side to the coast, bypassing the barriers to tidal surges. Massive flooding caused by Hurricane Floyd along the eastern seaboard in 1999 also demonstrated the need for better floodplain management in coastal lowlands where heavy rains can swell rivers and streams. Rainfall, rather than wind, caused most of the billions of dollars of damage from Floyd.

Following the devastating and lethal damage done by Hurricane Mitch in Central America in 1998, attention has been focused on measuring the potential of hurricanes so that communities can be better prepared. The Saffir-Simpson scale (see Table 3–3) rates hurricanes largely in terms of their sustained winds, with a force 5 hurricane having winds in excess of 155 mph. While the scale does indicate the potential damage, it does not factor in the terrain, the population and housing in the path of the storm, and the amount of rainfall being generated. Those variables may dramatically increase the level of damage from a storm. Satellite imaging, too, has shown that the height of the "towers of rain" indicate the intensity of the storm at particular times. A new scale may be developed to capture the potential impact of hurricanes and to encourage more effective mitigation and preparedness efforts.

Prior to Hurricane Andrew, there was considerable concern that many Florida residents had little experience with major hurricanes, and therefore they did not fully appreciate the destructive power of such storms. To some extent, the public seems to be taking hurricanes a bit more seriously. The graphic pictures of destruction during Hurricane Hugo and Hurricane Andrew, recent storm experience along the Outer Banks and in south Florida, and reports of deaths among "hurricane party" celebrants during several recent disasters have encouraged more attention to warnings. Better weather forecasting and reporting may be encouraging more cautious behavior, as well. Restrictions on sales of alcoholic beverages prior to expected landfalls also may be having an effect. Changing demographics, too, may be having an effect. More full-time residents in beach communities, more children, more social support for evacuation decisions, and older residents may be discouraging risk taking (Riad et al. 1999). A benefit of greater coastal development is the increase in permanent residents who take hurricane risks more seriously than tourists and those with vacation homes near the beach. Indeed, the apparent willingness of residents in south Florida and along the Gulf coast to evacuate quickly as Hurricane Georges approached in 1998 suggests that the risk is being taken more seriously than in the past. Reports of over 300 deaths in the Caribbean with dramatic news coverage of the devastation in the Dominican Republic, Haiti, Puerto Rico, and Cuba, as well as on other islands, certainly added credibility and emphasis to the warnings from U.S. emergency management agencies for residents to find secure shelter out of the reach of storm surges. However, dramatic satellite images of Force 5 Hurricane Floyd in 1999 encouraged evacuations of the Florida and Georgia coastlines, but Floyd weakened and did not make landfall until it reached North Carolina. Traffic away from the coast was so slow that some evacuees may not have found adequate shelter had Floyd made its expected landfall in Florida. Anger about the "false alarm" and evacuation problems may cause some coastal residents to be much less willing to comply the next time officials ask them to leave.

A situation report from the Office of Foreign Disaster Assistance, U.S. Agency for International Development (USAID), on the disaster relief effort in Central America following Hurricane Mitch in 1998 is given in Appendix 3–1. The extent of the damage and the complexity of the disaster operation are amply evident, although the report was issued during the event

CASE 3–8   Hurricane Andrew in 1992

Hurricane Andrew hit the Bahamas first, crossed southeastern Florida, and made landfall again along the Louisiana coast. The storm grew from a small tropical storm into a Category 5 hurricane as storm trackers followed it across the South Atlantic. Its strength ebbed before it hit the Bahamas, but it was still a Category 4 storm as it crossed the islands and made landfall again in south Florida. By the time it hit Louisiana, it was a Category 3 storm and still deadly. The maximum sustained winds were 145 miles per hour with gusts measured as high as 175 miles per hour. The leading winds blew the radar off the roof of the National Hurricane Center in Coral Gables, giving residents their first real measure of the storm's strength. The storm surge reached 23 feet in the Bahamas and 17 feet in Florida. A 30–mile path was cut across south Florida with hurricane-force winds stretching out an additional 30 miles (Greeson 1998). An estimated $30 billion in damage and at least 61 dead were left in the storm's wake. The damage to Homestead, Florida, and surrounding communities was staggering. Hospitals, fire stations, and other public facilities were severely damaged. Approximately 49,000 homes were left uninhabitable, 180,000 people were left homeless, and, of the 6,600 mobile homes in South Dade, only nine were left (Morrow 1997, 6). Hurricane Andrew was the costliest natural disaster in U.S. history until the Northridge earthquake in 1994.

The extent of the damage was uncertain for at least two days after the hurricane hit Florida. Debris-filled roadways hampered the damage assessment effort. Whole neighborhoods were flattened, and rescue workers had difficulty identifying landmarks, such as intersections and major buildings, so that victims could be directed to emergency shelters and food centers. Katherine Hale, the emergency management director for Miami–Dade County, had so few local resources left that she appealed for aid on national television, asking for the "cavalry" to come to the rescue. The disaster declaration process was expedited, cost-share waivers were granted, and the Federal Response Plan was implemented for the first time. National Guard units were activated, and active-duty units were brought in to provide emergency medical care, food and shelter, debris clearance, and other needed services. Early in the relief efforts, problems were evident in the state emergency management system, particularly relating to communication and coordination between local agencies and the governor's office. Problems also occurred in the federal response. When federal resources were slow in coming, President Bush assigned responsibility for coordinating the federal effort to the secretary of transportation, rather than to the FEMA director. With the national

(continued)

CASE 3–8 *(continued)*

election only 2–1/2 months away, there was a fear that the president would lose critical electoral votes because of the slow response.

Assessments of the disaster in south Florida generally concluded that it was fortunate that the storm did not score a direct hit on Miami Beach or downtown Miami. It was also fortunate that the keys were spared. Those were considered the most vulnerable areas in the region. Nonetheless, the damage was severe. Despite strong construction standards, building code enforcement had been lax and construction poor, consequently many structures fared far worse than they should have. Experts also noted the patterns of destruction that indicated that tornadoes and fierce updrafts, rather than the hurricane winds themselves, caused much of the damage in some neighborhoods. Better building design would have reduced the level of damage in some cases, but not in all.

---

rather than after. The involvement of nongovernmental organizations, as well as U.S. federal and local agencies, is described in some detail. The participation of the U.S. Department of Defense (DOD) and the U.S. Department of Agriculture (USDA) was important to the U.S. effort. The participation by emergency responders from Miami–Dade County, Florida, was also important. Tipper Gore, the wife of Vice-President Al Gore, surveyed the damage and reported back to President Clinton. The president of the American Red Cross (ARC), Elizabeth Dole, toured the disaster area and helped target ARC assistance.

Hurricane Mitch may give added impetus to a rethinking of how the power of hurricanes is measured. Because of the vulnerability of the population in Honduras and other Central American nations—given the low coastline, the hilly interior, the nature of housing in the area, and the heavy amount of rainfall—there was much more damage than might have been experienced had Mitch made landfall on the Yucatan Peninsula or elsewhere. Much of the damage in Central America was due to heavy rainfall in the hills, which caused massive flooding and landslides.

TORNADOES

There are 800 to 1,000 tornadoes a year in the United States, compared to 50 to 160 in Canada, and they kill 70 to 80 Americans annually (*National Geographic* 1998). Tornadoes occur in other parts of the world, but they are far more common in North America. While tornadoes occur in most parts of the continental United States, they are most common in the so-called "tornado alley" stretching from Texas to Michigan. Other "hot spots" with frequent tornado damage and deaths are in central Arkansas and an area stretching from central Mississippi through northern Alabama and Georgia. The most lethal tornadoes have been part of series that have hit wide stretches of countryside over extended periods of time. For example:

- In 1925, the Great Tri-State Outbreak struck across Missouri, Illinois, and Indiana killing 695 people, including 234 in Murphysboro, Illinois. Twenty-four people were killed in one school.
- In 1932, a series of tornadoes in Alabama killed 268.
- In 1936, a series of tornadoes in Mississippi and Georgia killed 454. Later that same year, a series in Georgia killed 203.
- In 1952, a series of tornadoes in Arkansas, Missouri, and Tennessee killed 208.
- In 1965, a series of tornadoes in Indiana, Illinois, Ohio, Michigan, and Wisconsin killed 271.
- In 1974, a series of storms, spawning at least 148 tornadoes in 13 states and Canada, killed over 400 people, including 350 in Xenia, Ohio.
- In 1985, a series of tornadoes in New York, Pennsylvania, Ohio, and Ontario killed 90.

Warning systems, including networks of tornado watchers, have reduced the number of deaths. The systems have improved tremendously as meteorologists have become better at predicting tornadic conditions, tracking thunderstorms, and using Doppler radar to identify the likely path of severe storms and tornadoes. The increasing use of Doppler radar, which identifies the signature "hook" caused by circular winds, is becoming a familiar topic on weather broadcasts. Meteorologists can pinpoint the location of possible tornadoes and issue warnings to communities that might be directly in their paths without having to issue a broad warning to communities that are not threatened. The new weather radios can issue focused warnings, and in the future, radios and televisions will be equipped with computer chips that can turn them on when weather and other emergency warnings have been issued. Structural mitigation efforts are also paying off. Stronger building codes have reduced the damage to structures not hit directly by tornadoes.

As the descriptions of damage by category on the Fujita tornado scale indicate, mobile homes are particularly vulnerable to even lesser storms. While mobile homes may not be the "natural food" of tornadoes as some

TABLE 3–4	Fujita Tornado Scale
Scale	*Description*
F0:	40–72 mph, chimney damage, tree branches broken
F1:	73–112 mph, mobile homes pushed off foundation or overturned
F2:	113–157 mph, considerable damage, mobile homes demolished, trees uprooted
F3:	158–206 mph, roofs and walls torn down, trains overturned, cars thrown
F4:	207–260 mph, well-constructed walls leveled
F5:	261–318 mph, homes lifted off foundation and carried considerable distances, autos thrown as far as 100 meters
F6:	Over 318 mph

Source: FEMA Web page http://www.fema.gov.

would suggest, they are generally more vulnerable to high winds than permanent structures and are often placed in locations that increase their exposure to storm damage, such as along the crests of hills. Higher standards for manufactured housing located in high wind areas, mandatory use of tie-downs to secure the homes, and greater regulation of the location of such housing are expected to reduce property losses and deaths, as well.

WILDFIRE

There are approximately 100,000 wildfires in the United States per year, most caused by people rather than nature (*National Geographic* 1998). The fires damage or destroy timber, ranch buildings, and, increasingly, subdivisions of homes built in heavily wooded areas. Until the early twentieth century, responsibility for fighting major fires in and around national parks was given to the U.S. Army. That responsibility was transferred to the National Park Service (NPS) when it was created in 1916. The U.S. Forest Service (USFS) provided assistance. By the 1960s, NPS adopted a more flexible fire suppression policy, recognizing the natural role of wildfires.

In 1965, the Boise Interagency Fire Center was created to coordinate and support activities by federal agencies. The center was staffed by NPS, USFS, Bureau of Land Management, Bureau of Indian Affairs, Fish and Wildlife Service, and National Weather Service. To facilitate intergovernmental and interagency cooperation, the National Wildfire Coordinating

CASE 3–9   Palm Sunday Tornado Outbreak of March 27, 1994

On Palm Sunday in March 1994, a series of tornadoes moved across the Southeast. The storms left a path of destruction from north-central Alabama through northern Georgia into the Carolinas. Forty-two people died and over 320 were injured. The property damage estimate was $107 million. The most devastating events were the destruction of the Goshen United Methodist Church in Cherokee County, Alabama, and a swathe of destruction through Pickens County, Georgia.

In Cherokee County, Alabama, an F3 tornado passed just north of the Goshen church causing the roof to collapse on the congregation. Twenty people died and 90 were injured. A warning had been issued 12 minutes before the tornado struck at 11:39 A.M., but the church did not have a National Oceanic and Atmospheric Administration (NOAA) weather radio and the warning was not received. A police officer saw the tornado just before it passed the church, but did not have time to warn the people.

There were two tornado events in Pickens County, Georgia. A mile-wide F3 tornado struck two mobile homes at 3:24 P.M. Family members were gathered for a reunion. Six of the 7 in one mobile home were killed. Seven others in an adjacent mobile home escaped serious injury, although their home was destroyed. Two more people were killed ten minutes later. The Weather Service Field Office had issued a warning 4 minutes before the mobile homes were destroyed, but the family did not have a weather radio and the warning was not received. One other person was killed in Pickens County at about 2:03 P.M.

The Pickens County storms were part of a relatively small system of supercells that had traveled 200 miles from east-central Alabama. The *Atlanta Journal* reported that a state employee in Rabun, in northeast Georgia, found a canceled check from a destroyed mobile home in Piedmont, Alabama, 130 miles away. The NOAA Weather Wire Service warnings did not reach many local emergency managers and law enforcement officials in time, in part because some were relying on their Law Enforcement Telecommunications System and not monitoring the weather radio. The fact that the storms started on a Sunday morning also made it difficult to get storm spotters into the field early. Many radio and television stations were slow to activate the Emergency Broadcast System because they were relying on manual reports from the National Weather Service, telephone calls from local emergency management

(continued)

CASE 3–9 *(continued)*

agencies, or a special announcement from the AP wire service. Automated messages would have been received much quicker and warnings could have been issued earlier. Still, the warning system saved lives.

A Disaster Survey Team was dispatched to assess the effectiveness of the warning system. They also investigated the destruction and concluded, among other things, that:

- All of those in the Goshen church might have survived the storm had they taken shelter in a hallway;
- Fifteen of the eighteen people killed in Georgia were in mobile homes;
- Many of those who survived in damaged homes did so because they took shelter in crawl spaces, center hallways, or bathrooms;
- The weather radars and other equipment worked very well, even though the storm system did not have the "classic" features associated with a tornado outbreak;
- The warnings might have been more effective if they had been more specific and emphatic about the danger to communities in the path of the storms;
- The warnings should have been issued earlier because of the likelihood that there would be delays in communicating them to communities;
- The media could have activated the Emergency Broadcast System sooner had the National Weather Service warnings been received directly, by radio; and
- Radio and television stations, public safety agencies, and other essential components of the warning system are understaffed and slower to react on Sunday mornings (NOAA 1994).

Group (NWCG) was established in 1976. NWCG created standards for the training of wildland firefighters and adopted the National Interagency Incident Management System, based on the Incident Command System (ICS) used by fire departments in the United States (Moskow-McKenzie and Freemuth 1990). ICS was created after a series of wildfires in California in 1970 demonstrated the need for better mechanisms to coordinate multiagency responses to emergencies.

The training of firefighters and the command system for fighting wildfires became issues in 1994 when fourteen, ten men and four women, died fighting a blaze on Storm King Mountain in Colorado. It was the worst wildfire disaster since a dozen smokejumpers were killed in Mann Gulch, Montana, in 1949. The South Canyon fire, as it is called, surprised a group of firefighters when a relatively small blaze turned into a windblown inferno, overtaking them as they tried to scramble to safety on the rocky mountainside. The tragedy was all the more compelling because 9 of the casualties were from the Prineville Hot Shots, a twenty-member firefighting team from a small town in Oregon. National attention was focused on the community of firefighters, who move from fire to fire across the United States each year, and official attention focused on the adequacy of training and supervision (Adler et al. 1994).

In 1988, wildfires ravaged Yellowstone National Park and surrounding forestland. National attention was focused on the fires as they consumed thousands of acres of parkland and threatened Old Faithful Lodge. The fires raised questions about Park Service policies of using natural fires and "prescribed" fires to lessen the buildup of combustible materials and, thus, lessen the likelihood of large, uncontrollable fires. Critics argued that putting out too many fires may have caused the buildup of dead trees and underbrush. However, under pressure from Congress, the Park Service put a temporary moratorium on such fires, requiring a more proactive fire suppression policy (Moskow-McKenzie and Freemuth 1990). While experts generally maintain the necessity for controlled burns to prevent large conflagrations, the policy is still controversial. Interestingly, the Yellowstone fires were finally extinguished more by the precipitation and cooler temperatures of the approaching winter than by the efforts of the firefighters. Property owners near national parks and forests generally oppose policies that might threaten their timber, buildings, and cattle and resist pressures to restrict building in high-risk areas. Also, development along the boundaries and within woodlands increases the risk of fire from electrical problems, brush burning, and other sources.

The risk of wildfire is not restricted to America's forestlands. In 1991, the Berkeley–Oakland Hills fire burned 3,300 homes overlooking San Francisco Bay and caused over $2 billion in losses. In 1993 and 1996 and, more recently, in 1998, there have been major wildfires in Malibu and elsewhere in southern California that have destroyed homes and businesses. In 1998, Mexico, Texas, and Florida experienced major fires that required hundreds of firefighters and took weeks to contain, as well. And, in 1999, Florida was again fighting major wildfires with some crossing the border into Georgia.

Several issues have been raised by wildfire losses. First, if people are going to be permitted to build in areas with significant histories of wildfire,

CASE 3–10 The Berkeley–Oakland Hills Fire of 1991

On October 20, 1991, fire broke out in an affluent residential area overlooking San Francisco Bay. As the fire spread, it became a firestorm, leaping eight-lane highways, sparing some homes as the wind pushed the flames on an erratic course. By the time that the fire was extinguished, approximately 1,500 acres were burned, 25 people were dead, and 3,000 homes were destroyed. There were approximately $2 billion in insured losses and over $44 million in costs to public agencies involved in the response.

The Berkeley–Oakland Hills area had experienced serious fires since the 1920s, at least, and the risk of fire on the heavily wooded hillside was known. Several years of drought had dried out the trees and brush and homes were surrounded by highly flammable vegetation. Many of the homes had been built in the 1920s, and many were of unique design with expensive furnishings. Narrow, winding streets slowed the fire trucks and low water pressure, fragile old water mains, and incompatible hydrant connectors further slowed the response. Coordination of the firefighting was made the more difficult because of differences in emergency radio frequencies.

The victims were largely affluent and had little need for government-sponsored emergency shelter or other disaster assistance. They often could begin rebuilding as soon as fire officials gave the "all clear" and moved their trucks and hoses. Indeed, some were seeking building permits before the ruins of their old homes quit smoldering. The city of Oakland hired a consulting firm to assist with the recovery process and created the Community Restoration Development Center as a clearinghouse for building permits. View management became a central concern very early in the recovery process. As new homes were built, some blocked neighbors' views of the bay, particularly when new setback requirements necessitated moving the structures away from their old locations on the property or the new structures were taller than the old.

Nicholas Petris, a state senator, was among the victims and he sponsored the bill to create the Statewide Emergency Management System (SEMS). The Petris Bill of 1992 was designed to facilitate intergovernmental, multi-jurisdictional disaster responses. The local response was an effort to improve fire protection. A citizen group helped city and utility officials to create an assessment district to upgrade and expand the water system (Sutphen 1996; Jordan 1998).

how can they be encouraged (or even forced) to mitigate the risk. Homeowners frequently surround their homes with highly flammable landscaping. Shade trees overhanging roofs, bushes next to houses, dry grasses and brush near structures, and building materials that are not resistant, or not as resistant as they should be, to fire all contribute to the hazard. Second, what kinds of policies should be adopted to reduce the risk of fire in wooded and grassy areas. In Kansas and other states with tall grass prairies, grasslands are periodically burned to reduce the likelihood of larger, uncontrollable fires that might threaten livestock, farms, and communities. The Yellowstone National Park fire in 1988 raised the issue in terms of woodlands. NPS had a policy of using prescribed fires to reduce the buildup of underbrush, dead trees, leaves, and other materials to reduce the fire hazard and to encourage new tree growth. Fires caused by lightning, accident, and arson were generally contained, but not necessarily extinguished if they served the same purpose as the prescribed fires. However, despite the arguments of scientists, there was a loud public outcry when the fires threatened the historic lodge next to Old Faithful geyser and other facilities. Opposition to the policy of using prescribed fires also developed when fires threatened private property along the fringes of the park. The Park Service was encouraged to reconsider its policy. Similarly, the use of prescribed fires in the state of Florida became controversial as developers built subdivisions in wildfire areas. As a consequence, the buildup of flammable materials fed the fires in 1998 that threatened a wide area of east central Florida. While firefighters did a heroic job protecting homes and businesses, the state's tourism industry suffered millions of dollars in losses because potential visitors assumed that the fire was much more widespread.

SNOW AND ICE STORMS, HEAT WAVES, AVALANCHES, LANDSLIDES, AND LESSER HAZARDS

Heat waves typically do not last more than a week or two. Heat-related deaths in the United States generally range from 175 to 200 persons per year. However, in 1901, over 9,500 people died from heat in the Midwest. In 1980, over 1,200 Americans died (Weather Channel 1998). In 1988, a major drought in the central United States brought heat that directly or indirectly killed an estimated 5,000 to 10,000 people (*National Geographic* 1998). Another Midwest heat wave in 1995 killed over 1,000 people, including over 450 people in Chicago (Weather Channel 1998). Particularly vulnerable were the elderly who lived without air-conditioning and did not open windows for fear of intruders. Young children left in automobiles, joggers and other athletes exercising with too little regard for dangerously high temperatures, and those working construction and other jobs out in the heat were also highly vulnerable.

Windstorms are relatively common and cause considerable damage. New

CASE 3–11 The Washington State Inaugural Day Windstorm of 1993

High wind warnings were issued for western Washington on January 19, 1993. On the morning of January 20, local and tribal governments were reporting high winds with gusts up to 90 miles per hour, and damage reports began coming in. Power lines were downed and buildings were damaged. Emergency operations centers were opened by city and county governments and by the Washington State Emergency Management Division. By midafternoon, as many as 750,000 homes were without power. Downed power lines were blocking roads, and private utilities were estimating that it would take as long as a week for power to be restored to all. Snow blocked highways through the mountains, further complicating the emergency operations (Washington Emergency Management Divison n.d.).

As power was being restored, melting snows caused rivers to rise and warnings were issued for thirteen rivers in western Washington. The National Guard distributed sandbags and generators. Fortunately, there was little flooding and little property damage. Recovery efforts were stepped up with assistance given to the state insurance commissioner and damage assessment teams. On January 28, the state emergency management agency ended the state of emergency (Washington Emergency Management Division n.d.).

Five people were killed, 870,000 customers were without power, 110 single-family homes were destroyed and 976 were damaged, 584 businesses were damaged, public facilities (including hospitals and shelters) were without backup power, avalanches and flooding stranded motorists, and there was extensive power line damage. The crisis provided an opportunity to assess the preparedness of state and local agencies and community groups so that weaknesses could be addressed (Washington Emergency Management Division n.d.).

England, in particular, has experienced severe winter storms with strong winds, Nor'easters. A 1962 storm raged for five days along the northeastern coast bringing damaging winds and flooding. In 1991, the "Halloween Storm" damaged over 1,000 homes along the eastern seaboard (Weather Channel 1998). In 1993, the so-called Storm of the Century shut down airports, brought down trees and power lines, and damaged homes from Florida to Maine. In November 1998, a similar storm moved across the plains, bringing extremely high winds and cold temperatures from the Dakotas eastward. In Chicago, the gusts were so strong that they blew bricks and roofing off buildings.

Snowstorms can paralyze cities, as well. The Blizzard of 1888 brought snow to the eastern United States from Tennessee to New England. New York City received almost 2 feet of snow, White Plains received almost 3 feet, and cities farther north received over 4 feet of snow. Bitter cold and strong winds caused over 400 deaths. A blizzard in the northeastern United States in 1958 killed 171, and one in the southwestern United States in 1967 killed 51. In Chicago, a 1967 blizzard brought 2 feet of snow in a little over 24 hours. The city was paralyzed and O'Hare International Airport was shut down for 3 days. In 1969, New York City and Boston experienced a similar catastrophe, with each receiving over 2 feet of snow. Major blizzards in 1978 and 1983 again paralyzed cities along the East Coast. While snowstorms bring cold temperatures and make travel difficult, there are more serious consequences. Motorists may be stranded along roadways, residents may be snowbound without heat or food, power lines may be cut, roofs may collapse from the weight of snow, and elderly residents may suffer heart attacks trying to shovel snow. Officials in Wyoming and other western states block off Interstate highways and other major roads to prevent motorists from becoming stranded and to reduce the risk to law enforcement officers who are responsible for patrolling the highways. Street clearance and snow removal can become very important political issues, particularly in large cities. The 1969 blizzard in New York City is still referred to as the "Lindsay storm," since Mayor John Lindsay lost his bid for reelection because city crews were slow to clear the streets (Weather Channel 1998).

Ice storms, too, are common in the United States. In January of 1973, Atlanta and north Georgia experienced up to 4 inches of ice. Downed power lines left 300,000 residents without power for as long as a week. In 1994, a very large storm wreaked havoc from Louisiana to Virginia. Communities can usually cope with snowstorms, although residents of the deep South may not have warm clothing for periods of extreme cold and may not even have heated homes, but ice storms can bring life to a virtual standstill. Fortunately, ice storms are relatively uncommon, and schools and businesses often shut down when there is a high probability of an ice storm. However, Texas has a long history of "blue northers," in which cold fronts moving south from the Rockies bring freezing rain and sleet (Weather Channel 1998), and other parts of the United States have similar histories. In early 1998, an ice storm in the northeastern United States and eastern Canada left approximately 4 million people without power. Extreme cold made it dangerous for families to remain in their homes without electricity, even if they had fireplaces and kerosene heaters.

Droughts often have devastating effects on agriculture, causing millions of dollars in crop and cattle losses, and on communities that may find themselves with too little water for drinking, washing, and watering lawns. Businesses may have to be shut down to conserve water. The "Dust Bowl" of the 1930s affected

CASE 3–12 The Southeast Ice Storm of 1994
In February 1994, a severe ice storm struck the Southeast. As warm moist air
overran a near-stationary cold front, an unusually large ice storm formed. The
storm moved from the west on February 9, and then spread into Tennessee,
Mississippi, and Alabama. In northern Mississippi, the ice was 6 inches deep,
and there was flooding in some areas as the ice melted. By February 13, the
storm had moved into North and South Carolina, Virginia, and Kentucky.
Heavy ice brought down power lines, leaving hundred of thousands of customers without electricity. Power company officials called the ice storm the worst
on record, and some customers were without power for as long as a month.
Tree limbs and even whole trees blocked roadways and damaged homes and
automobiles (Lott and Ross 1994).

virtually all the central United States. Precious topsoil became blowing dust,
creating clouds that choked people and cattle, and covered crops. Residents
of Stratford, Texas, were suffocated in a 1935 storm. The young and the
elderly, in particular, were made ill or killed by the pervasive dusting.
Droughts associated with La Niña, El Niño's sibling, are a growing concern.
Changing climatic patterns have caused major droughts in central Australia,
just as they have caused catastrophic flooding in Chile and other parts of
South and North America. Predicting drought, as well as larger climatic
changes, is a high priority. Some areas of the United States are already
experiencing droughts and some are experiencing periodic water shortages
that are affecting development. The regulation of lawn watering is common
in some communities.

Sinkholes in Florida, avalanches in the Rockies, and lesser storms (e.g.,
lightning storms) can all have catastrophic effects, as well, but they are
generally more localized than the major disaster types discussed above. Local
officials commonly include such events in their disaster planning, depending
upon the frequency of their occurrence. Communities in western Colorado and
elsewhere in the Rockies may have a significant risk of avalanches. Ski resorts
commonly have programs to monitor avalanche zones, warn skiers and snow
mobilers, and reduce the buildup of unstable snow, as well as have search-and-
rescue capabilities. Explosives are often used to encourage avalanches at times
when hillsides and valleys are clear of hikers and skiers.

The International Scale of Avalanche Hazard Ratings lists risk as low
(green), moderate (yellow), considerable (orange), high (red), or extreme
(black), generally with less risk from naturally caused avalanches than from
human-triggered ones. While avalanches causing multiple deaths are relatively rare in the United States, there have been recent tragedies elsewhere

in the world. For example, in 1996, 35 people were killed in Kashmir when an avalanche hit a small village. In 1997, 100 were buried by snow, ice, and rocks as they walked along a highway in northern Afghanistan, and up to 46 were killed in vehicles on a highway in Tajikistan. Groups of soldiers and police were killed in separate avalanches in India and Turkey in 1998. By far the most common fatalities are hikers, climbers, and skiers. In 1998, 6 backcountry skiers were killed in British Columbia and 11 snowshoers in a group of schoolchildren on holiday were killed in the French Alps. In both cases, there was warning of the danger (Colorado Avalanche Information Center 1998). In 1999, unusually heavy snows in the Alps stranded about 60,000 in their homes or hotels in Switzerland, 20,000 in Austria, and tens of thousands elsewhere. Avalanches killed dozens in resort communities in Austria and prompted an evacuation to prevent further deaths (Drozdiak 1999). Climatic change may well increase snowfall and speed snowmelt, thus creating more avalanche and flood hazards, and monitoring systems are all the more important.

Sinkholes may be more difficult to predict, but because of increased property loss in areas prone to sinkholes, more attention is being given to the problem, along with increased monitoring of areas that may be susceptible to collapse. Florida, Texas, and southeastern Minnesota are particularly prone to sinkholes because they have limestone or other soluble rock, karst, formations. When groundwater levels drop, caverns may be formed, and underground rivers or streams can create caverns or tunnels that then can collapse. Cars, houses, and roads have been swallowed up. Because sinkholes are difficult to identify before they appear, care has to be taken in building roads, parking lots, and buildings. Sinkholes also appear when underground water pipes burst and the soil is washed away. Some cities—Atlanta, for example—have serious sinkhole problems because their water systems are old and poorly maintained.

Landslides can be caused by earthquakes, floods, volcanoes, and other natural disasters. On average, they cause $1.2 billion in property losses and 25 deaths each year. They occur in all U.S. states but particularly in the Appalachian region, which has soils with high clay content (causing sliding), on the Great Plains, and in the Rocky Mountains (where slopes are steep, rainfall may be heavy, and vegetation may be burned off by wildfires). The problem has been severe enough for the U.S. Geological Survey to implement the National Landslide Hazards Program (NLHP) to study the causes of landslides and develop mitigation measures. The eruption of Mount St. Helens in 1980 caused a tremendous landslide and the Northridge earthquake in 1994 caused thousands of smaller landslides in the mountains.

CASE 3–13 The San Leandro Landslide of 1998

San Leandro is a community of about 75,000 residents in the East Bay, between Oakland and San Jose. It is close to the Hayward fault, as well as to lesser faults. Heavy rains and other weather phenomena were anticipated as a result of El Niño, and the city initiated a program to prepare. When the rains arrived in February 1998 and flooding began, the city activated its emergency management system, declared a local emergency, and monitored areas that might be prone to landslides. The rains continued. When a homeowner asked city inspectors to examine a hill above and below his property in the Bay-O-Vista area, small breaks were found. As the day wore on, the breaks became larger and more building officials were brought in to assess the problem. There were twelve homes at the bottom of the hill and twelve at the top (Lunsford 1998).

By the next morning, it was apparent that the hill was moving. Residents were evacuated from three homes and the residents of three other homes were warned that evacuation was recommended. The rain continued and the movement of the hill accelerated. City officials suggested moving homes and contracted to have them moved for the homeowners. During a break in the rain, two homes were moved approximately 20 feet away from the hillside. By March 2, the rain abated and the emergency was called off. However, in May, the hill was still moving and was threatening the relocated homes and other city infrastructure. City officials took a very proactive role in protecting private property, and the city is still seeking financial assistance from state and federal agencies to fund a mitigation program so as to anchor the hillside with shearing pins and prevent further movement (Lunsford 1998).

A landslide in Thistle, Utah, in 1983 blocked two state highways and a railroad track, and caused a lake to flood the town and a railyard. The slide caused $400 million in losses. Heavy rainfall in the San Francisco Bay area in February 1998 caused landslides and mudslides in many communities, and the soggy ground was expected to cause slides several months after the storms (U.S. Geological Survey 1998b). Recommended mitigation measures include avoiding highly hazardous areas; building structures to stop or divert slides; and reducing the slope, removing unstable materials, or stabilizing the slope (California Department of Conservation 1998).

CONCLUSION

Natural disasters are common occurrences, albeit more common in some parts of the United States than others. Fortunately, the loss of life and property is usually small and, because of mitigation efforts, is getting smaller. In some measure, the good fortune is due to our efforts to reduce risk. Public awareness of hazards, scientific and technical knowledge about hazards and how to reduce them, and the technology and practice of emergency management are reducing the vulnerability of communities to disasters. However, as we have learned in the 1990s, natural disasters are not predictable and our exposure is growing as population concentrates along coastlines and development proceeds with too little attention to appropriate mitigation measures.

The 1998 fires in central Florida highlighted the problem of unregulated development. While the major cause of the fires was a severe drought, building in wooded areas and permitting highly flammable landscaping increased the risk. Clearly, the "lessons learned" from past disasters are not all being heeded. One has only to drive along the U.S. Gulf Coast to see the decay of mitigation efforts. Buildings raised on pilings after Hurricane Camille and other catastrophic storms, to protect them from future storm surges, now have new walls as owners enclose the pilings to create storage areas and garages. When the next hurricane makes landfall, the new walls will provide resistance to the storm surge and the buildings may be pushed over. Similarly, in the hills and canyons of southern California, residents still plant highly flammable bushes and trees close to their homes and thereby increase the vulnerability of their property to wildfire. Residents in coastal communities still build homes too close to the shoreline. Motorists attempt to ford streams even when flooding is imminent. But, the hazards are better understood and the means to reduce risk are more available.

The declining numbers of casualties and property losses in the United States in recent decades may also be due to simple luck. Hurricane Andrew narrowly missed a direct hit on the most heavily populated areas of south Florida. The Loma Prieta and Northridge earthquakes did not occur during rush hour when there would have been thousands more motorists on the highways and bridges and thousands more workers in office buildings and garages. Mount St. Helens's eruption principally affected a sparsely popu-lated area of Washington State, although the ashfall significantly affected cities and towns over several states. Our recent disasters could have been much worse, in other words. At the same time, other nations have suffered massive loss of life and property. The estimated 10,000 deaths in the Caribbean and Central America due to Hurricane Mitch in 1998 provide grim reminder of the possibilities. The floods and landslides caused by Hurricane Mitch in Honduras and Nicaragua were due to the heavy rainfall and a hilly terrain prone to flooding. While the population was all too exposed to flooding, particularly in the valleys along the rivers, the amount of rainfall was so unusual as to be virtually unpredictable. The unusual rainfall in the upper Midwest in 1992–1993 that caused floods from the Dakotas to Louisiana was a similar case. Sometimes the unexpected happens.

Sometimes it may be possible to prevent or reduce the effects of natural disaster. More often, however, it may be easier to get out of nature's way. Buyouts of flood-prone property, regulation of development along hazardous coastlines and near volcanic hazards, spot zoning in areas with high risk of seismic activity and liquifaction, stringent land-use regulations in areas prone to landslides and other movements of the earth, public education concerning wildfire hazards, and similar actions can be effective mitigation measures. But they cannot remove all risk.

DISCUSSION QUESTIONS

1. Should the federal and state governments regulate development on the barrier islands to discourage the expansion of resident populations and any activities that may reduce the natural barriers to tidal surges provided by sand dunes, vegetation, and wetlands?
2. Should search-and-rescue agencies decline to help hikers, climbers, surfers, and others who put themselves in danger when the operations may endanger the lives of the search and rescue personnel? Should governments charge victims for the cost of search-and-rescue operations when they knowingly put themselves in danger?
3. Should the government provide disaster assistance to people who choose to live on floodplains, near volcanoes, in wildfire areas, along beachfronts prone to storm surges, and on seismic fault lines?
4. What should FEMA and other disaster agencies do, if anything, to address the needs of people (i.e., the poor and the homeless) who were without adequate shelter, food, and other necessities prior to the disaster?

REFERENCES

Adler, Jerry; Karen Springen; Sherry Keene-Osborn; Patricia King; and Debra Woodruff. 1994. "Blowup." *Newsweek* (July 18): 28–31.

Bolin, Robert, and Lois Stanford. 1998. "The Northridge Earthquake: Community-Based Approaches to Unmet Recovery Needs." *Disasters* 22, no. 1 (March): 21–38.

California Department of Conservation. 1998. "Mitigation of Earthquake-Induced Landslide Hazards." http://anaheim-landslide.com/mitigation1.htm.

Center for Coastal and Land-Margin Research. 1998. "Science for Society: Impact of Tsunamis on Oregon Coastal Communities." http://www.ccalmr.ogi.edu/projects/ oregonian.

Colorado Avalanche Information Center, Web site. www.caicstate.co.us.

Drozdiak, William. 1999. "Growing Wave of Snow Disasters Worst in Decades in Alps." *Atlanta Journal-Constitution* (February 25): A13.

Ewert, John W.; C. Dan Miller; James W. Hendley, II; and Peter H. Stauffer. 1997. *Mobile Response Team Saves Lives in Volcano Crises*. U.S. Geological Survey Fact Sheet 064–97. http://vulcan.wr.usgs.gov.

Federal Emergency Management Agency/National Flood Insurance Program. *NFIP* (brochure).

Federal Interagency Floodplain Management Task Force. 1991. *Floodplain Management in the United States: An Assessment Report, Executive Summary*. Washington, DC: Task Force.

Fuller, Myron L. (1912) 1988. *The New Madrid Earthquake*. U.S. Geological Survey Bulletin 494, as reprinted, 1988. Washington, DC: Government Printing Office, 1912.

General Accounting Office. 1990. *Loma Prieta Earthquake: Collapse of the Bay Bridge and the Cypress Viaduct*. Washington, DC: USGAO, GAO/RCED-990–177, June.

Godschalk, David R.; Timothy Beatley; Philip Berke; David J. Brower; and Edward J. Kaiser. 1999. *Natural Hazard Mitigation: Recasting Disaster Policy and Planning*. Washington, DC: Island Press.

Greeson, Cary. 1998. "Hurricane Andrew." Paper prepared for Public Administration 836, Emergency Management, Georgia State University, Atlanta, Spring.

Gruntfest, Eve. 1996. "Twenty Years Later: What We Have Learned Since the Big Thompson Flood." *Proceedings of a Symposium on the Big Thompson Flood, Boulder, Colorado, July 13–15, 1976*. Boulder: University of Colorado, Natural Hazards Research and Information Center, Special Publication 16.

Gruntfest, Eve, and Marc Weber. 1998. "Internet and Emergency Management: Prospects for the Future." *International Journal of Mass Emergencies and Disasters* 16 (March): 55–72.

Jordan, Mary. 1998. "The Berkeley-Oakland Hills Fire." Paper prepared for Public Administration 836, Emergency Management, Georgia State University, Atlanta, Spring.

Lott, Neal. 1993. "The Summer of 1993: Flooding in the Midwest and Drought in the Southeast." National Climatic Data Center, National Oceanic and Atmospheric Administration, http://www.ncdc.noaa.gov/cgi-win/wwcgi. dll?WWNolosProductPB-012.

Lott, Neal, and Tom Ross. 1994. "1994 Weather in the Southeast: The February Ice Storm and the July Flooding," National Climatic Data Center, National Oceanic and Atmospheric Administration, http://www.ncdc.noaa.gov/cgi-win/wwcgi.dll? WWNolosProductPB-015.

Lunsford, Dan S. 1998. "The San Leandro Landslide: A Community's Response." *Disaster Recovery Journal* (Fall): 14–16.

Morrow, Betty Hearn. 1997. "Disaster in the First Person." In *Hurricane Andrew: Ethnicity, Gender and the Sociology of Disasters*, eds. Walter Gillis Peacock, Betty Hearn Morrow, and Hugh Gladwin, 1–19. London: Routledge Press.

Moskow-McKenzie, Diane, and John C. Freemuth. 1990. "Wildfire Hazards." In *Handbook of Emergency Management,* eds. William L. Waugh, Jr., and Ronald John Hy, 129–147. Westport, CT: Greenwood.

National Geographic Society. 1998. "Natural Hazards of North America" (Map). July.

National Oceanic and Atmospheric Administration, U.S. Department of Commerce. 1994. *National Disaster Survey Report: Southeastern United States Palm Sunday Tornado Outbreak of March 27, 1994*. Silver Spring, MD: National Weather Service, NOAA, August.

National Wildlife Federation. 1998. *Higher Ground*. Washington, DC: NWF.

Nuttli, Otto W. 1983. "1886 Charleston, South Carolina, Earthquake Revisited." In *Proceedings of Conference XX: A Workshop on "The 1886 Charleston, South Carolina, Earthquake and Its Implications for Today," Charleston, S.C., May 23–26, 1983*, 44–50. Washington, DC: U.S. Geological Survey.

Pacific Tsunami Museum. 1998. "Frequently Asked Questions" and "Archives." http://planet-hawaii.com/tsunami/faq.htm.

Reed, Ed. 1998. "Pierce County, Washington, Preparation for Mt. Rainier Eruption." Presentation at the National Conference of the American Society for Public Administration, Seattle, WA, May 11.

Riad, Jasmin; William L. Waugh, Jr.; and Fran H. Norris. 1999. "The Psychology of Evacuation and Policy Design." In *Handbook of Crisis and Emergency Management*, ed. Ali Farazmand. New York: Marcel Dekker, forthcoming.

Simpson, Robert H., and Herbert Riehl. 1981. *The Hurricane and Its Impact*. Baton Rouge: Louisiana State University Press.

Sokolowski, Thomas J. 1998. "The Great Alaskan Earthquake and Tsunamis of 1964." West Coast and Alaska Tsunami Warning Center, Palmer, Alaska, http://www.alaska.net/atwc/64quake.htm.

Street, Ronald, and Otto Nuttli. 1984. "The Central Mississippi Valley Earthquakes of 1811–1812." In *Proceedings of the Symposium on "The New Madrid Seismic Zone," Reston, Virginia, November 26, 1984*, 33–63. Washington, DC: U.S. Geological Survey.

Sutphen, Sandra. 1996. "California Wildfires: How Integrated Emergency Management Succeeds and Fails." In *Disaster Management in the U.S. and Canada*, eds. Richard T. Sylves and William L. Waugh, Jr., 161–188. Springfield, IL: Charles C. Thomas.

Toner, Mike. 1986. "Quake Hit Charleston in 1886—Will It Strike Again?" *The Atlanta Journal/Constitution* (August 31): A1, A12.

Uphaus, Mallion. 1998. "Emergency Management for a Mt. Rainier Volcanic Event." Presentation at the National Conference of the American Society for Public Administration, Seattle, WA, May 11.

U.S. Geological Survey. 1998a. "The July 17, 1998 Papua New Guinea Tsunami." http://walrus.wr.usgs.gov/docs/tsunami/PNGhome.html.

————. 1998b. "The National Landslide Hazards Program." http://landslides.usgs.gov/html_files/landslides/program.shtml.

Washington, State of, Emergency Management Division. n.d. "Inaugural Day Windstorm Summary." Olympia, WA: State of Washington.

Waugh, William L., Jr. 1990a. "Hurricanes." In *Handbook of Emergency Management: Policies and Programs for Dealing with Major Hazards and Disasters*, eds. William L. Waugh, Jr., and Ronald John Hy, 61–80. Westport, CT: Greenwood.

————. 1990b. "Volcanic Hazards." In *Handbook of Emergency Management: Policies and Programs for Dealing with Major Hazards and Disasters*, eds. William L. Waugh, Jr., and Ronald John Hy, 52–60. Westport, CT: Greenwood.

Weather Channel. 1998. "Weather Channel Encyclopedia." http://www.weather.com.

Wolfe, Ed. 1998. "USGS Preparation for a Mt. Rainier Eruption." Presentation at the National Conference of the American Society for Public Administration, Seattle, WA, May 11.

APPENDIX 3–1 U.S. Agency for International Development (USAID)
Bureau for Humanitarian Response (BHR) Office
of U.S. Foreign Disaster Assistance (OFDA)
Hurricane Mitch Fact Sheet #21, December 4, 1998

Background

On October 24 Atlantic Tropical Storm Mitch was upgraded to a hurricane
that developed into one of the strongest and most damaging storms to ever hit
the Caribbean and Central America. At its height on October 26 and 27, the
hurricane had sustained winds of 180 mph and dumped heavy rains over
Central America. Although the winds diminished as Hurricane Mitch traveled
inland over Honduras on October 30, the storm continued to produce torrential
rains, reaching a rate of more than 4 inches per hour, which caused
catastrophic floods and landslides throughout the region. After its slow,
destructive march north and west across Honduras and Guatemala, Mitch
dissipated over southeastern Mexico but briefly regained tropical storm
strength as it moved northeasterly across Mexico's Yucatan Peninsula, the
Gulf of Mexico and southern Florida. By November 5 all tropical storm
warnings were discontinued as Mitch's remnants tracked out into the
Atlantic. Prior to Mitch making landfall, USAID/OFDA prepositioned
assets throughout the region along the storm's forecasted course, and
quickly launched its emergency relief efforts as the hurricane passed
overland. The USAID/OFDA Disaster Assistance Response Team (DART)
was established to coordinate the U.S. Government relief effort for Central
America. Senior Regional Advisor and DART leader Paul Bell has managed the DART personnel and its operations in Belize, Costa Rica, El
Salvador, Guatemala, Honduras and Nicaragua from the USAID/OFDA
Regional Office at the U.S. Embassy in San Jose, Costa Rica.

USG Assistance

On November 5, President Clinton announced a $70 million U.S. Government
(USG) assistance package for Central America in response to Hurricane Mitch.
This package has been augmented and now totals $263 million, to be channeled
largely through USAID, the Department of Defense (DOD), and the U.S.
Department of Agriculture (USDA). Of this package, $30 million in assistance

will be provided by USAID's Office of Foreign Disaster Assistance (OFDA), $35 million by USAID/Food for Peace (USAID/FFP), $130 million by DOD, $63 million by USDA, and the remaining $5 million will be for development assistance and micro-enterprise credits. The assistance by USAID will provide immediate disaster relief, including health and water/sanitation needs, food, shelter, and other emergency relief commodities as well as airlift support and logistics. USAID/OFDA assistance to date, described below, is part of this overall package, which is being closely coordinated with DOD.

Honduras

Storm Impacts

Honduras suffered the brunt of Hurricane Mitch. After being stalled for more than two days off the country's northern coast, the storm traveled inland during October 30 and 31. Extensive wind damage and devastating floods occurred nationwide, but particularly on the northern seaboard and in the Bay Islands. As of December 1, the National Emergency Committee of Honduras (CONEH) reported that 5,657 persons were killed, 8,052 were missing, 11,762 were injured while approximately 1.9 million were affected. The U.N. Office for the Coordination of Humanitarian Affairs (OCHA) estimated at least 70,000 houses had been damaged and the USAID/OFDA DART estimated that more than 92 bridges had been damaged or destroyed. Damage to the nation's infrastructure isolated entire communities which made access by emergency aid workers extremely difficult and it hampered efforts to supply the larger cities with food, water and other essentials.

Immediate USG Response

On October 27, the U.S. Ambassador to Honduras James F. Creagan declared a disaster due to the effects of Hurricane Mitch. USAID/OFDA responded immediately by providing a total of $125,000 to the USAID Mission in Honduras for the local purchase and transport of critical relief supplies, including food, simple cooking stoves, blankets, and medical supplies. USAID/OFDA also provided a total of $750,000 for the deployment of DOD aircraft to assist in aerial assessments, search and rescue operations, and delivery of relief supplies. Initially grounded by poor visibility, the USAID/OFDA-funded aircraft missions have been operating since November 1.

As of December 3, 9 Black Hawk (UH-60 or MH-60) and 6 Chinook (CH-47) helicopters, and 2 C-27 and 1 C-12 cargo planes were distributing relief supplies from Soto Cano air base. By December 3, the DOD aircraft had flown 293 helicopter missions and 238 cargo plane airlifts. These flights carried 2,264,000 pounds of food, 117,900 gallons of water and 862,900 pounds of medicine, supplies and equipment. The flights also transported 4,132 people to medical centers. USAID/OFDA has deployed a total of 1,038 rolls of plastic sheeting, 32 10,000–liter water bladders, 25,500 five-gallon water jugs, and 1,004 body bags to Honduras at a total estimated cost of $523,999 including transport. The first airlift carrying USAID/OFDA relief supplies arrived at La Ceiba on October 31, the second arrived at Soto Cano airbase on November 1, the third airlift arrived at Soto Cano on November 2, the fourth arrived at Soto Cano on November 9, and the fifth arrived at Tegucigalpa on November 22. Supplemental relief commodities were transported by DOD on November 9 and 10.

To date, USAID/OFDA has provided $400,000 to the USAID Mission for the local purchase of food and emergency supplies, and for other response activities. Additionally, USAID/OFDA provided $800,000 to the USAID Mission, which granted funding to resident Private Voluntary Organizations (PVOs) in Honduras for the purchase and delivery of local relief supplies. USAID/OFDA has also purchased and airlifted plastic food storage bags from Costa Rica that will allow for the distribution of critical food stocks to 100,000 families in Honduras. USAID/OFDA provided $2 million to USAID in Tegucigalpa to fund projects to repair the nation's water supply system. On November 20, USAID/OFDA provided $2,133,000 through USAID in Tegucigalpa to CARE. This grant is to assist approximately 70,000 families for up to four months with basic livelihood needs such as: sanitation and health, agriculture, construction, food and shelter. On November 25, USAID/OFDA provided an additional $3,164,000 to USAID in Tegucigalpa to support grants with non-governmental organizations (NGOs) for disaster response projects that will provide assistance in the following sectors: water/sanitation, emergency shelter, housing, roads and bridges, medicine, food, hygiene, and agriculture.

USAID/OFDA had disaster specialists on the ground in Honduras since October 27. A total of fifteen DART members from USAID, Miami-Dade County Fire Rescue Department (Miami-Dade), and the U.S. Forest Service (USFS) operated out of Tegucigalpa, San Pedro Sula, La Ceiba, Danli, Choluteca and Soto Cano airbase. USAID/OFDA DART personnel in Honduras assisted CONEH's Emergency Operations Center, conducted field assessments, coordinated aircraft and transport logistics, and performed other disaster relief activities.

Assessment Reporting and Recovery

USAID/OFDA DART reports that people are beginning to move out of shelters and return home. The staple crops did not sustain as much damage as the cash crops because the former are grown on higher ground. Because staple crops were relatively undamaged, there is an ample supply of local food on the market. In terms of infrastructure, the water systems and the roads networks are in need of repair. Hurricane Mitch devastated the Honduran road network and in the early days of the response, air transport was the only means to transport emergency relief supplies, including food and non-food items. The USG used the air assets of DOD for emergency rescue and to provide access to areas and people that were isolated. Now, however, the response has entered into the next phase. Over 90 percent of the bridges that were damaged by Mitch are now passable with provisional repairs or by-passes. Road access has improved dramatically, and all areas to which DOD had been flying relief supplies over the past weeks (La Ceiba, the Bay Islands, Trujillo, Olanchito, Isletas, Yoro, Danli, Catacamas, Choluteca, Mocoron, etc.) are now open by surface transportation. In addition to improved road access, all Honduran ports are now functional at some level and are also accessible by road. At last report, the port at Mocoron was cut off by road from Tegucigalpa but was accessible from Puerto Lempira.

USAID in Tegucigalpa and the USAID/OFDA DART continue to be in contact with the Government of Honduras concerning areas that might still require emergency assistance. However, as a result of the dramatically improved capabilities of ground transport, the projected need for DOD air support is diminishing. Limited needs may surface for air support to distribute commodities from local hubs to inaccessible rural areas. As the region has not fully entered its dry season, severe rains could again close some roads temporarily. The Honduran Government and USAID are in the process of building up stocks of critical supplies in vulnerable areas. Additionally, USAID and the DART continue to monitor the progress of road rehabilitation and other reconstruction and rehabilitation efforts.

Nicaragua

Storm Impacts

Mitch inflicted its greatest damage in Nicaragua through severe rains that caused extensive flooding and landslides. As of November 19, the Nicaraguan National Emergency Commission estimated that 2,863 people had died, 884 were missing, and 867,752 were affected as a result of the disaster, many after a large mudslide inundated ten communities situated at the base of the Casitas Volcano. A Nicaraguan transportation official reported as of November 6 that 71 bridges are either destroyed or heavily damaged, and OCHA estimated that 70% of roads were impassable immediately after the storm. On November 19, the Government of Nicaragua estimated that 31,750 houses were destroyed and 113,950 were damaged. Further the National Emergency Commission estimates that total losses were $400 million in housing, $605 million in the transportation network, $185 million in other infrastructure and $170 million in agriculture.

Immediate USG Response

On October 29, U.S. Ambassador to Nicaragua Lino Gutierrez declared a disaster due to continued flooding. USAID/OFDA has provided $175,000 for the local purchase and transport of critical relief supplies, including medicines, food and shelter material. On November 2, USAID/OFDA provided $250,000 for the deployment of DOD UH-60 and CH-47 helicopters to assist with search and rescue efforts and the delivery of relief supplies. As of December 3, 4 UH-60 and 2 CH-47 helicopters were operating in Nicaragua. By December 3, 128 helicopter missions have transported 755,000 pounds of food and 68,200 pounds of medicine, supplies and equipment within Nicaragua.

Airlifts of USAID/OFDA relief supplies to Nicaragua consisted of 679 rolls of plastic sheeting, 10,000 polyester blankets, 4,000 wool blankets, three 10,000–gallon water bladders, and 15,500 five-gallon water jugs, at a total estimated cost of $419,267 including transport. The first airlift arrived in Managua on November 4, a second on November 8, and a third on November 19. On November 19, USAID/OFDA provided $4 million to USAID/Managua to fund relief grants to reduce hunger and the threat of disease for thousands of victims in rural areas.

USAID/OFDA has operated in Nicaragua since October 29. A total of eleven DART personnel from USAID, Miami-Dade, and DOD have conducted assessments, assisted national search and rescue operations, and performed other response activities throughout the country.

Assessment Reporting and Recovery

All major roads in Nicaragua are open, with a few exceptions. Although most roads are passable, there are some detours and temporary measures to allow access. The delivery of emergency supplies by DOD helicopter continues, but as roads open more and more relief commodities are moved overland. Since

November 3, DOD has carried more than 500,000 pounds of supplies on more than 135 flights to 66 affected communities in Nicaragua.

On November 30, the Pan American Health Organization (PAHO) reported epidemic levels for cholera, leptospirosis and dengue. Local health teams have conducted extraordinary prevention and outbreak control efforts.

Guatemala

Storm Impacts

The storm moved northwestward across Guatemala on November 1, causing heavy rains and severe flooding. The national emergency office (CONRED) took steps to evacuate 5,969 people prior to the storm's arrival. The Red Cross estimated that 27,000 people were still housed in shelters as of November 4. As of November 9, officials reported a total of 258 deaths and 120 people missing in Guatemala. The most recent reporting from OCHA indicated that 32 bridges and 40 roads had been severely damaged or destroyed by flood waters and CONRED reported that about 19,000 homes were either destroyed or heavily damaged. On November 5 the U.S. Embassy estimated that 95% of the nation's banana crop was damaged, 25–60% of the corn, bean, coffee, and sugar crops were destroyed, and 30% of the cattle herd was lost.

Immediate USG Response

On October 31, Ambassador Donald J. Planty declared a disaster for Guatemala. In response, USAID/OFDA provided $25,000 through the U.S. Embassy to Catholic Relief Services for the local purchase of food. USAID/OFDA has delivered 290 rolls of plastic sheeting, 3,000 polyester blankets, 7,350 five-gallon water jugs, and four 3,000–gallon water bladders to Guatemala, at a total estimated cost of $182,013 including transport. The first airlift arrived in Guatemala City on November 4, and the second on November 9. USAID/OFDA has also provided $ 50,000 for the rental of local helicopters for aerial assessments of disaster-affected areas. As of December 3, 6 UH-60 and 4 CH-47 helicopters were operating in Guatemala to facilitate USAID/OFDA relief efforts. On November 18 USAID/OFDA provided $1 million in funding to USAID/Guatemala to support grants with non-governmental organizations (NGOs) for disaster response projects that will provide assistance in the following sectors: water/sanitation, emergency shelter, medicine, hygiene, and agriculture.

USAID/OFDA disaster relief personnel have operated in Guatemala since October 27. They have assisted CONRED in coordinating the national relief effort, and have conducted damage assessments and oversight of USAID/OFDA assistance. A total of five USAID/OFDA DART members have operated in Guatemala, and as of November 24 there are three remaining.

Assessment Reporting and Recovery

The DART reports indicate that northeastern Guatemala was most severely affected, including Isabal, Zacapa and Alta Verapaz. On November 12 the DART reported that in Panzos, Alto Verapaz, there are 10,000–12,000 displaced persons from 30 communities that suffered from flooding, landslides, and swollen rivers. Dead animals have infected the water supply, and most aqueducts have been destroyed. The lack of potable water has resulted in the first cases of diarrhea, amoebas, and undernourishment. Some communities are still totally isolated, and many houses have extensive roof damage. Sand flows in the water have affected rice, maize, bean, and coffee crops. It is estimated that it will be six months before replanting can take place. Community leaders indicate an urgent need for salt, sugar, soap, vegetable oil, chlorine tablets, water jugs, and plastic sheeting. The DART also reported that in Izabal there are 18,350 people in shelters, mainly from banana plantation communities, who are expect to remain displaced for the next 60–90 days. The DART also reports that all major roads are passable and the bridges damaged along the Atlantic Coast Highway are operable.

The DART recommends that the international donor community continue to focus on the following relief and recovery priorities during the next 60 days: food and water distribution to displaced persons continue for the next 60 days; environmental sanitation, including distribution of tools; massive campaign for disease prevention and control; reconstruction of water supply systems; provision of agricultural inputs and tools; and provision of building materials and tools for home reconstruction.

El Salvador

Storm Impacts

As of November 9, the National Emergency Committee (NEC) of El Salvador reported that 239 deaths and 135 people missing as a result of flash floods, and the Red Cross estimated that 400 people had died and 600 were missing. As of November 6, the Government of El Salvador estimated that 55,864 people had been displaced and had established 107 emergency shelters. The government also estimates that 10,000 houses have been destroyed and thousands more were seriously damaged.

Immediate USG Response

Ambassador Anne W. Patterson declared a disaster in El Salvador on November 1. In response, USAID/OFDA provided $25,000 for the immediate needs of flood victims. In addition, on November 5 USAID/OFDA airlifted 117 rolls of plastic sheeting, 5,150 polyester blankets, 6,000 five-gallon water jugs, and four 3,000–gallon water bladders, at a total estimated cost of $98,451 including transport. On November 18 USAID/OFDA provided $1 million to USAID/San Salvador to support grants with NGOs for disaster response projects that will distribute recovery packages to the areas of greatest need. As of December 3, 8 CH-47 and 4 UH-60 helicopters were operating in El Salvador to facilitate USAID/OFDA relief efforts.

A total of four USAID/OFDA DART members have been based in San Salvador to assist in the ongoing assessment of relief needs and priorities, and as of November 24 one member was still in the country.

Assessment Reporting and Recovery

The USAID/OFDA DART conducted a complete assessment of the southeastern portion of El Salvador from November 13–19. The most adversely affected communities were in Usulatan and San Miguel departments. The DART reported that only 1,000–2,000 homes were destroyed, which is fewer than previously reported by official sources. Most of the displaced population has returned home and only a few hundred people remain in emergency shelters. Many inhabitants of the Usulatan and San Miguel departments raise livestock and fish and no significant losses were sustained to any of the areas. Assessment reports indicate that only three major roads in El Salvador are still in need of major repair, while all seaports and airports are operational. The lack of potable water and sanitation are major concerns. Many people are drinking contaminated water because well covers were not an established practice. The Ministry of Health and PAHO have done an outstanding job preparing for, and responding to, the health needs of the affected population.

Belize

Storm Impacts

The Government of Belize established an Emergency Operations Center in Belize City to prepare for the storm's arrival and evacuated over 75,000 people from Belize City and the coastal islands to temporary shelters in Belmopan. Contrary to initial forecasts, the hurricane did not directly strike Belize. Nonetheless, heavy rains caused flooding throughout the coastal areas, particularly in Belize City. The Government of Belize has since granted permission for residents to return to Belize City, however according to the Red Cross thousands had opted to remain in emergency shelters long afterward.

Immediate USG Response

On October 29, U.S. Charge d'Affaires Joel Danies declared a disaster for Belize due to the impacts of Hurricane Mitch. In response, USAID/OFDA immediately provided $25,000 for the local purchase of food for distribution to displaced populations inhabiting emergency shelters. In addition, USAID/OFDA provided funding for two DOD Black Hawk helicopters based in Honduras to conduct overflight assessments and evacuations. Weather conditions during the storm's peak never permitted these aircraft to fly and as Hurricane Mitch turned and tracked away from Belize the helicopters were deployed to support emergency logistics requirements in Nicaragua. A four-person USAID/OFDA assessment team (comprised of a USAID/OFDA/LAC Regional Advisor and three Miami-Dade disaster specialists) was in Belize from October 29 to October 31. The team assessed needs of the evacuated population and reported that food stocks were adequate in Belmopan, but in short supply at Belize City. The team also reported that sanitation and hygiene were poor in all flood-affected areas. No additional USAID/OFDA assistance is anticipated for Belize.

Costa Rica

Storm Impacts

Heavy rains along the entire Pacific coast of Costa Rica prompted the National Emergency Commission to evacuate at-risk populations. The Government of

Costa Rica (GOCR) has since granted permission for people to return to their homes although approximately 1,700 people remained in temporary shelters up to a week after the storm had passed. Four people are reported dead as a result of the storm while four are still missing.

Immediate USG Response

On October 23, the U.S. Charge d'Affaires to Costa Rica Richard L. Baltimore III declared a disaster due to severe flooding caused by Hurricane Mitch. USAID/OFDA responded by providing a total of $45,000 to the U.S. Embassy in San Jose. Funds were used to rent local helicopters to provide overflight assessments and the delivery of food, water, and medicine to affected populations. No additional USAID/OFDA assistance is anticipated for Costa Rica.

Region

USAID/OFDA has provided $5 million to DOD for reconstruction activities in Honduras, Nicaragua, El Salvador and Guatemala. These funds will support the purchase of reconstruction and engineering materials and supplies, including gravel for road repair. USAID/OFDA has provided an additional $4 million to DOD for continued aircraft support in Honduras, Nicaragua, Guatemala and El Salvador, which contributes to the positioning of more than 40 DOD helicopters in Central America. As of November 12, these aircraft had flown over 400 missions in support of USAID/OFDA relief efforts. To date, USAID/OFDA has provided $2 million to the PAHO to address emergency water and sanitation needs of Hurricane Mitch victims. USAID/OFDA has also provided $160,000 to the U.S. Embassy in San Jose for the regional deployment of emergency supplies and personnel. On December 2, USAID/OFDA provided a $500,000 grant to the International Center for Tropical Agriculture (CIAT) for agricultural rehabilitation projects in Honduras and Nicaragua. The USAID/OFDA DART personnel stationed at the DART Headquarters in San Jose continue to coordinate the disaster response in the region.

USAID/OFDA Assistance in Honduras	$ 9,895,999
USAID/OFDA Assistance in Nicaragua	$ 4,844,267
USAID/OFDA Assistance in Guatemala	$ 1,257,013
USAID/OFDA Assistance in El Salvador	$ 1,123,451
USAID/OFDA Assistance in Costa Rica	$ 45,000
USAID/OFDA Assistance in Belize	$ 25,000
USAID/OFDA Assistance to the Region	$11,660,000
Total USAID/OFDA Assistance for Hurricane Mitch (to date)	$28,850,730

Public Donation Information for Victims of Hurricane Mitch

Disasters often generate an outpouring of interest and concern by the American people which lead to spontaneous collections of relief supplies i.e. food, clothing, medical supplies, etc. In the interest of effective coordination of such public response we encourage concerned citizens to provide monetary donations to appropriate organizations.

As transportation of relief supplies is limited by capacity, infrastructure damage and continuing weather constraints, it is difficult to move supplies into the affected countries. Unsolicited commodity donations often place an unnecessary burden on relief workers and local governments to store, transport and distribute supplies to those affected populations in need. This can also detract from the provision of more urgently needed relief assistance. USAID/OFDA can not provide assistance for the transport of donated goods.

USAID encourages the public to contact directly those private voluntary organizations (PVOs) who are currently working in, or with local affiliates, in Guatemala, Honduras, Nicaragua, Belize, Costa Rica and El Salvador to provide monetary donations. A list of PVOs may be obtained by contacting InterAction directly at 202–667–8227 x106, or via the internet at www.interaction.org. Those interested in providing specific relief services or supplies should contact Volunteers in Technical Assistance (VITA) for information and guidelines. VITA can be reached at 703–276–1914, or via the internet at www.vita.org.

4

MANAGING
MAN-MADE HAZARDS
AND DISASTERS

In many respects, the categorization of disasters as "natural" or "man-made" is very ambiguous. Too often, people become victims of "natural" disasters because they choose to live or work too close to natural hazards. The hazards are natural, but the disasters that occur are of human design. For example, people are causing "natural" disasters like droughts by failing to manage water resources effectively. Decertification due to overgrazing of cattle or sheep and flooding and landslides due to deforestation are other examples of man-made threats to the environment. However, notwithstanding the looseness of the categorization, the distinction made here is principally in terms of whether the disaster is largely the result of direct human action. In essence, "man-made disasters" occur because people misuse technology, ignore critical environmental processes, construct complex systems (such as structures and equipment) that fail, or even intentionally cause harm to the environment or to other human beings. Sometimes the disasters are purposeful, sometimes they are the result of human error, and sometimes they are simply failures of complex systems or what the economist Charles Perrow calls "normal accidents" (1984) and, thus, are beyond the effective control of the creators of the system. Moreover, sometimes the level of risk is known and sometimes it is not.

For most Americans, the kinds of man-made disasters that are the most familiar are those related to structural fires and transportation accidents. Nightly news broadcasts often run the gamut from murders to automobile accidents. "If it bleeds, it leads," as the saying goes, and house and apartment fires provide dramatic footage of emergency responses to attract viewers. Unfortunately, the media coverage usually stops before local Red Cross workers arrive with clothing, food, and vouchers for temporary shelter in local motels. Public attention is short-lived, unless the event contains compelling human tragedy. For example, the deaths of 6 children in a house fire in Detroit on December 28, 1998, drew national attention. The children were being cared for by their grandmother while their mother was in the hospital having a baby. The grim irony gave the event more media appeal than it might otherwise have had. Such tragedies are all too common in the United States. Approximately 5,000 people are killed each year by fires. While the death rate from fires in the United States is declining, it continues to be one of the highest among the industrialized nations (FEMA 1998). The United States has experienced its share of major hotel and theater fires, as well. Structural fires are usually human in origin, resulting from faulty wiring, smoking in bed, unattended space heaters and stoves, kids playing with matches or lighters, arson, or any number of other human acts or failures to act. While wildfires or lightning strikes may cause structural fires, as was common in earlier centuries, such events are relatively rare these days.

Similarly, automobile and truck accidents sometimes result in dozens of casualties, although large wrecks are seldom considered disasters by emergency managers unless they involve vehicles carrying hazardous materials. However, emergency management agencies typically are mobilized when trains wreck, aircraft crash, ships sink, and dozens of vehicles collide on the highway as a result of smoke or fog or ice. The massive wreck in Michigan early in 1999, when the blowing snow from a winter storm caused a "whiteout," was just such a case. Over 100 vehicles were damaged, 4 people were killed, and dozens more needed emergency medical assistance. The storm stranded motorists, and rescuers had to search vehicles along the sides of highways for victims.

Collapses of bridges, buildings, and other structures are relatively uncommon, as are failures of oil and gas pipelines, but releases of hazardous materials at chemical and nuclear plants and storage areas may be more common than we really want to know. System failures may be preventable, but, as Perrow suggests, some failures will occur despite our best efforts to prevent them. Even with primary and secondary safety mechanisms, complex systems fail. Indeed, as technologies become more complex and we become more and more reliant upon them, society becomes more fragile. Power outages, computer failures, and even accidents that shut down transportation networks can be devastating. A power failure in Auckland, New Zealand, in 1997 effectively shut down major parts of the city's downtown for weeks. The impacts of such failures can be devastating. People may die, property may be damaged, economic losses may be suffered, and lives may be disrupted for long periods of time. The Y2K issue is important for just that reason. Shutting down computer systems can affect everything from the water supply to police and emergency medical responses.

There are also increasing risks of social disruption, property loss, and human casualties from acts of random and purposive violence. Riots, large-scale street and workplace violence, low intensity terrorism, and terrorism involving so-called "weapons of mass destruction," as well as war, require mitigation and preparedness efforts just like natural and other man-made hazards. Even rather unsophisticated terrorist groups have the capacity to develop and use nuclear, biological, and chemical weapons and, as the Aum Shinrikyo sarin nerve gas attack on the Tokyo subway system in 1995 demonstrated, the willingness to use them. Cyberterrorism is also a growing threat as society becomes more and more dependent upon computers. Disruption of computer networks can have devastating effects both in terms of the loss of essential community life support systems and the loss of critical public and private data. There is tremendous potential for mass casualties and billions of dollars in economic losses when government services and private sector operations are disrupted.

The potential for public health emergencies due to natural causes and/or human error or action cannot be overlooked, as well. Terrorists may use biological weapons, infecting individuals and even whole populations with such dreaded agents as anthrax, or chemical weapons, contaminating subway systems and even cities with toxic materials. Fortunately, while there have been credible threats to use biological and chemical weapons and some incidences involving such weapons, such as the sarin (a lethal nerve agent that caused hyperactivity in muscles, glands, and nerves) attack in the Tokyo subway, catastrophic disasters involving such weapons have been prevented thus far. The potential for health emergencies of more natural origin cannot be discounted either. Smallpox and many of the other scourges of earlier centuries have largely been eradicated, but cholera still remains a major killer. The Spanish flu outbreak of 1918, which killed over 600,000 Americans and about 30 million more elsewhere in the world, is getting more attention as medical researchers and scientists trace the development of epidemics. The swine flu scare of 1976 conjured up images of that earlier epidemic as officials tried to immunize the entire U.S. population (Neustadt and Fineberg 1983, xix).

STRUCTURAL FIRES

It was common in centuries past for fires to get out of control and quite literally burn down cities. A fire in New York City in 1835 destroyed 500 buildings. The Great Chicago Fire of 1871 destroyed much of the city and caused 250 deaths. A fire in Boston in 1872 destroyed 800 buildings. And the firestorm that followed the Great San Francisco Earthquake of 1906 leveled much of that city. Large city fires were common when construction was largely of wood, houses were located very close to one another, and the technology of firefighting and the training of firefighters were much less sophisticated than they are today.

The risk of urban fires has remained with us, however. In Atlanta, for example, the Great Fire of 1917 burned for 1 1/2 miles through some of the city's close-in residential areas. The fire began in a hospital storage area and spread through an adjacent shantytown to a neighborhood of large homes. Fire engines were brought in from Macon and Augusta, Greenville, South Carolina, and Knoxville and Chattanooga, Tennessee. Soldiers from Fort McPherson, south of the city, were mobilized to fight the fire and put to dynamiting homes to create a fire break. By the time the fire was contained and extinguished, it had consumed 73 blocks of homes (Patureau 1987). Atlanta has experienced several large fires because the city has tree-lined residential areas and large patches of woodlands. The city's experience with fires is not unusual. The same pattern is common in cities and towns with a lot of trees and wooden homes. While tree-lined streets and wooden homes are less common in our larger cities now, many small towns still have shady old neighborhoods that may fuel large fires.

While new building standards and materials and increased regulation of residential and business construction have reduced the hazard tremendously, fires are still all too common in the United States. Buildings still burn, and large buildings can burn with a great many people in them. A church fire in Birmingham in 1902 killed 115, the Coconut Grove club fire in Boston in 1942 killed 491, a nightclub fire in Kentucky in 1977 killed 164, the Dupont Plaza hotel fire in Puerto Rico in 1986 killed 96, a New York City social club fire in 1990 killed 87, and a chicken-processing plant fire in North Carolina in 1991 killed 25, to name but a few of the more catastrophic fires in the 1900s (*World Almanac 1999,* 234–235). In these cases, the victims were trapped in crowded facilities when the fires broke out. Fire exits were blocked, locked, or nonexistent. Better fire codes and inspections have reduced the number of mass casualty fires in the United States, but violations of the regulations continue to pose significant risks.

The social club that burned in 1990 in New York City was an illicit, unregulated establishment. The operators of the chicken-processing plant in Hamlet, North Carolina, had locked exit doors, in violation of fire code, and workers were unable get out when the fire started. The effectiveness of regulation is evident from the decreasing numbers of casualties in hospital, nursing home, hotel, store, theater, jail, and apartment building fires in the United States.

By contrast, over 260 people were killed in a fire in Ethiopia in 1991, 213 were killed in a toy factory fire in Bangkok in 1994, 300 were killed in a theater fire in China in 1994, over 500 were killed in a school fire in India in 1995, and 90 were killed in a hotel fire in Thailand in 1997 (*World Almanac 1999*, 235). In most of those cases, the fatalities resulted from too few or locked exits. In countries without effective regulation of building design and construction, including requirements for fire exits, the potential for catastrophic fires is very high. To be sure, hotel fires are a serious concern for Americans traveling overseas, and it is recommended that they check the fire alarm and evacuation systems as soon they check in. Because of the perceived risk of hotel fires, some travelers in the United States and elsewhere refuse to take rooms on floors above the level that can be reached by fire ladders.

High-rise building fires pose even more problems. The design of high-rise buildings exacerbates the risk. Having stairways, elevators, electrical systems, and water systems located in or near the center of the building complicates access by firefighters, ventilation, and the evacuation of residents. The very height and complexity of the buildings complicates fire response. Firefighters may have to climb many floors before reaching the fire. Offices are often arranged differently on each floor, so that personnel unfamiliar with the building may have a difficult time locating particular rooms or simply moving from one part of the floor to another. Steel and concrete construction may interfere with radio communications and the distance from the command center to the fire floor may further distort communications. In effect, tall buildings may become "smokestacks," with smoke rising through stairwells and elevator shafts to the upper floors. While automatic sprinkler and other fire suppression systems may reduce the likelihood of large fires, system failures may occur and building owners and local fire officials have to monitor the systems to ensure that they are functional (see USFA 1999).

STRUCTURAL FAILURES

Structural failures are somewhat unusual events in the United States. Building collapses occur in older urban areas, such as New York City, but

CASE 4–1   The Winecoff Hotel Fire of 1946

The Atlanta fire that is perhaps more remembered than all but the 1865 conflagration immortalized in *Gone With the Wind* involved a hotel. On December 7, 1946, in the middle of the night, a fire broke out on the third floor of the fifteen-story Winecoff Hotel in downtown Atlanta. The hotel was advertised as "fireproof" and had no fire escapes, sprinklers, fire doors, or enclosed stairways. Elevators went up the middle of the building, and the open stairway containing the only stairs to the ground level, wound around the elevator shaft. Once the fire broke out, the open stairs and shaft acted like a chimney causing the fire to spread rapidly to the upper floors. The fire department's ladders were too short to reach beyond the first several floors and the fire nets were inadequate for a fifteen-story building. Guests trapped on the upper floors attempted to use sheets to reach the ground or the roofs of surrounding buildings or, finding no routes to safety, jumped to their deaths to escape the flames. By the time the fire was extinguished, 119 of the hotel's approximately 300 guests were dead. The Winecoff was the worst hotel fire in American history, and remained the worst hotel fire anywhere until a 1971 fire in Seoul, Korea, left 162 dead.

In the investigation of the Winecoff fire, arson was rumored, but the official finding was that a cigarette had been dropped onto a mattress in the hallway. There was little incentive to pursue the arson rumors and to do so might have jeopardized legal claims against the owners. The $3 million to $4 million in claims brought only about $350,000 from the hotel's insurers. The Winecoff fire drew public attention to the issue of fire safety and encouraged state and local governments to require fire escapes and other safety precautions in the building of hotels. Subsequent hotel fires, particularly the MGM Grand Hotel fire in Las Vegas in 1980 in which 84 people died, have encouraged officials to mandate sprinkler systems, smoke detectors, and fire alarms and to regulate building standards and materials (Thompson 1986; Heys 1986).

they are usually associated with fires and other factors that weaken supports for roofs, walls, and floors. Collapses also occur during earthquakes, landslides, and other disasters. Despite the relative infrequency of building collapses and other structural failures, concerns have been raised by professional associations, such as the American Institute of Architects (AIA), about the increasing pressure to build quickly and cheaply using exotic materials and designs. There have been some failures of long-span designs, in particular, that have resulted in deaths and injuries of construction workers during the building of structures and users after structures have been put into use (Waugh 1990; Waugh and Hy 1996).

In large measure, the adoption and implementation of building codes are left up to local governments in many states with state officials providing little guidance, technical assistance, or financial support for enforcement of the codes. Some communities have no building codes, some have codes but no inspectors, some have inadequate codes, some have strong codes and ill-qualified or too few inspectors, and some have strong codes and good enforcement. The very unevenness of local capabilities to regulate building makes it difficult to evaluate the hazard and poses a significant problem for insurers who may not be able to gauge their own exposure to losses. Building codes, like land-use regulations, are sometimes intensely opposed by builders because they can increase the cost of building. As recent hurricanes have demonstrated, some communities have long traditions of nonregulation. Residents may well build their own homes, garages, businesses, dams, bridges, and other structures without professional designs, licensed craftspeople, or local oversight. While communities with significant seismic risk, particularly in California, require strict compliance with appropriate codes, communities that have had few major disasters in recent memory may have little inclination to adopt appropriate codes (Waugh and Hy 1996).

Building regulators are having increasing difficulty adequately monitoring construction to assure safe design and conformity with building standards, as well. Budgetary limitations make it difficult for many local governments to hire enough adequately trained inspectors. Large projects, complex and exotic designs, and very large numbers of subcontractors contribute to the difficulty. Construction management firms often find it difficult to monitor their own subcontractors on very large projects (Waugh 1990; Waugh and Hy 1996). In the aftermath of a major disaster, such as Hurricane Andrew, building regulators simply cannot keep up with the reconstruction. Also, because some of the repairs and major construction may be done by unscrupulous and/or unqualified people, the likelihood that construction will be substandard may be even greater.

Dam failures have also caused deaths, injuries, and property losses. There are over 80,000 dams in the United States, and over 95 percent are owned by state and local governments, private individuals or firms, and condominiums (e.g., resort community associations). Failures typically result from erosion of the embankment, leakage, deterioration of structures around the dam, overtopping when spillway capacity is inadequate, faulty construction, instability of the ground around the dam, and earthquakes (FEMA 1987).

CASE 4–2   The Hyatt Skywalk Disaster in 1981

On July 24, 1981, approximately 1,500 people were attending an informal tea dance in the lobby of the Hyatt Regency Hotel in Kansas City. Dancers crowded the lobby floor, with about 100 onlookers on a skywalk suspended over the floor and another 50 or so on a skywalk above that. Many of the onlookers were swaying with the music. When the support gave way, the 120–foot section of the upper skywalk collapsed onto the lower and both fell on the dancers in the lobby; 113 people were killed and about 200 more were injured.

Fortunately, a group of about 20 radiologists were having a dinner in the hotel, and the medical response was very quick. An aid station, then a triage area and morgue were set up. Unfortunately, the nature of the injuries and the fact that many people were still trapped under the concrete walkways complicated the rescue. The entrance to the hotel had to be opened up so that heavy equipment could be brought in. A remarkable aspect of the emergency response was the number of volunteers who converged on the scene. It was estimated that 250 police, 250 fire service personnel, and over 100 paramedics responded, along with volunteers from local hospitals and community organizations. Victims were transported by ambulance, helicopter, taxi, and private car to hospitals.

The identification of victims was difficult because their relatives and friends often did not know that they were at the hotel. In some cases, authorities had to match unidentified victims with automobiles parked around the hotel. In other cases, families noticed that members were missing and realized that they might have gone to the dance.

Structural failures are relatively uncommon, but the American Institute of Architects had warned of the possible danger from "long span construction." The AIA had expressed concern that the complexity of construction projects, pressures to use light materials and exotic designs, the lack of redundancy in supports, pressure to keep costs low, and inadequate monitoring of construction might lead to such failures.

Following the collapse, the Federal Bureau of Standards (FBS) examined the concrete walks and supports, the Occupational Health and Safety Administration (OSHA) reviewed construction records, a "blue ribbon" committee appointed by the mayor investigated the design approval process, and several state agencies did their own investigations. Eventually, blame was laid on the subcontractors who made the steel supports. The design deviated from the

(continued)

original engineering drawings, and the engineer who signed off on the supports was not licensed to do so by the state of Missouri. Questions were also raised about the adequacy of city building inspection, particularly with exotic designs and the sheer number of designs that the codes office had review. The skywalks, too, were not built with the expectation that large numbers of people might dance or sway on them. They were built for walking rather than for "dynamic loads," and the "harmonic motion" created by swaying may have caused the failure. Other issues included the capability of the general contractor to oversee such a large project (Waugh 1988; Waugh and Hy 1996).

The most infamous dam failure in U.S. history is that which caused the Johnstown flood in 1889. A poorly designed and maintained dam on a resort lake failed during heavy rains and the waters swept through Johnstown miles downstream. The flood hit the town with little warning and wiped out entire families. The dead numbered 2,209, and the massive relief effort that followed included Clara Barton and her fledgling organization, the American Red Cross. In more recent years, dam failures have been less common, but there have still been deadly events. In 1972, the Buffalo Creek dam in West Virginia failed and caused 125 deaths. In 1976, the Teton Dam in Idaho failed, causing 14 deaths and over $1 billion in property losses. In 1977, the Laurel Run Dam in Pennsylvania failed, killing 40 people. In 1977, the Kelly Barnes Dam failed in Georgia and left 39 dead (FEMA 1987). In recent flood disasters, including the south Georgia floods caused by Tropical Storm Alberto in 1994, failures of private earthen dams, in particular, have exacerbated the flood problem and increased the amount of property damage.

Although there are federal, state, and local laws regulating dam design, construction, maintenance, and operations, primary responsibility for dam safety rests with the owners. FEMA and other agencies provide technical support to those who seek it, as well as public information programs to raise awareness of the hazard, but state and local regulation tends to be lacking or lax. Simply holding owners legally liable for failures is a poor substitute for regulations to prevent or mitigate the effects of failures. While equitable compensation may be provided for property losses, financial compensation is a poor substitute for a lost life.

CASE 4–3   The Buffalo Creek Dam Failure in 1972

A coal company used a pile of wastes from its mining operation to dam up a stream in Middle Fork Hollow, West Virginia. In February 1972, the dam collapsed, releasing water through the long, narrow valley of Buffalo Creek. The water and debris rushed through 16 communities in the valley, killing 125 people immediately and destroying approximately 1,000 homes. Survivors of the disaster formed a committee and decided to sue the Buffalo Mining Company.

Company officials called the disaster an "act of God" and beyond their control. Heavy rains had caused flooding and had added to the wastewater held by the dam. Pittston, the parent company, sought to focus attention on its West Virginia subsidiary in order to assure that the lawsuit would be brought in a state court. A suit against Pittston, a New York corporation, would go to a federal court that would likely be less sympathetic. The Federal Coal Mine Health and Safety Act of 1969 set specific standards for mining refuse and dams and the act assigned responsibility for deaths and injuries to the mining company when standards were not met. An initial issue was whether the act covered only miners working in or around the mine and those working in the immediate vicinity and not other victims downstream who were not working at the mine. The narrowest interpretation of the act was that it covered only employees of the company actually working at the time.

The Buffalo Mining Company was blamed for failing to do something about the dam when it was apparent that it was unsafe. Officials also blamed the state of West Virginia for not letting the company release some of the wastewater into the stream. The state also was blamed because it had not inspected the dam despite its own regulations that should have covered the structure. Some blamed the victims themselves because they had been warned that the dam was unsafe and chose to remain in their homes despite the risk. A sad irony of the disaster was that there had been numerous catastrophic mining disasters in the state that involved men working in mines, and this disaster killed miners and their families in their own homes (Stern 1976, 3–18).

As well as documenting damages suffered by the victims, including mental suffering, the plaintiffs' lawyers discovered that another dam owned by a subsidiary of Pittston had failed in 1955, destroying a home and almost killing a family. They argued that the owners of the Buffalo Creek dam should have known the danger it posed to communities downstream and acted to reduce the risk of failure (Stern 1976, 218–221). Rather than go to trial, the parties settled out of court for $13.5 million (Stern 1976, 298–299).

HAZARDOUS MATERIALS ACCIDENTS

Hazardous materials accidents are almost too frequent to enumerate. The manufacture, storage, and transport of hazardous chemicals pose numerous risks to handlers and those nearby. There have been cases in which thousands of people have died from single events, such as the tragic gas leak at Union Carbide's Bhopal, India, insecticide plant in 1984. Gas built up in a storage tank, safety systems failed, and warning was not given until well after the leak. Residents near the plant had nowhere to run to escape the poison cloud. Over 6,400 people were killed and 30,000 to 40,000 were seriously injured by the methyl iso cynanate. More have died from injuries to lungs and nervous systems since the disaster and the human costs are still being assessed. The legal battle continues as almost 900,000 claims for personal injury and death have been filed against Union Carbide and the Indian government. There have been major chemical leaks in the United States, but nothing comparable to the Bhopal disaster.

There are concerns about the transport of hazardous materials through major metropolitan areas, and state and local governments are increasingly requiring that vehicles carrying such materials take routes around the downtown areas and avoid tunnels and other more dangerous routes. Studies of the trucking industry have found significant percentages of the vehicles with serious mechanical problems and cases of drivers being impaired because of too little sleep or because of alcohol and/or drugs.

Communities have been contaminated with hazardous chemicals, as well. The Love Canal disaster involved a community being affected by toxic wastes buried by Hooker Chemical Company which leeched into the groundwater. The community experienced long-term health problems with deaths directly attributable to contact with the wastes. After a long legal battle, homes were bought out and a cleanup program was initiated. It is uncertain how many communities suffer from similar kinds of undefined hazards from old storage areas that may be long forgotten, groundwater contamination, old landfills or fills from construction sites, and other sources. In October 1998, there were about 1,200 severely contaminated hazardous waste sites being cleaned up under the Superfund program of the Environmental Protection Agency (EPA). State governments are cleaning up thousands more sites. EPA maintains the National Priorities List of the most serious sites and has a process for identifying hazardous waste sites, assessing conditions, and determining alternative approaches for cleanup. Superfund is part of the Comprehensive Environmental Response, Compensation, and Liability Act (CERCLA) (GAO 1998).

Oil spills from ships run aground, damaged in collisions with other ships or piers or bridges, and simply sunk in heavy seas have also been the source of major environmental damage. The most infamous case in recent U.S. history has been the Exxon Valdez disaster in the Gulf of Alaska in 1989. The extent of the damage done to wildlife and fish hatcheries and the slowness of Exxon to respond to the disaster has raised serious concerns about any expansion of oil exploration in fragile areas. In particular, the disaster increased opposition to oil exploration in the Alaska National Wildlife Refuge on the North Slope of Alaska, despite oil company assurances that their operations would cause little or no environmental damage.

NUCLEAR ACCIDENTS

Nuclear accidents are most closely associated with problems in nuclear power plants, but they may also occur in facilities where nuclear materials are produced and used, in nuclear weapons production plants and storage facilities, in storage facilities for nuclear wastes, and in the transport of nuclear materials. Nuclear materials are used in a wide variety of agricultural, industrial, research, and health care facilities. Until 1975, the Atomic Energy Commission (AEC) was responsible for monitoring and regulating nuclear facilities. The Nuclear Regulatory Commission (NRC) was created with the passage of the Energy Reorganization Act of 1974 and charged with regulating the use of nuclear energy. When accidents or lesser events occur, the NRC sends a site team to the location and the commission's response is directed from its Headquarters Operations Center (NRC 1998).

The NRC's listing of responses includes events ranging from losses of off-site power and equipment failures to breaches of security and natural disasters. The responses are normally categorized as "information," "transient events," "alerts," "site area emergencies," and "unusual events." The impact of Hurricane Gloria in 1985, for example, was assessed at eight separate nuclear power plants. Earthquakes, fires, and other largely external threats to plant operation and safety are monitored closely, and the NRC also responds to accidents when nuclear materials are being transported (NRC 1998).

Two events that have had profound effects on the U.S. federal government's regulation of power plants are the Three Mile Island disaster in 1979, which caused the evacuation of residents near the Pennsylvania plant, and the Chernobyl disaster in the Ukraine (then part of the Soviet Union) in 1986. The two events have also affected public opinion on the production and use of nuclear energy. Opponents of nuclear energy, in

CASE 4–4   The Exxon Valdez Oil Spill of 1989

On March 24, 1989, the Exxon Valdez, carrying 1,260,000 barrels of crude oil, ran aground in Prince William Sound, 25 miles from the port of Valdez and the terminus of the Alyeska pipeline. The vessel hit Bligh Reef, a hazard clearly marked on navigational maps and well off its intended course. The hull of the vessel was damaged, and approximately 240,000 barrels of crude oil spilled into the sea. In several days, the spill spread over a 100–square-mile area (Lutrin and Settle 1992, 265–272).

The captain of the Exxon Valdez, Joseph Hazelwood, was not on the bridge when the vessel hit the reef, and the officer on duty, the third mate, was not certified to pilot the vessel in the Gulf of Alaska. Checked by the Coast Guard nine hours after the vessel hit the reef, the captain still had unacceptably high levels of alcohol in his blood. The response to the disaster was slow and inadequate. By the time the effort was stepped up, the weather worsened and made containment operations very difficult.

The Alyeska Pipeline Service Company, a consortium of oil companies, activated its contingency plan as required by state regulations and began the containment effort. On the 25th, Exxon took over responsibility but, by the 28th, Exxon's containment effort was judged inadequate and state officials took over. In the meantime, local fishermen attempted to protect salmon hatcheries along the coast (Lutrin and Settle 1992, 265–272).

A study of the Exxon Valdez disaster response by the U.S. General Accounting Office in 1989 concluded that it was "clearly inadequate" and that "it is not surprising that major problems were encountered because no one had realistically prepared to deal with a spill of this magnitude in Prince William Sound" (1989, 1). The report went on to state that the United States "may be similarly unprepared elsewhere in the nation" (1989, 1) and that the federal government should assume a leadership role in this area. Prevention is the best strategy. Specialized equipment, skilled personnel, clear leadership, adequate planning, and money were the pressing needs. Alyeska was prepared for a spill of 42,000 to 84,000 gallons, and the Exxon Valdez spilled 10 million gallons. Alyeska had not conducted field exercises to test its plan and personnel. Emergencies were to be handled on an *ad hoc* basis, as an extra duty for Alyeska personnel, so it took time to assemble the response team (GAO 1989, 3–4).

The cost of the cleanup was considerable. The Exxon Corporation also had to pay the state and federal governments over $1 billion in damages. Attempts

(continued)

CASE 4–4 *(continued)*

to rescue oil-covered birds and mammals had very little effect, and the disaster continues to affect many of the wildlife populations in the Prince William Sound. Fishing and other industries have also continued to suffer. Exxon has appealed the judgments against it, and affected communities are still trying to recover from the disaster (Mitchell 1999).

The Exxon Valdez disaster also revealed serious weaknesses in the federal and state emergency response systems. U.S. Coast Guard officials did not feel that they had authority to require preparedness efforts (GAO 1989). As a consequence, the system was reorganized. New procedures include keeping pilots on tankers longer, extending radar coverage, reducing the speed of the tankers, keeping emergency response vessels on standby, and stockpiling cleanup and containment supplies in coastal communities so that they can be readily accessed in the event of a spill (Mitchell 1999, 117). The Oil Pollution Act of 1990 strengthened preparedness and regulatory requirements but some of its provisions have yet to be implemented because of limited funding. The double hulling of ships was also mandated, although that requirement will not be fully met until 2015 (Sylves 1998).

---

particular, point out the danger inherent in using technologies that are not well understood and are so risky. Proponents point out the relative infrequency of serious events, the need for "clean" sources of electrical power, and the human errors that led to the Three Mile Island and Chernobyl disasters.

While the design of the Chernobyl nuclear plant is significantly different from the designs of American and European plants, the disastrous core meltdown and massive release of radioactive material offer lessons for Western planners and policymakers. The tragic consequences to residents near the Ukrainian plant site are still being assessed. The radioactive contamination has caused long-term health problems, particularly high rates of some cancers and birth defects, and there are still deserted communities that once housed families and supported the local economy.

AVIATION DISASTERS AND OTHER TRANSPORTATION DISASTERS

Aviation disasters generally result from mechanical failure, pilot error, air traffic controller error, terrorist action, or bad weather. There have been

CASE 4–5   Three Mile Island Nuclear Accident of 1979

On March 27 and 28, 1979, a series of events, some mechanical and some resulting from human error, precipitated a serious nuclear power plant accident at the Three Mile Island facility outside of Harrisburg, Pennsylvania. Unit 2 was operating at near full capacity when problems began to develop. The polisher, which removes resins so that the water is pure enough not to damage the turbines, was the source of the problem initially. However, a small leak from the polisher caused the turbine to shut down automatically. This, in itself, would not have been a problem if the emergency feed water pumps had come on. That secondary cooling system was supposed to compensate for the shut down of the primary system. Unfortunately, valves in each pipe had been left closed during maintenance two days earlier and the operator did not notice that the water was being fed into a closed pipe rather than into the cooling system (Perrow 1984, 17–31).

There were indicators on the control panel that showed that the valves were closed, but the operators did not notice them early enough to prevent damage to the unit. The water in the steam generator boiled out. An automatic safety device, a pilot-operated relief valve (PORV), was supposed to relieve pressure in the core by diverting some of the hot, radioactive water into a drain pipe to a storage tank with the excess going into a sump. That valve opened but did not close, and roughly one-third of the water around the core escaped. The warning light that would have alerted the operators did not work. At this point, the operators were not making the connection between the series of mechanical problems and the drop in the water level within the core. In short, the readings of radioactive water outside of the core were not associated with the water drop within the core. The operators expected to find a leak in the plant's complex of water pipes, not a leak from the reactor core itself (Perrow 1984, 17–31).

The containment building was flooded with radioactive water, the reactor core was uncovered and overheating, and operators were still unsure of the status of the core. Fortunately, one of the operators checked the PORV and, finding it open, shut another valve to stop the flow of water from the core. That act prevented a complete core meltdown and likely a breach of the containment area. Thirty-three hours after the accident began, a hydrogen bubble appeared as oxygen from the water reacted with the lining of the fuel rods. The explosion could be heard in the control room (Perrow 1984, 17–31).

(continued)

CASE 4–5 (continued)

With radioactive water escaping the containment building into one of the plant's auxiliary buildings, radiation alarms sounding, and mounting evidence of serious damage done to the core, officials sealed the buildings and declared a site emergency. The public was informed of the emergency and communities around the plant were evacuated. Subsequent studies of the disaster blamed it on operator error, a series of mechanical failures, or a combination of human and system errors. Charles Perrow characterized it as the kind of "normal accident" that occurs in complex processes with "tightly coupled" systems. A failure in one system affects others which, in turn, affects yet others (Perrow 1984, 93–100).

thousands of crashes involving general aviation since the Hindenberg disaster in 1937. As the skies have become more crowded and aircraft have become larger, the risk of major disasters has increased. Crashes normally occur as aircraft take off or land, although mechanical failures may occur at any time. There have been recent crashes caused by weather, particularly wind sheers or microbursts that push aircraft into the ground, including the crash of a Delta aircraft landing at the Dallas–Fort Worth airport in 1985. The Federal Aviation Administration (FAA) has developed a system to warn pilots of such hazards and procedures for pilots to follow if they encounter such winds without warning. Icing of aircraft and runways also creates hazards that the FAA is addressing. The crash of an American Airlines MD-82 in Little Rock, Arkansas, in June 1999, in which 9 people were killed, may have been due to a combination of weather (in this case a severe thunderstorm) and mechanical problems. Sorting out the causes of crashes may take some time.

Mechanical failures have also been problematic. Recent fatal disasters resulting from mechanical failures include the 1985 crash of an Arrow Air charter flight carrying members of the 101st Airborne Division in Gander, Newfoundland; the 1989 crash of a United Airlines jet in Sioux City, Iowa, after a long, dramatic effort to land the aircraft despite a hydraulic failure that caused steering problems; and, the 1996 crash of a TWA flight off Long Island after an apparent explosion in its fuel system. Following a series of crashes involving Boeing 737s, the most widely used jet aircraft in the world, the National Transportation Safety Board (NTSB) concluded that there were rudder design problems. The rudder system was not "reliably redundant," according to the NTSB, because the aircraft's two control systems relied on a single valve that might fail. Rudder problems were determined to be the likely cause of a USAir crash outside Pittsburgh in 1994, which killed 131 passengers and crew; the possible cause of a United Airlines crash outside Colorado Springs in 1991, which killed 25; and the near crash of a Eastwind Airlines aircraft in 1996 in Richmond. To redesign the system would have cost the airlines over $100 million, but NTSB recommended installing a new power control unit that would lessen the likelihood of the rudder's jamming (Johnson 1999b, A4; 1999a, A3).

Sometimes the problem is the cargo. In 1996, a ValuJet DC-9 crashed into the Everglades after taking off from Miami International Airport. A fire had broken out in the aircraft's cargo hold and caused damage to its steering mechanism. The firm responsible for the cargo was ultimately held liable for the crash. There had been a series of problems involving fires ignited by oxygen generators, like those that caused the ValuJet crash. In most cases, fires broke out while the aircraft were on the ground or while the cargo containers were outside of the aircraft. The FAA and air carriers had ample warning of the danger in transporting such equipment, but failed to reduce the hazard (Charles 1999).

Pilot and air traffic controller errors have also contributed to fatal crashes. One of the worst aviation disasters ever was the March 27, 1977, collision of a KLM 747 and a Pan Am Airlines 747 on the runway in Tenerife, Canary Islands. The cause was due to a miscommunication between the control tower at the airport and one of the aircraft. The result was that the pilot of one aircraft attempted to land while another was attempting to take off. The collision killed 582 people on the two jumbo jets. English is the language of air traffic controllers, but flight crews do not always speak and understand the language very well. Misunderstandings do occur.

While terrorist attacks on civil aviation are far less common than they were in the late 1960s and early 1970s, airports and aircraft are still logical targets of terrorism because such attacks attract international media attention, access to airport facilities is relatively easy (in comparison to buildings that limit public access), and the aircraft provide a means of escape. There are international conventions against attacks on civil aviation, but some so-called rogue nations have little regard for international law and, apparently, for human life. The terrorists responsible for the bombing of the Pan Am 747 over Lockerbie, Scotland, in 1988 have not been brought to justice yet, but arrangements have been made for the trial of two Libyans by the International Court of Justice at The Hague, Netherlands. When the TWA 747 exploded off Long Island in 1996, officials initially assumed that it was

TABLE 4–1   Selected Air Crashes Involving U.S. Carriers Since 1979

Date	Aircraft	Site	Deaths
May 25, 1979	American Airlines DC-10	O'Hare Airport, Chicago	275
January 13, 1982	Air Florida Boeing 737	Washington/Potomac River	78
July 9, 1982	Pan Am Boeing 727	Kenner, Louisiana	153
August 2, 1985	Delta Air Lines Jumbo Jet	Dallas–Ft. Worth Airport	133
December 12, 1985	Arrow Air DC-8	Gander, Newfoundland	256
August 16, 1987	Northwest Airlines MD-82	Romulus, Michigan	156
December 21, 1988	Pan Am Boeing 747	Lockerbie, Scotland	270
July 19, 1989	United Airlines DC-10	Sioux City, Iowa	111
September 8, 1994	USAir Boeing 737–300	Aliquippa, Pennsylvania	132
October 31, 1994	American Eagle ATR-72	Near Roselawn, Indiana	68
December 20, 1995	American Airlines 757	North of Cali, Colombia	160
May 11, 1996	ValuJet DC-9	Everglades, Florida	110
July 17, 1996	TWA Boeing 747	Off Long Island, NY	230

Source: World Almanac 1999, 230.

due to a terrorist bomb and there are persistent rumors that it could have been caused by a missile fired by a military aircraft in the area or by someone on the ground. Under federal law, the FBI, rather than the Federal Aviation Administration, became the lead agency in the suspected terrorist bombing of the TWA flight. Complaints concerning the poor communication between the investigators and the families of the victims and the slowness of authorities in releasing the remains encouraged the passage of legislation to protect the families of victims.

Although studies by the U.S. General Accounting Office and other public and private agencies have found serious weaknesses in the security systems of many major U.S. and foreign airports, the precautions implemented since the early 1970s have been very successful in reducing the number of hijackings and bombings. The metal detection devices and newer devices most frequently find weapons carried by people who have simply forgotten that they have guns or knives in their purses, briefcases, or hand baggage. While terrorists may still be able to sneak a bomb aboard a flight, the likelihood of it happening is relatively small. The possibility that most concerned officials following the explosion and crash of TWA Flight 800 off Long Island in 1996 was that the aircraft had been shot down with a hand-carried surface-to-air missile, such as a Stinger, Redeye, or Dragon missile. Many of the Stinger missiles provided to Afghan rebels by the United States during the 1980s are still unaccounted for and preventing attacks on civil or military aviation with such weapons would be extremely difficult. Aircraft taking off or landing or in a low-level holding pattern around a major airport would be vulnerable. It was with some relief that the explosion was determined to be a mechanical problem, rather than a missile.

Responding to air crashes is different from other kinds of disaster response. When aircraft crash there are generally no survivors or many serious casualties. The force of impact and fire can result in grievous injuries. The crash at the Sioux City, Iowa, airport in 1989 was a remarkable case because of both the drama of the flight as pilots struggled to steer the aircraft to that airport and the response on the ground to the crash. Emergency managers had run a disaster drill before the crash and corrected perceived deficiencies, the airport was easily accessible from the interstate highway which facilitated the emergency response, and emergency personnel had considerable time to prepare for the crash. A similar situation might have occurred on September 2, 1998, when a Swissair MD-11 crashed offshore from Halifax, Nova Scotia, after leaving New York's Kennedy Airport. Halifax is the center for Canada's maritime rescue operations in the Atlantic, and a full range of emergency response resources could have been brought to bear. Unfortunately, the pilots could not get the aircraft to Halifax after dumping fuel over the water. None of the 229 people aboard the Swissair airliner survived the crash into the sea.

Shipwrecks are relatively rare in the United States or involving U.S.-flagged vessels. The sinking of the *Edmund Fitzgerald,* an American cargo ship, in a storm on Lake Superior in 1975, in which 29 crew members were lost, is perhaps the most notable recent case, although it is perhaps best remembered because the wreck was immortalized in song by Gordon Lightfoot. In 1976, a tanker collided with a ferry on the Mississippi River and 77 were killed; and, in 1983, a freighter sank off the coast of Virginia and 33 were killed (*World Almanac 1999,* 228–229). More recently, a freighter lost propulsion and hit a shopping pier in the Port of New Orleans. Fortunately, no one was killed (see Sylves 1998). Recent cruise line disasters have also been largely casualty free. Cruise ships have had serious fires, become grounded, and suffered hull damage. Inspections by the U.S. Coast Guard have revealed serious problems with some cruise lines and specific ships. They have found crews ill prepared to deal with disasters and ships with serious safety violations. Regulating safety on foreign vessels is difficult, however, even if they are in American ports and carrying American passengers.

Shipwrecks are far more common in the developing world. Over the past two decades, major wrecks killed 580 in Indonesia in 1981, 357 on the Nile River in 1983, 262 in Bangladesh in 1986, 398 on the Black Sea in 1986, 4,341 in the Philippines in 1987, over 400 on the Ganges River in 1988, 161 on the Danube River in 1989, 140 in Italy in 1991, 462 in Egypt in 1991, over 500 in Haiti in 1993, 285 off South Korea in 1993, 1,049 in Estonia in 1994, approximately 500 on Lake Victoria (Africa) in 1996, 280 in Nigeria in 1997, over 200 in the Congo in 1998, and 97 in the Philippines in 1998 (*World Almanac 1999,* 228–229). Most of these tragedies involved overloaded and/or ill-maintained ferries, and not all involved bad weather or heavy seas. American travelers were involved in several of the shipwrecks, which points out the problem of traveling in nations that do not have effective safety regulations and have few alternative modes of transportation.

Train wrecks are common occurrences in the United States, but they usually involve trains hitting automobiles or trucks when roadways cross the rails or trains derailing. However, notwithstanding the wreck of an Amtrak train in Bourbonnais, Illinois, in March 1999, which killed 11 passengers, major derailings or collisions resulting in more than a few casualties are very unusual in the United States today. Part of the reason for the rarity of mass casualty wrecks is the decline of passenger train service. Not many passenger trains are operating now. The Bourbonnais crash involved a tractor-trailer loaded with steel rods. The driver of the truck was believed to have attempted to cross the tracks despite warnings of the approaching train (Robinson 1999). Such collisions between trains and automobiles and trucks are relatively common. In 1997, for example, there were 183 such accidents involving Amtrak trains and motor vehicles, and most, 114, were at crossings with warning devices such as flashing lights and gates. Impatient and inattentive drivers are the biggest problem. It can take trains a mile or more to stop, and crew members are the most frequent casualties of collisions (Johnson 1999c, A8). While slowing trains down as they pass through urban areas is often suggested, there are so many small towns along rail lines that rail service would be seriously impaired.

There have also been crashes involving two trains, such as the collision of two commuter trains in Chicago in 1972, which killed 45 people and injured over 200 more, and the collision of two commuter trains in Maryland in 1996, which killed 11. The crash of a train at the Big Bayou Conot in Alabama in 1993, which resulted in 47 deaths (*World Almanac 1999,* 231), was more unusual. In this case, a barge had damaged a bridge over the bayou earlier, and the bridge collapsed under the weight of the train. Train cars fell into the water, and passengers struggled in the dark to find safe ground. Although mass casualty train wrecks are very uncommon, there are concerns that high-speed train lines, development of which is under study in several parts of the United States, might be vulnerable to terrorist attack and/or mechanical failure. There have been terrorist attacks on trains in the United Kingdom, as well as on the London subway system, the Underground, and there was a serious crash of a high-speed train in Germany in 1998, in which 102 people were killed. There are also concerns that terrorists might strike the "Chunnel," the tunnel that connects southern England with France, by placing a bomb on a train or in a motor vehicle. Much the same hazard exists in the United States where rail lines cross bridges or pass through tunnels.

WORKPLACE VIOLENCE

Workplace violence takes many forms, including violent attacks by workers on their coworkers and managers, by spouses and other intimates on workers, by criminals from outside the workplace, by people with psychological and/or substance abuse problems, by clients frustrated over poor service or program cuts, by patients and inmates, and by domestic and international terrorists. Workplace violence is a relatively new concern for emergency managers. Their interest can be traced to a number of factors, including (1) the potential for large-scale terrorist attacks, particularly following the bombing of the Murrah Federal Building in Oklahoma City in 1995; (2) the growing threat from so-called weapons of mass destruction; and (3) the fact that a large proportion of the violence has been directed at public workplaces and public employees (i.e., the emergency managers' friends and colleagues).

According to a 1997 survey of city and county officials, just over one-third of local governments have formal workplace violence policies, and slightly fewer have programs in place (Nigro and Waugh 1998, 4). Statistics are more difficult to find on state and federal policies and programs because many large agencies have their own, but a 1999 study of state governments found that over half have workplace violence policies, but only about a third have programs in place (Nigro and Waugh 1999). Large agencies tend to have their own policies and programs, however. This is particularly true of law enforcement agencies, corrections facilities, and health care facilities that routinely deal with violent inmates or patients and

TABLE 4–2   Selected Train Wrecks in the United States in the Twentieth Century

Date	Location	Fatalities
August 7, 1904	Eden, Colorado	96
September 4, 1904	New Market, Tennessee	56
December 30, 1906	Washington, DC	53
March 1, 1910	Wellington, Washington	96
March 21, 1910	Green Mountain, Iowa	55
June 28, 1918	Ivanhoe, Indiana	68
July 9, 1918	Nashville, Tennessee	101
November 1, 1918	Brooklyn, New York	97
June 16, 1925	Hackettstown, New Jersey	50
June 19, 1938	Saugus, Montana	47
July 31, 1940	Cuyahoga Falls, Ohio	43
September 6, 1943	Philadelphia, Pennsylvania	79
December 16, 1943	Between Rennert and Buie, North Carolina	72
August 4, 1944	Near Stockton, Georgia	47
December 31, 1944	Bagley, Utah	50
April 25, 1946	Naperville, Illinois	45
November 22, 1950	Richmond Hill, New York	79
February 6, 1951	Woodbridge, New Jersey	84
September 15, 1958	Elizabethport, New Jersey	48
October 30, 1972	Chicago, Illinois	45
September 22, 1993	Big Bayou Conot, Alabama	47

Source: World Almanac 1999, 231.

have to be concerned about legal liability for inappropriate responses to violence or inadequate security for their own employees (Nigro and Waugh 1999). The more telling statistics, however, may be those that indicate that 26.1 percent of local government personnel officers reported having felt in personal danger, 32.7 percent reported being threatened, and 54.7 percent reported knowing someone in their agency or building who had been attacked, although only 2.7 percent had been attacked themselves. Much larger percentages of the officials have their own plans to escape if violence erupts in their offices (Nigro and Waugh 1998, 7).

Certainly the history of violent attacks on public workplace and employees suggests that all agencies should be prepared. Domestic terrorists have attacked law enforcement officials and facilities, women's clinics and health care providers, forest rangers, tax officials and offices, military personnel and facilities, and other political targets. Comprehensive workplace violence policies and programs are being recommended for most public agencies by the National Institute of Occupational Safety and Health (NIOSH) and agencies such as the Federal Protective Service (FPS), and those recommendations generally include liaison with local law enforcement and emergency management agencies (Nigro and Waugh 1998, 1999).

There is also a threat of violence by disgruntled employees, angry clients (including patients and prisoners), angry spouses and other intimates, street criminals, and others. The image of employees "going postal" is now a familiar one, and certainly there have been a number of tragic shootings in U.S. Postal Service (USPS) facilities. On the whole, however, the USPS is a very large agency and has not had an inordinately large number of violent incidences for its size. Also, the USPS and increasing numbers of other public and private organizations are adopting comprehensive policies and programs to address the threat of workplace violence. Budget cuts have reduced the capacities of many public agencies to deliver services, and as a consequence, clients more often become frustrated and aggressive. Privatization and service contracting have increased the levels of stress on many public employees, as well. Agencies are understaffed, workloads have increased, and employees are under stress when their agencies have too few resources to perform their missions effectively. Workplace violence can also result from substance abuse and psychological problems, and can be associated with sexual harassment and spousal abuse. The levels of anger and frustration in American society as a whole have contributed to the hazard, as well. As one might expect, much of the impetus for workplace violence policies and programs in state and local governments has been from their human resource offices, rather than from their security offices (Nigro and Waugh 1998, 1999).

Recent incidences of violence in America's schools are being noted by emergency managers, as well. The shooting of 13 teachers and students and the suicides of the 2 teenaged attackers in Littleton, Colorado, in 1999 followed a series of school attacks by students. An attack at a suburban middle school outside Atlanta in May 1999, in which 6 students were wounded, served to underscore the danger. The threat of violence has prompted many schools to use surveillance cameras in hallways and outside buildings, post armed security guards at entrances, and use metal detectors to prevent students from bring guns, knives, bombs, and other dangerous objects into buildings. While most of the incidences of school violence have only involved a few students, there is the potential, as the Littleton case demonstrated, for more casualties. Mass casualty incidences can require a broad emergency management response. Had any of the bombs taken into Columbine High School in Littleton been detonated the tragic toll might have been considerably worse. A comprehensive workplace or school violence program should involve the local emergency management agency to coordinate the efforts of facility officials and local emergency response and law enforcement agencies management agencies.

Terrorism and Civil Disorder

The potential for terrorism has never been greater and the potential for civil disorder is always present. Politically motivated violence against public and private individuals, facilities, and complex communications, power, and transportation networks is of increasing concern. The hazard is not new, but the potential consequences have grown tremendously. In fact, terrorism has been a common political tactic since humans began walking the earth and has been used frequently throughout American history. The Sons of Liberty were using terrorism when they tossed boxes of tea into Boston Harbor and attacked supporters of the king. The scale of political violence has increased since that time. Attacks and attempted attacks on women's clinics, police stations, tax offices, law enforcement officers, forest rangers, aircraft and airports, and other targets have increased public awareness of domestic and international threats and encouraged Congressional and presidential action to assess, monitor, and mitigate the risk of such violence.

Since World War II, there have been several cycles of political violence directed against Americans in the United States and overseas, and directed against foreign individuals and firms in the United States. Few Americans were killed during the violence of the 1950s. In fact, bombs were often designed to create considerable noise without lethal shrapnel. The willingness of terrorists to maim and kill increased during the 1960s, however. Aircraft hijackings became a common occurrence and increasingly resulted in passenger and crew deaths. The escalation of the violence has been attributed to a variety of factors ranging from a shift in terrorist motives from ideological idealism to more fanatical ethnic and religious separatism, copying the shift in national nuclear warfare strategies from political and economic targets to civilian populations, the focus on psychological warfare in conventional military doctrine, and the growing frustration among terrorists about their lack of political success and their inability to draw broad popular support. The need to create ever larger spectacles to attract and keep media attention may also be a factor. Whatever the reasons, terrorism moved from nonlethal violence, to murders of one or a few individuals, to mass casualty events from the 1950s to the 1980s. There were successes in mitigating the violence. Airport security, particularly the use of metal detectors and x-ray machines, reduced the incidence of hijackings. It also helped that officials in Cuba, the destination of many American hijackers in the 1950s and 1960s, decided that such guests were more trouble than the minor propaganda value they generated, and Palestinian groups, for whom hijacking became high art in the mid- to late 1960s, also chose not to continue using the tactic in the early 1970s. By 1972, hijackings were uncommon events, although there were still a few dramatic and long hostage takings during the 1980s, such as the hijacking of a TWA flight in 1985 that involved weeks of negotiations on the tarmac in Beirut, Lebanon. Such events can become very difficult to manage because of the number of actors involved and unclear legal jurisdiction. In the Beirut case, the aircraft was American and many of the passengers were American, but the site was Lebanese. The terrorists had boarded the aircraft in Greece. U.S. authorities had no means of gaining control of the location, particularly after the hostages were moved to other locations by the terrorists and their supporters (see Waugh and Sweeney 1988).

Responsibility for domestic antiterrorism programs was largely in the hands of the FBI, with the Federal Aviation Administration being responsible for airport security, the Nuclear Regulatory Commission being responsible for security within nuclear plants, and other agencies having similar responsibilities regarding other sensitive facilities. The focus was on guarding facilities, limiting access, and apprehending suspected terrorists. Some programs were very simple—for instance, removing luggage lockers from the parts of airport terminals with high pedestrian traffic (to reduce the risk to innocent travelers) and increasing surveillance of secure areas. Other programs were more complex, such as using psychological profiles to identify potential terrorists.

Despite objections to baggage searches by some travelers concerned with privacy, delays caused by the heightened security precautions, and the cost of security personnel and equipment, the public has largely adjusted to the new regulations. More sophisticated explosive detection equipment may delay passengers further, however. Prohibiting parking outside air terminals and other public facilities to reduce the risk of car bombs, matching passengers and luggage prior to flights to assure that all are accounted for, and occasional restrictions on access to gate areas by nonpassengers still confuse and frustrate some people, but such extraordinary precautions are seldom taken unless there has been a credible threat of violence. Similarly, the American public appears to be adjusting to the increasingly restricted access to public buildings and the inconvenience of facility security procedures (Waugh 1990). The mitigation programs appear to be working, although recent violence suggests that precautions should be strengthened and/or expanded. There is also a natural tendency for security to become lax when there are long periods of time between incidences of violence. Low pay also may not encourage diligence or attract capable people.

The bombing of the World Trade Center towers in New York City by international terrorists in 1993 and the bombing of the Murrah Federal Building in Oklahoma City by domestic terrorists in 1995 have encouraged a new look at the hazard of terrorism. While there have been relatively few deaths from terrorist violence in the United States, notwithstanding the 168 killed in the Oklahoma City bombing, the willingness of terrorists to kill hundreds or thousands of innocent bystanders suggests a further escalation in the level of violence. Many of the constraints that dissuaded groups and nations from killing thousands or even millions of people have been loosened. Soviet and Eastern European intelligence and military officers left unemployed at the end of the Cold War; nuclear and chemical weaponry and materials, left over from the Cold War, which may be sold to or stolen by terrorist organizations; international tension caused by "rogue regimes" not constrained by concerns for human rights or international law and with histories of investment in chemical and biological weapon research; and the fact that even relatively unsophisticated international and domestic terrorist organizations can produce "weapons of mass destruction" increase the level of risk. Bombs are relatively easy to make. The directions for building pipe bombs, fertilizer and fuel oil bombs, and even nuclear, biological, and chemical weapons can be downloaded from the Internet by virtually anyone.

In the United States, the general availability of military-type weapons increases the potential for mass casualty incidences of terrorist violence. High rates of fire make automatic weapons much more dangerous than traditional hunting and target shooting weapons and the semiautomatic weapons commonly carried by law enforcement officers. In fact, the firepower of terrorists and other criminals may well exceed that of the police. Terrorists, too, are generally far less concerned than the police about endangering bystanders with a spray of bullets from automatic weapons or high-powered bullets that may penetrate buildings or travel long distances. However, the use of automatic weapons poses a danger to the public no matter whether the shooters are terrorists, criminals, or law enforcement officers.

Antigovernment violence is as old as the nation. In recent years, ultra-conservative groups, including members of the Ku Klux Klan, Aryan Nations, Christian Identity groups, the numerous militia movements, "free-men" organizations, and even separatist movements, have attacked federal, state, and local officials and facilities. Their grievances range from fears of world government and international conspiracies to federal gun control legislation and the tax system. Antigovernment violence is also being committed by people unassociated with organized groups, some identifying themselves and their religious war with the so-called Phineas Priesthood. Antigovernment attacks or attempted attacks since 1992 (U.S. Department of Energy 1997) include:

- An attempted bombing of the National Association for the Advance-ment of Colored People (NAACP) headquarters in Tacoma, Washing-ton, and a gay bar in Seattle by a group called the American Front Skinheads in 1993.
- The bombing of a Bureau of Land Management facility in Reno, Nevada, in October 1993.
- The pipe bombing of a U.S. Forest Service facility in Carson City, Nevada, in March 1995.
- The attempted bombing of the federal courthouse in Spokane, Wash-ington, in April 1995.
- The truck bomb that destroyed the Murrah Federal Building in Okla-homa City in April 1995, killing 168 people and wounding 400 more.
- A plot to kill federal officials with ricin, a toxin extracted from castor beans, by the Patriots' Council, a terrorist group in Minnesota, in May 1995.
- A plot to bomb the Internal Revenue Service (IRS) processing center in Austin, Texas, by a tax protester in 1995.
- The crude bombing of the federal courthouse in Seattle, Washington, in June 1995.
- The bombing of machinery belonging to the U.S. Forest Service in Buffalo Creek, Colorado, in October 1995.
- The attempted bombing of the IRS office in Reno, Nevada, in Decem-ber 1995.
- A plot by a three-member "patriot" group to bomb the Southern Poverty Law Center in Atlanta, the Anti-Defamation League office in Houston, federal buildings, women's clinics, and other targets in April 1996.
- The pipe bombing of the Valley Planned Parenthood Clinic in Spokane, Washington, in July 1996. The bombing was a diversion designed to

enable a group associated with the Phineas Priesthood and other extremist groups to rob a nearby bank.

- A plot by members of the Mountaineer Militia of West Virginia to bomb the FBI fingerprint center in Clarksburg, West Virginia, in October 1996.

Law enforcement agencies have also uncovered large caches of weapons, including stolen assault rifles, hand grenades, rocket launchers, and toxic biological agents, in raids on extremist groups and individuals (U.S. Department of Energy 1997). Even rather unsophisticated groups have the capability of constructing and detonating pipe and other bombs, although the bomb builders themselves are often casualties of their own devices. The teenagers who attacked their classmates and teachers in Littleton, Colorado, in April 1999, for example, built dozens of explosive devices (as many as 50 at last report). Some were crude pipe bombs, but others were much more sophisticated and capable of destroying the high school.

The attacks on women's clinics by antiabortion extremists have included bombings, arson, assassinations of doctors and other clinic workers, and physical attacks, as well as terroristic threats against workers, their families, and patients. While the Freedom of Access to Clinic Entrances Act and increased federal and local law enforcement efforts to protect clinic personnel and facilities have reduced the number of attacks, bombings and shootings continue (U.S. GAO 1998a). Eric Robert Rudolph, the suspected bomber of a women's clinic in Birmingham that killed an off-duty police officer, Centennial Olympic Park in Atlanta during the Olympics, and a gay club and women's clinic in Atlanta was still a fugitive in late 1999. Law enforcement agencies were also searching for an antiabortion extremist who was suspected of stalking and shooting doctors in their homes in Canada and the United States. The Atlanta bombings, in particular, put emergency responders on notice that they may also be targets of extremists. In the Centennial Olympic Park bombing, a threat was called into the city's 911 center, but the bomb exploded prior to the time given by the caller. It is assumed that the intent of the bomber or bombers was to injure or kill police officers who did not expect the bomb to go off that soon. In subsequent bombings of a gay club and a women's clinic, small bombs exploded initially and, after emergency responders arrived on the scene, larger secondary devices exploded. Emergency medical responders have adopted the "burning car" protocol, to pick up and transport victims very quickly so that they might get away from the site of the bombing before a secondary bomb goes off.

CASE 4–6   The Murrah Federal Building Bombing in 1995

On April 19, 1995, a large blast shattered the Alfred P. Murrah Federal Building in downtown Oklahoma City. The bomb killed 168 people, including 19 children, and injured 674 more. Over 300 buildings were damaged, 25 severely. Automobiles, glass, and other debris were strewn over a 10-block area. A side of the Murrah building was laid open and floors collapsed. The rescue and recovery effort lasted until May 4, over two weeks after the blast (Oklahoma City 1996, 1–5).

Local first responders, as well as civilians who converged on the site to help, rescued victims from the upper floors, dug victims out of the rubble, and treated the injured as they made their way out of the collapsed building and surrounding buildings. Firefighters responded first to the walking wounded, gradually working their way to the Murrah building through the debris-filled street. The incident command system (ICS) was implemented with a shift commander taking charge of the incident and creating a command center near the federal building (Oklahoma City 1996, 10–13). With the implementation of the ICS, additional resources were brought in and a more systematic response was possible.

Because the facility was a federal building, federal authorities had principal responsibility for the operation, but the Oklahoma City Fire Department remained in charge of the rescue operation. The FBI was responsible for the crime scene. By afternoon, clergy volunteers were organized to counsel victims and their families and the disaster workers, the State Funeral Directors' Association had implemented its disaster plan for mass casualty events, mental health workers were organized, National Guard chaplains were assigned to death notification services, the American Red Cross had assumed responsibility for the Family Assistance Center, the Salvation Army and Feed the Children had helped set up temporary shelter and food programs for those evacuated from damaged buildings, and public information mechanisms had ben set up to assure accurate information for the media (Oklahoma City 1996, 28–31). FEMA brought in Urban Search and Rescue task forces and other agencies brought in law enforcement and rescue personnel.

The bomb was a 4,800-pound ammonium nitrate fuel oil device that had been transported to the north entrance of the building in a Ryder rental truck (Oklahoma City 1996, 10). The media coverage was compelling, particularly as the search for survivors gained momentum and rescuers focused on the location of the day care center on the first floor.

President Clinton declared a "National Day of Mourning" on Sunday, April 23, and a memorial service was held at the Oklahoma State Fairgrounds (Oklahoma City 1996, 60).

The biggest concern today is the potential for terrorists to use nuclear, biological, chemical, and radiological agents (i.e., "weapons of mass destruction"). Nuclear materials are available from a number of sources, including the "rogue" nations. The miniaturization of nuclear weapons may also make them vulnerable to theft and relatively easy to transport. Bomb-grade materials may also be available from the newest members of the "nuclear club." Biological weapons are certainly within the capabilities of some domestic and international terrorist groups, as well (Foxell 1997). In fact, in early 1999, there were threats of anthrax contamination virtually every week. Letters containing powder were sent to women's clinics, a news media office, and government offices. Emergency response personnel had no choice but to treat the incidents as real emergencies and put those exposed to the powder through complex decontamination processes. Thus far, fortunately, the threats have been hoaxes. Nonetheless, there is an imperative to develop biological agent detectors, vaccines, and other medical countermeasures for the most likely biological agents, in addition to more effective security measures to make it more difficult to loose a biological or chemical agent on the population (see Siegrist 1998). Fire-fighters and emergency medical personnel (alluding to the use of canaries to warn against methane and other gases in mines) do not want to become "red canaries" and law enforcement officers do not want to become "blue canaries" so that authorities can determine whether there are lethal agents in the area.

Presidential Decision Directive 39 outlines federal responsibilities for terrorist attacks involving weapons of mass destruction (WMD), with the FBI as the lead agency for crisis management and FEMA as the lead agency for consequence management. The organizational structure is described in Chapter 2. What is notable in policy terms is the expectation that there will be similarities between WMD events and other kinds of disasters and differences. WMD events will be similar in terms of potentially involving mass casualties, damage to buildings, the need for warnings, and the need to evacuate. The differences are that such events are caused purposely by people, the disaster areas will be treated as crime scenes, the weapons may not be immediately recognizable as such, there may be multiple sites or events, responders are at higher risk of becoming targets, critical facilities (e.g., hospitals) may be contaminated, the disaster area may expand as the agent spreads, and the public will likely respond strongly (FEMA 1998, 2-1–2-5). Moreover, residents in and around the disaster scene may panic and, in fleeing the area, spread the contagion (especially if it is a biological agent). Fear management in WMD events is a growing concern of federal officials (Waugh 1999a and b, 2000).

Terrorism is the bigger threat, but the potential for civil disorder should not be underestimated. The most recent major civil disorder was the so-called Rodney King riots in Los Angeles in 1992. The riots broke out on April 29, after a court did not find police officers guilty of beating King, an African American. Outrage concerning the verdict precipitated the violence, and over 50 people were killed as stores were looted and burned. Violence also erupted in other cities as the news of the verdict and the Los Angeles riots spread. The mayor of Los Angeles imposed a curfew, and the governor called out the National Guard to patrol the streets of the city. Over $1 billion in property damage resulted. Miami experienced riots in the 1980s following the death of a black resident by a police officer, and many cities experienced racial and antiwar disorders during the 1960s and 1970s. Civil disorder is common enough to warrant serious preparedness efforts in major cities and for public officials to be attentive to the need to lessen tensions (i.e., mitigate the hazard) when there are conflicts involving the police, ethnic groups, and others. There is often increased risk of violence during hot summer days when people and tempers are overheated. Increased violence has been associated with higher barometric pressures, as well (see Waugh 1990).

CIVIL DEFENSE

The threat of a catastrophic disaster wrought by a "rogue nation" or a rogue official with access to nuclear weapons and the necessary codes cannot be discounted, even though the Cold War has effectively been over for a decade or more. U.S. agencies still monitor the security and maintenance of nuclear weapons in the newly independent states, the nuclear capabilities of nations that are unfriendly to the United States, and the potential for nuclear devices to be lost, stolen, or sold to parties who might use them in a campaign of terrorism or an act of war.

Much of the current U.S. emergency management system was created as part of our national civil defense network, although the system has become far more oriented during the 1990s toward natural and man-made disasters not associated with war. The civil defense network was set up in the late 1940s and early 1950s, after the Soviet Union exploded its first atomic bomb and the United States became embroiled in the Korean War. The Federal Civil Defense Act of 1950 provided the authority to develop crisis plans and to train state and local officials to protect their constituents. The central focus of the program was bomb shelters. When the Soviet Union exploded its first hydrogen bomb in 1953, mass evacuation plans were added to the program (see, e.g., Smith 1990).

A nationwide system of fallout shelters was the centerpiece in President John F. Kennedy's civil defense program. The Cuban Missile Crisis and the Berlin Crisis fueled concern about a Soviet attack, and civil defense became a serious program. But interest in civil defense waned as the crises cooled. President Richard Nixon tried to reinvigorate the program, but local officials evidently were more interested in natural disasters. In 1979, President Jimmy Carter transferred the civil preparedness program from the U.S. Department of Defense to a new agency, the Federal Emergency Management Agency (FEMA).

While civil defense capabilities have certainly deteriorated considerably since the 1960s, the old programs are still having an impact on the national emergency management system. Many state and local emergency management agencies still have "civil defense" in their names. Most federal, state, and local emergency management agencies still employ former military personnel and some still have military-type organizational structures. But the system is changing rapidly as the field of emergency management professionalizes, and the organizational cultures of agencies are becoming much less hierarchical and formal. The changes are paralleling organizational changes in other public agencies and in the private sector (Waugh 1993).

HUMANITARIAN RELIEF

Increasingly, DOD and other federal agencies are being called upon to assist in humanitarian relief operations. While the Office of Foreign Disaster Assistance is a very small office with limited staff and other resources, it relies heavily on nongovernmental organizations to deliver U.S. disaster aid. The roles of NGOs and government agencies in such operations are well illustrated in Appendix 3.1, an Office of Foreign Disaster Assistance's situation report on the Hurricane Mitch disaster operation. Appendix 4–1 contains a situation report from the relief effort for Kosovo, prior to agencies of the United Nations and other agencies leaving that province. The interaction with foreign NGOs was similar to the Hurricane Mitch effort. A major difference, however, occurs when humanitarian relief is being provided in areas that are essentially war zones. The risk to disaster workers can be very great. CARE workers were accused of being spies and were arrested by the Serbian government in 1999. International relief workers in Somalia and other African nations have been killed in recent years. In such situations, there are strong pressures to use the military to deliver aid and to preserve order. In some cases, as in Somalia, for instance, the situation can be dangerous for military personnel as well. Disaster workers, civilian and military alike, can find themselves caught between two or more warring factions, having to defend food and other material from thieves and even from corrupt government officials, and prey to criminals and terrorists. Famine and other disasters often create chaos when governments are too weak to maintain order or disinclined to try. Relief organizations are making their own judgments concerning acceptable risk and are increasingly choosing to stay out of situations in which their workers will be in danger.

CONCLUSIONS

This chapter addresses only the major man-made hazards and disasters that may occur. The list could include everything from acid rain to the biohazards that might result from genetic engineering gone awry. The beginning of the new millennium also brings new hazards, the Y2K problem perhaps being the biggest, although, in the past, human society has experienced all sorts of madness as it has moved from one millennium to another. "Millennium madness" has taken the forms of mass hysteria, religious violence, and lethal exuberance. Fear, fervor, and excitement have caused people to burn their homes and villages, and to attack neighbors and strangers. While human society is less ignorant and superstitious and there are more constraints on behavior now than there were on December 31, 999, one should not overestimate the rationality of individuals and collectives.

Computer failures may be the most anticipated issue of the new millennium and, given that computer problems may continue for months after January 1, 2000, there will certainly be anxiety about the integrity of financial records, transportation safety, food and water availability, and other essential services and products for some time. It is likely, however, that concerns will continue after the computer transition is complete. Sophisticated computing systems are increasingly vulnerable to casual hackers, thieves, and terrorists. Viruses, information theft, and other threats to interconnected data networks prompted President Bill Clinton, on the advice of the President's Commission on Critical Infrastructure Protection, to create the National Infrastructure Protection Center and the Critical Infrastructure Assurance Office. Cyberterrorism is certainly a threat, but the larger hazard may be from hackers who break into computer networks for nonpolitical reasons (Peters 1999). In any case, computer security is one of the biggest issues of the new millennium.

Technological advancements create hazards and make societies more fragile because they are vulnerable to disruptions of critical systems. In that respect, it is difficult to anticipate all the kinds of disasters that may occur.

In terms of known hazards, there are literally thousands. There have been recent cases of food and water contamination in which thousands of people have been made ill. Biological and chemical contamination of processed meats, vegetables, milk, fruit, and other foodstuffs seems on the increase, although the incidences may seem larger because products may be sold regionally or nationally rather than in one or two communities as they were earlier in American history. There is growing concern that the public is paying too little attention to food recalls, as well. Even when contaminated foods are discovered, they may be consumed before the warnings are received.

There is a growing problem with so-called "road rage" in which aggressive drivers kill other motorists with their cars or with firearms. On congested urban roadways, such behavior can cause multivehicle wrecks and endanger dozens of drivers and passengers. In response to the problem, cities and states are implementing traffic monitoring programs to identify aggressive drivers before they cause accidents or use violence against other motorists.

The cleanup of hazardous materials sites (e.g., the Superfund sites) has been very slow and some communities are experiencing serious health problems. Higher than normal cancer rates, birth defects, nervous disorders, and other conditions have been found in communities situated on or near old industrial sites. The "Emergency Planning and Community Right to Know" law assures that residents will be informed of hazards in their communities and that authorities will develop appropriate emergency plans, but there are still old hazards that have not yet been discovered and evaluated. In some cases, there are no records of the materials that were buried or spilled on the sites and no individuals or firms responsible for cleaning them up. The companies have long since disappeared or moved on to other sites.

Mitigating man-made disasters is essentially a function of protecting people from themselves and one another. Individualism is a core American value, and there is a notion ingrained in the American psyche that people should be able to do whatever they wish as long as they do not hurt other people. Despite periodic efforts to protect us from ourselves, such as Prohibition and current antidrug laws, Americans have a remarkable amount of freedom. As population grows, however, it is becoming more and more dangerous for people to behave as they did when the nation was largely rural. Debates are raging about the regulation of private property to protect larger community values or to protect people from their neighbors or themselves. Land-use regulations, building codes, gun control laws, environmental regulations, and other restrictions on personal prerogatives are generally designed to prevent or lessen the likelihood that individuals will hurt someone else. Depletion of aquifers encourages the regulation of water use on private and public property, the threat of structural failures encourages the regulation of building, terrorism and workplace violence encourage discussion of gun control and other security measures, aircraft crashes encourage efforts to improve aircraft design and pilot training, and so on. Regulations are implemented in response to specific disasters and often are less applicable to future events, however.

DISCUSSION QUESTIONS

1. Why do developers and builders oppose stricter building codes?
2. What is the problem in holding owners financially liable for building, dam, and other structural collapses, rather than regulating the building and maintenance of such structures?
3. Why might clients attack public employees?
4. Why do extremists attack government offices and public employees? What kinds of agencies might be the major targets of violence?

REFERENCES

Charles, Richard. 1999. "Evaluating the Performance of the FAA: An Application of Herbert Simon's *Administrative Behavior*." Ph.D. Dissertation, Atlanta: Georgia State University, draft.

Federal Emergency Management Agency. 1987. "Dam Safety: Know the Potential Danger," Pamphlet L152. Emmitsburg, MD: FEMA, May.

————. Emergency Management Institute. 1998. *Senior Officials' Workshop Manual: Preparedness and Response for Terrorist Incidents.* Emmitsburg, MD: FEMA, September.

Foxell, Joseph W., Jr. 1997. "The Prospect of Nuclear and Biological Terrorism." *Journal of Contingencies and Crisis Management* 5 (June): 98–108.

Heys, Sam. 1986. "Winecoff Fire Seared Memories of the Survivors." *Atlanta Constitution* (December 5): 1B, 4B.

Johnson, Glen. 1999a. "Board Points to Faulty Rudders in Air Crashes." *Atlanta Journal-Constitution* (March 24): A3.

————. 1999b. "NTSB Urges More 737 Changes." *Atlanta Journal-Constitution* (March 25): A4.

————. 1999c. "Scores Killed in Track Crossing Wrecks Yearly." *Atlanta Journal-Constitution* (March 17): A8.

Lutrin, Carl E., and Allen K. Settle. 1992. *American Public Administration: Concepts and Cases.* 4th ed. St. Paul, MN: West.

Mitchell, John G. 1999. "In the Wake of the Spill: Ten Years After *Exxon Valdez*." *National Geographic* 195, 3 (March): 96–117.

Nigro, Lloyd G., and William L. Waugh, Jr. 1999. "The Human Resources Perspective on

Workplace Violence." In *Strategic Public Personnel Administration: Managing Human Capital for the New Century,* ed. Ali Farazmand. Westport, CT: Greenwood, forthcoming.

———. 1998. "Workplace Violence Policies and Programs in American Local Government." In *Municipal Yearbook 1998.* Washington, DC: International City/County Management Association, 3–8.

Neustadt, Richard E., and Harvey Fineberg. 1983. *The Epidemic That Never Was: Policy-Making and the Swine Flu Affair.* New York: Vintage Books.

Nuclear Regulatory Commission. 1998. "NRC Response to Events." http://www.nrc.gov. December.

Oklahoma City, City of. 1996. *Final Report: Alfred P. Murrah Federal Building Bombing, April 19, 1995.* Stillwater, OK: Fire Protection Publications.

Patureau, Alan. 1987. "Atlanta's Other Great Fire." *Atlanta Constitution* (May 17): 1H, 5H.

Perrow, Charles. 1984. *Normal Accidents: Living with High-Risk Technologies.* New York: Basic Books.

Peters, Katherine McIntire. 1999. "Information Insecurity." *Government Executive* (April): 18–22.

Robinson, Katherine McIntire. 1999. "Information Insecurity." *Government Executive* (April): 18–22.

Siegrist, David W. 1998. "Advanced Technology to Counter Biological Terrorism." Presentation to the International Conference on Threats in the Technological Age, Hohon, Israel, March 18.

Smith, Loran. 1990. "Civil Defense." In *Handbook of Emergency Management,* eds. William L. Waugh, Jr., and Ronald John Hy, 271–292. Westport, CT: Greenwood.

Stern, Gerald M. 1976. *The Buffalo Creek Disaster.* New York: Vintage Books.

Sylves, Richard T. 1998. "How the Exxon Valdez Disaster Changed America's Oil Spill Emergency Management." *International Journal of Mass Emergencies and Disasters* 16 (March): 13–43.

Thompson, Tracy. 1986. "Winecoff Hotel Fire Remains a Mystery." *Atlanta Constitution* (December 5): 1A, 9A.

U.S. Department of Energy, Office of Safeguards and Security. 1997. *Anti-Government Terrorism and Related Activities in the U.S., 1992–96.* Washington, DC: DOE, January.

U.S. Fire Academy. 1999. "Operational Considerations for High-Rise Firefighting." Technical Report 082. http://usfa.fema.gov/techreps/tr082.htm.

U.S. General Accounting Office. 1998a. *Abortion Clinics: Information on the Effectiveness of the Freedom of Access to Clinic Entrances Act.* Washington, DC: GAO, GAO/GGD-99-2, November.

———. 1998b. *Hazardous Waste Sites: State Cleanup Practices.* Washington, DC: GAO, GAO/RCED-99-39, December.

———. 1989. *Coast Guard: Adequacy of Preparation and Response to* Exxon Valdez *Oil Spill.* Washington, DC: GAO, GAO (RCED-90-44), October.

Waugh, William L., Jr. 2000. *Terrorism and Weapons of Mass Destruction.* New York: Marcel Dekker, forthcoming.

———. 1999a. "Managing Terrorism as an Environmental Hazard." In *Handbook of Crisis and Emergency Management,* ed. Ali Farazmand. New York: Marcel Dekker, forthcoming.

————. 1999b. *Terrorism and Emergency Management: An Instructor Guide*. Emmitsburg, MD: Federal Emergency Management Agency, Emergency Management Institute, Higher Education Project.

————. 1993. "Co-ordination or Control: Organizational Design and the Emergency Management Function." *International Journal of Disaster Prevention and Management* 2 (December): 17–31.

————. 1990. *Terrorism and Emergency Management*. New York: Marcel Dekker.

————. 1988. "The Hyatt Skywalk Disaster." In *Crisis Management*, eds. Michael Charles and John Kim, 115–129. Springfield, IL: Charles C. Thomas.

Waugh, William L., Jr., and Nigro, Lloyd G. 1999. "Workplace Violence Policies in American State Governments." Paper presented at the National Conference of the American Society for Public Administration, Orlando, FL, April 10–13.

Waugh, William L., Jr., and Ronald John Hy. 1996. "The Hyatt Skywalk Disaster and Other Lessons in the Regulation of Building." In *Disaster Management in the U.S. and Canada*, eds. Richard T. Sylves and William L. Waugh, Jr., 253–269. Springfield, IL: Charles C. Thomas.

Waugh, William L., Jr., and Jane P. Sweeney. "International Law and the TWA Hijacking of 1985." In *Crisis Management*, eds. Michael Charles and John Kim, 130–146. Springfield, IL: Charles C. Thomas.

World Almanac and Book of Facts 1999. Mahwah, NJ: World Almanac Books, 1998.

APPENDIX 4–1 USAID/OFDA Kosovo Disaster Assistance Response Team (DART) Update, December 2, 1998

Dart Visits Village of Llausha

On November 28, Kosovo DART members visited the village of Llausha, two kilometers south west of Kosovska Mitrovica. DART Kosovo talked to a family working on the roof of their home. The family said that most of the 300 homes in Llausha suffered severe damage. The UNHCR IDP/shelter survey reported that 85% of the houses in Llausha had no roofs and fall into category four or five. In addition, in their section of the village there are forty houses but only three families have returned. The twelve-member family, which is living in a two-room structure next to their burned out house, said they had received assistance just two days before of 50 kilograms of flour, 1 liter of vegetable oil, sugar, salt, beans, a CRS hygiene pack two pair of children's boots and some winter clothes from a local distribution site. (WFP had requested the addition of the village of Llausha to the list of convoys for the week of November 24–30, since the village reportedly had not received assistance for some time.)

Kosovo DART Visits Village of Murge

Kosovo DART members also visited the village of Murge, 15 kilometers west of Klina. The DART was following up on a report by the German NGO Kinderberg dated November 23, 1998, which reported there were 310 people living in a railroad tunnel near Murge who had not received assistance. Several villagers stated that a few months ago there were people in the railroad tunnel, but they had all returned to the area of Donje Obrinje. The villagers in Murge said they had received wheat flour earlier in the week from the Mother Teresa Society (MTS).

Kosovo DART Visits Village of Donje Obrinje

Kosovo DART members proceeded to the village of Donje Obrinje, 15 miles north west of Klina. The DART visited a family of eighteen people (seven adults and 11 children) living in a two room structure. The structure had a mud floor, brick and mud walls, and a roof made of corn stalks and plastic sheeting.

The family reported they had been living under plastic sheeting next to their house only two days before. The family had received relief commodities including wheat flour, milk, beans, and soap at the local distribution site in Likovac. The family had only a two day supply of food left and was not sure when the next delivery of aid would occur. Kosovo DART members plan to return to the village next week to see if additional commodities arrive.

UNHCR Escorting Convoys Containing P.L. 480 Title II Food

A Catholic Relief Services (CRS) representative told the Kosovo DART that Montenegrin drivers are refusing to deliver P.L. 480 Title II food commodities from the port of Bar to Prizren or from Pristina to Prizren without an escort, due to security concerns. The CRS representative, however, said UNHCR is meeting the needs for daily convoy escorts from Bar and Pristina to Prizren. The CRS representative also said that UNHCR has agreed to provide a convoy leader in Prizren for convoys delivering P.L. 480 Title II and other non-food commodities. The CRS did note they would begin sending out a total of six convoys a day from Prizren and Pristina by the middle of December and would therefore require additional convoy escorts.

Curfew for UNHCR-Plated Vehicles

Due to an increase in vehicle vandalism, the head of the UNHCR office in Pristina announced that all vehicles with UNHCR license plates are now required to be off the streets and in garages by 10:00 P.M. This curfew affects both vehicles owned by UNHCR and vehicles owned by NGOs, which have UNHCR license plates. Earlier in the week, KDOM, OSCE, WFP, and several NGOs reported slashed tires and broken windows on vehicles parked either in front of their headquarters or in downtown Pristina. In addition, the UNHCR declared that all UNHCR plated vehicles must have an international staff member aboard during all travel around Kosovo.

NGOs and IOs Report Delays in Visa Approvals

Several NGOs and international organizations reported to the DART Kosovo information officer that they are experiencing delays in the approval of visas for international staff members. A World Food Program representative reported that they have a person in Rome who has been waiting four weeks for a visa. The WFP representative also reported having a similar problem in August. IRC reports that several of their employees are having to wait up to a month or more for approval of visas. They currently have two individuals who submitted their visa applications over three weeks ago. IRC is submitting visas applications in Nairobi, London, Rome, and Washington. In total, IRC said they have seven people with applications still pending. In addition, Medecins du Monde/France (MDM/F) says that when applying for visas through Paris they are experiencing delays of six to eight weeks. A Danish Refugee Council representative reports no delays in their visa applications but did say when international staff are applying for multiple entry visas the FRY visa office is asking for information on the type and number of vehicles they are bringing in, and the salaries and home addresses of their local and international staff.

CONVOY REPORTS FOR NOVEMBER 26–DECEMBER 2, 1998

November 26, 1998

1. Location: Zur—municipality of Pec
   Beneficiaries: 700 IDPs
   Escort: UNHCR
   Commodities: MCI—1 truck (500 kg sugar, 300 kg salt, 300 kg milk powder, 400 kg beans, 1100 packs of soup, 400 kg detergent, 1500 bars of soap, 1100 pair of footwear/boots and shoes, 200 kg supplemental food, 100 bags of clothes)
      CRS—1 truck (90 packs of soap, 10 bags of footwear, 30 blankets, 1430 kg of clothes)
      UNHCR—1 truck (256 hygienic napkins, 10 bales of clothes, 100 shelter kits, 192 HDRs)

   Total food items: 2 MT
   Total non-food: 7.9 MT

2. Location: Urosevac—municipality of Urosevac
   Beneficiaries: 13,000 IDPs
   Escort: UNHCR
   Commodities: MCI—1 truck (3000 kg sugar, 170 kg rice, 1500 kg salt, 2004 kg milk powder, 2010 kg beans, 14400 packs of soup, 2340 kg detergent, 3000 bars of soap, 4000 pair of footwear/boots, 1000 blankets, 150 bags of clothes, 60 packs of cheese)

CRS—1 truck (90 packs of soap, 10 bags of footwear, 30 blankets, 1150 kg of clothes)

UNHCR—1 truck (512 packs of hygienic napkins, 100 shelter kits, 15 bales of blankets, 20 bales of clothes)

WFP—1 truck (4.5 MT wheat flour, 500 kg vegetables)

Total food items: 15.7 MT
Total non food: 21.4 MT

3. Location: Vucitrn—municipality of Glogovac
   Beneficiaries: 50,500 IDPs
   Escort: UNHCR
   Commodities: MCI—1 truck (3500 kg sugar, 2000 kg rice, 1800 kg salt, 2004 kg milk powder, 2010 kg beans, 14400 packs of soup, 2340 kg detergent, 3000 bars of soap, 5000 pairs of footwear/boots and shoes, 60 blankets, 60 packs of cheese)

   CRS—1 truck (90 packs of soap, 10 bags of footwear, 30 blankets, 1328 kg of clothes)

   DOW—1 truck (1050 family packs of food)

   WFP—1 truck (5 MT wheat flour)

   UNHCR—1 truck (256 hygienic napkins, 120 mattresses, 10 bales of blankets, 10 bales of clothes, 100 shelter kits)

   Total food items: 19.4 MT
   Total non food: 16.6 MT

4. Location: Llausha—municipality of Srbica
   Beneficiaries: 4,000 IDPs
   Escort: UNHCR
   Commodities: MCI—1 truck (30 stoves, 500 kg sugar, 300 kg rice, 100 liters of vegetable oil, 300 kg milk powder, 400 kg beans, 1200 packs of soup, 400 kg detergent, 1500 bars of soap, 1100 pairs of footwear/boots and shoes, 90 blankets, 300 kg salt, 3000 kg wheat flour, 70 packs of cheese)

   Total food items: 5.7 MT
   Total non food: 3 MT

November 27, 1998

1. Location: Polac—municipality of Srbica
   Beneficiaries: 3,000 IDPs

Escort: UNHCR
Commodities: MCI—2 trucks (5 MT wheat flour, 30 stoves, 240 liters of vegetable oil, 2295 kg cheese, 400 kg salt, 840 kg milk powder, 500 kg rice, 405 kg beans, 720 kg detergent, 2500 bars of soap, 2000 pair of footwear/boots, 432 packs of high protein biscuits)

CRS—1 truck (45 packs of soap, 10 bags of footwear, 1370 kg of clothes)

Cad—1 truck (44 packs of clothes/children and adult, 26 packs of footwear/children and adult, 30 bales of blankets, 60 bags of baby plastic bags)

UNHCR—1 truck (512 hygienic napkins, 10 bales of clothes, 256 packs of soap, 32 packs of blankets)

Total food items: 10.1 MT
Total non-food: 15.9 MT

2. Location: **Magura**—municipality of Lipljan
Beneficiaries: 3,000 IDPs
Escort: UNHCR
Commodities: MCI—1 truck (600 kg sugar, 400 kg salt, 400 kg rice, 229.5 kg cheese, 600 kg milk powder, 400 kg beans, 432 packs of high protein biscuits, 1872 packs of soup, 612 kg detergent, 1500 bars of soap, 2000 pair of footwear/boots, 4 MT wheat flour)

CRS—1 truck (45 packs of soap, 10 bags of footwear, 1010 kg of clothes)

UNHCR—1 truck (512 hygienic napkins, 10 bales of clothes, 256 packs of soap, 32 packs of blankets)

Total food items: 7.2 MT
Total non-food: 7.6 MT

3. Location: Patacane—municipality of Orahovac
Beneficiaries: 4,000 IDPs
Escort: UNHCR
Commodities: MCI—1 truck (700 kg sugar, 400 kg rice, 300 kg salt, 153 kg cheese, 360 kg milk powder, 300 kg beans, 288 packs of high protein biscuits, 360 kg detergent, 1500 bars of soap, 1500 pair of footwear/boots, 1723 packs of soup, 2000 kg wheat flour)

CRS—1 truck (45 packs of soap, 10 bags of footwear, 1060 kg of clothes)

Total food items: 4.6 MT
Total non-food: 3.6 MT

November 28, 1998

1. Location: Gornja Luka—municipality of Decane
   Beneficiaries: 6,800 IDPs
   Escort: UNHCR
   Commodities: MCI—1 truck (3205 kg sugar, 2196 kg milk powder, 2500 bars of soap, 1800 pairs of footwear/boots, 4924 packs of soup, 1296 kg detergent, 930 kg rice, 600 kg salt, 230 kg cheese, 432 packs of hygienic kits, 240 blankets, 744 liters of vegetable oil, 350 kg macaroni, 405 kg beans, 300 pairs of footwear/shoes, 10 mattresses, 300 pairs of underwear, 800 kg baby food, 408 packs of hygienic napkins, 150 packs of used clothes)
   Total food items: 9.9 M
   Total non-food: 6.6 MT

2. Location: Domanek—municipality of Malisevo
   Beneficiaries: 13,616 IDPs
   Escort: UNHCR
   Commodities: MCI—2 trucks (10 MT wheat flour, 3000 kg sugar, 1100 kg rice, 600 kg salt, 306 kg cheese, 1800 kg milk powder, 300 packs of hygienic napkins, 810 kg detergent, 1500 bars of soap, 3200 pair of footwear/boots, 4896 packs of soup, 30 rolls of plastic sheeting, 210 bags of blankets/clothes)
   CRS—6 trucks (190 m3 of firewood)
   WFP—1 truck (5 MT wheat flour)
   DOW—1 truck (1000 family packs of food)
   Total food items: 23.2 MT
   Total non-food: 6.8 MT, 190 m3

3. Location: Petrovo—municipality of Lipljan
   Beneficiaries: 3,000 IDPs
   Escort: UNHCR
   Commodities: MCI—1 truck (2000 kg wheat flour, 1000 bars of soap, 1504 pairs of rubber boots, 1000 kg sugar, 288 packs of hygienic napkins, 539 kg rice, 400 kg salt, 720 kg milk powder, 200 kg beans, 1400 packs of soup, 630 kg detergent, 153 kg cheese, 6 bags of used footwear/shoes, 180 sets of bed linen, 20 stoves)
   CAD—1 jeep (5 packs of used clothes)
   Total food items: 4.9 MT
   Total non-food: 4.8 MT

November 30, 1998

1. Location: Golubovac—municipality of Klina
   Beneficiaries: 16,454 IDPs
   Escort: UNHCR
   Commodities: MCI—1 truck (396 liters of vegetable oil, 690 kg sugar, 530 kg rice, 306 kg cheese, 600 kg milk powder, 1440 packs of soup, 450 kg detergent, 1000 bars of soap, 288 packs of hygienic napkins, 1000 pairs of footwear/rubber boots, 27 rolls of plastic sheeting, 1250 bags, 300 kg baby food, 240 kg beans, 100 blankets, 58 packs of used clothes/shoes)
   UNHCR—1 truck (256 packs of hygienic napkins, 86 packs of soap, 15 bales of blankets, 225 mattresses)
   Total food items: 2.9 MT
   Total non-food: 9.2 MT

2. Location: Dobrosevac—municipality of Glogovac
   Beneficiaries: 8,770 IDPs
   Escort: UNHCR
   Commodities: MCI—1 truck (27 rolls of plastic, 1500 bars of soap, 2000 pairs of footwear/rubber boots, 1260 kg sugar, 432 packs of hygienic kits, 530 kg rice, 840 liters of oil, 840 kg milk powder, 300 kg baby food, 2592 packs of soup, 612 kg detergent, 306 kg cheese, 6 bags of used clothes, 1259 school bags, 140 blankets)
   UNHCR—1 truck (256 packs of hygienic napkins, 86 packs of soap, 15 rolls of blankets, 125 mattresses)
   Total food items: 4.3 MT
   Total non-food: 7.4 MT

3. Location: Sverke—municipality of Klina
   Beneficiaries: 6,800 IDPs
   Escort: UNHCR
   Commodities: MCI—1 truck (792 liters of vegetable oil, 1155 kg sugar, 530 kg rice, 306 kg cheese, 756 kg milk powder, 2016 packs of soup, 594 kg detergent, 1300 bars of soap, 432 packs of hygienic napkins, 1300 pairs of footwear/rubber boots, 30 rolls of plastic sheeting, 1250 bags, 300 kg baby food, 235 kg beans, 60 packs of used clothes/shoes)
   Total food items: 4.2 MT
   Total non-food: 4.6 MT

December 1, 1998

1. Location: Glogovac—municipality of Glogovac
   Beneficiaries: 17,000 IDPs
   Escort: UNHCR
   Commodities: MCI—1 truck (70 stoves, 15 bags of used clothes/ shoes, 1200 liters of vegetable oil, 4005 kg sugar, 459 kg cheese, 2404 kg milk powder, 7200 packs of soup, 576 packs of hygienic napkins, 2500 pairs of footwear/rubber boots, 706 pairs of footwear/shoes, 40 pairs of jeans, 10 bags of clothes, 150 blankets, 16 mattresses, 480 pairs of underwear/ children)
   Total food items: 8.7 MT
   Total non-food: 7.9 MT

2. Location: Djakovica—municipality of Djakovica
   Beneficiaries: 48,000 IDPs
   Escort: UNHCR
   Commodities: MCI—3 trucks (3959 kg milk powder, 50 medical packs, 100 kg paper, 100 packs of clothes, 21 hospital beds, 21 mattresses, 30 medical packs for disabled, 10 kg kitchenware, 6000 liters of vegetable oil, 7005 kg sugar, 5000 kg salt, 1800 kg cheese, 11400 packs of soup, 3600 kg soap, 864 packs of hygienic napkins, 3000 bars of soap, 200 blankets, 2000 pairs of footwear/rubber boots, 3 bales of clothes, 1030 pairs of shoes, 30 packs of footwear/shoes)
   Total food items: 24.9 MT
   Total non-food: 8.3 MT

December 2, 1998

1. Location: Brolic—municipality of Pec
   Beneficiaries: 3,000 IDPs
   Escort: UNHCR
   Commodities: MCI—2 trucks (4 MT wheat flour, 1200 liters of vegetable oil, 1200 kg sugar, 800 kg salt, 300 kg milk powder, 288 hygienic packs, 1440 packs of soup, 306 kg detergent, 152 blankets, 1000 pairs of footwear/ boots, 950 kg rice, 120 bags of clothes, 390 kg supplemental food, 30 plastic sheets)
   CRS—1 truck (10 bags of shoes, 30 blankets, 90 packs of soap, 1400 kg clothes)
   DOW—1 truck (500 food packs)
   Total food items: 9.4 MT
   Total non-food: 2.9 MT

2. Location: Decane—municipality of Decane
   Beneficiaries: 1,500 IDPs
   Escort: UNHCR
   Commodities: MCI—3 trucks (4 MT wheat flour, 1200 liters of
   vegetable oil, 153 kg cheese, 800 kg milk powder, 567 kg detergent, 1440
   packs of soup, 576 hygienic packs, 180 blankets, 920 kg rice, 20 packs of
   plastic sheets, 300 kg supplemental food, 40 bags of clothes)
      CRS—1 truck (10 bags of shoes, 30 blankets, 90 packs of soap, 1400 kg
   clothes)
      Total food items: 7.5 MT
      Total non-food: 1.9 MT

3. Location: Junik—municipality of Decane
   Beneficiaries: 3,000 IDPs
   Escort: UNHCR
   Commodities: MCI—3 trucks (40 stoves, 4 MT wheat flour,
   1200 liters of vegetable oil, 1500 kg sugar, 800 kg salt, 400 kg milk powder,
   288 hygienic packs, 306 kg detergent, 150 blankets, 1000 pairs of footwear/
   boots, 120 bags of clothes, 1000 kg rice, 20 packs of plastic sheets, 198 kg
   supplemental food)
      CRS—1 truck (10 bags of shoes, 30 blankets, 90 packs of soap, 1500 kg
   clothes)
      DOW—1 truck (500 food packs)
      Total food items: 9.7 MT
      Total non-food: 5.6 MT

5

POLICY ISSUES
IN EMERGENCY
MANAGEMENT

Epidemics, wars, floods, hurricanes, earthquakes, and other major natural and technological or man-made disasters present government leaders with both challenges and opportunities. Crises may tax technical and administrative capacities, exhaust resources for disaster response and even for day-to-day operations well after the disaster, and exact a political price whether the effort is successful or not. It is seldom the case that a government is overwhelmed by a natural or technological disaster, but it is usually the case that a government finds weaknesses in its preparation for that event. By their very nature, disasters present unanticipated problems and an effective response requires administrative flexibility. As a consequence, disaster operations are usually followed by an exercise to identify the "lessons learned" to improve operations for the next disaster. Perhaps more so than officials in other policy areas, emergency managers and other officials involved in disaster operations are forced to examine their own performances and evaluate their policies and programs. Emergency managers are seldom anonymous bureaucrats because they frequently operate in the glare of television lights and almost always under the close scrutiny of elected officials and the public. Accountability is difficult to avoid, in other words. The attention of political constituents, the media, and even neighbors and coworkers is focused on the response, and failures are hard to hide.

Hazard management activities, on the other hand, are seldom monitored closely by public officials, the media, or the public at large. While special interest groups, such as environmental organizations, may be very much involved in the hazard management effort or may be monitoring it very closely, relatively little attention is paid to hazard policies and programs until a crisis occurs. Disaster acts as a "triggering event," drawing public attention and public resources to the issue. In public policy terms, disasters create an imperative to act. Public agencies and other community organizations are charged with responding to the social and economic needs of victims. Disasters also create "policy windows" in terms of sensitizing the public and its elected leaders to the need to act and to prepare for future events, although those "windows" may close rather rapidly as the memory of disaster fades. Unfortunately, policy responses typically address the specific needs created by a catastrophic event or series of events, rather than anticipating needs that may arise in future but somewhat dissimilar events.

As public officials find out quickly, there can be great political costs if they fail to respond effectively, and conversely, there can be great political rewards if they appear successful. Whether elected or career officials, they have to weigh the potential costs against the gains. They may be held personally, politically, and (for local officials) legally accountable, even if the disaster is so catastrophic as to be beyond the capabilities of even the best-prepared government. Failures can result in election losses, lawsuits, and public humiliation. The dilemma, however, is that there may not be enough money to pay for effective hazard management programs, regardless of the attention of public officials. Many local governments have very limited capacities to raise revenue specifically for hazard management, because of antitax measures that make it difficult to pass new taxes, limited tax authority due to the nature of local tax systems (e.g., reliance upon property taxes), and opposition to new programs by influential political interests (e.g., developers, property owners, and ultraconservative groups that oppose government programs generally). As a result, officials who see the need for hazard management programs simply may lack the wherewithal to design and implement them. If the choice is to invest in emergency management policies and programs to reduce the likelihood of catastrophic losses, officials still face daunting challenges in order to design and implement effective programs. The prospects for effective action are not entirely grim, however. Federal and state governments may encourage and support the development of hazards programs and even provide financial and technical support. In some cases (e.g., the National Flood Insurance Program), they may require action. The community, too, may realize that the risk of disaster is too great to ignore and will support appropriate investments to reduce that risk.

It is not so difficult to find political and economic support for disaster operations. Public officials cannot afford to appear insensitive to the plight of the victims of disaster. While there may be every reason to blame the victims for their stupidity or ignorance, for putting themselves in harm's way, the camera and pen frequently capture their misery and pain and communicate a compelling image of need. The "CNN effect" makes it difficult to practice "tough love" by forcing individuals, organizations, and private firms to act responsibly when a hazard is known and lives and property are at risk. While it may not be reasonable to expect public officials to ignore the plight of victims who put themselves in danger, it is reasonable to provide incentives for risk reduction that will encourage desired behaviors. Moreover, reducing the availability of federal disaster assistance may encourage more state and local action to reduce hazards. The award of presidential disaster declarations is a political process. As Richard Sylves has pointed out, declarations are too often issued for relatively minor events (Sylves 1996). Forcing states and communities to rely more on their own resources for minor disasters is perhaps a starting place.

THE POLITICS OF EMERGENCY MANAGEMENT

Tip O'Neill's observation "All politics is local" is particularly apt in the case of emergency management. Much of the responsibility for reducing disaster losses rests with local governments and their constituents. While FEMA and state emergency management agencies may provide technical assistance, training, and financial resources, local authorities generally determine what will or will not be done. Land-use and construction regulation are good examples.

Developers, builders, and other economic interests, including individual property owners, often oppose the adoption of strict land-use regulations and building standards and too often successfully prevent their adoption. They argue that such regulations will increase the cost of building, reduce the value of property, limit the prerogatives of property owners in terms of what they can and cannot do with their property, and make it more difficult to sell the property to others. In large measure, their arguments are valid. The question, however, is whether those concerns outweigh the potential costs of not mitigating disasters. The lack of appropriate regulations and standards can result in tragic losses if a disaster occurs. Unexpected property losses can cause economic hardship for property owners who were unaware of the hazard or assumed that measures had been taken to minimize damage. Disasters can cause serious losses for mortgage and insurance companies that finance the purchase of the property and whose investment is generally backed up by the property itself. Ultimately, the failure to have appropriate land-use regulations and building standards can affect a community's capacity to survive and recover from major disasters and can jeopardize the investments of individual property owners and the financial institutions that helped them purchase their property.

Third, the costs of disaster response and recovery efforts are growing at a rapid rate. The ten most expensive disasters experienced by the United States have been in the last decade or so. For that reason, FEMA and its state and local counterparts are increasingly focusing their energies on mitigation programs to reduce the risk of disasters and to minimize their effects. Similarly, insurance companies and mortgage banks stand to lose millions of dollars and may well face bankruptcy when property damage liabilities exceed reserves and/or the value of properties. As a consequence of heavy losses in south Florida from Hurricane Andrew in 1992, the insurance industry has begun to focus on ways to encourage the adoption and enforcement of appropriate building codes.

IMPEDIMENTS TO EFFECTIVE DISASTER POLICIES AND PROGRAMS

The second chapter ended with a lengthy list of obstacles to effective emergency management, ranging from the state of scientific knowledge about the causes and effects of hazards to the current political milieu which is characterized by declining public support for taxes, regulations, and expanded government programs. For the most part, the obstacles are political and economic. The biggest problems for emergency managers are less technical than they are the obvious difficulties of gaining and maintaining political and economic support for mitigation efforts. More funds for research and the development of technologies to deal with hazards and to respond to disasters would also help. However, it would be naive to argue that more funding of basic and applied research would produce all the needed answers to questions about seismic, volcanic, meteorological, chemical, and other natural and technological hazards. But more funding would encourage researchers to address those important questions.

A central political issue is whether the hazards represent more of a risk to society than other problems. Is the need to reduce the risk of building collapses during earthquakes more compelling than, or even as compelling as, the needs for job training programs or prisons to house the human threats to society or more mass transit and transportation infrastructure? Historically, emergency management agencies have not competed well for scarce public moneys. The probability of a disaster generally weighs less heavily on the minds of officials and voters than the more immediate problems of potholes and large class sizes.

To be effective emergency management programs must be in place prior to the occurrence of disasters. But low probability events do not carry great weight in policymaking unless the consequences are so great that they cannot be ignored. Stronger political constituencies supporting emergency management programs might help overcome the strong opposition to building codes, land-use regulations, and other efforts. Consensus-building approaches to planning and regulation might overcome some of the distrust of government intentions. A more professional cadre of emergency managers with technical expertise, political skill, and interpersonal skills might also help. More partnership among federal, state, and local agencies and officials, rather than regulatory or even authoritarian relationships, might go a long way in encouraging consensus and commitment to hazard mitigation and other efforts. Money would certainly help. More scientific knowledge, technical expertise, and administrative capacity would also help. In short, the major obstacles to effective emergency management can be overcome.

The national emergency management system is shaped by a plethora of social, economic, political, and even cultural factors. The impetus for change is the social and economic costs of disasters. The limits of decision making are defined by the state of scientific and technical knowledge about hazards and their effects. The structure and organization are dictated by the fragmented political system from which policy is derived and programs are implemented. The fabric on which the system is woven is our sociocultural values. In short, disasters exact a high toll on communities, but it is difficult to design and implement effective emergency management policies and programs (to lower that toll) because it is often uncertain how that might be done, the political process is complex and the federal system creates a labyrinth of organizational and administrative variables, and communities are not always willing to do what is necessary to reduce losses even when experts know how to do it and there are ample resources to support the effort.

DESIGNING EFFECTIVE POLICIES AND PROGRAMS

Effective emergency management policies and programs can literally save lives and reduce property losses. To be effective, policymakers and program administrators need a broad view of emergency management. The implementation of effective policies and programs will require cooperation at all levels of government and among public, private, and nonprofit sector organizations.

First, there is a genuine economic need for regional and national support for communities that may face, or may have suffered, major disasters. Catastrophic events can simply overwhelm the resources and capabilities of a community, a substate region, or even a state, and can cause long-term economic problems if outside assistance is not forthcoming. While local governments are typically the "first responders" to natural and technological disasters, they generally have the fewest resources available for dealing with such events. Although some local governments have far more experience with particular kinds of hazards and disasters than their state and federal counterparts, local governments need technical assistance in most major disasters. Catastrophic disasters can tax the financial and technical resources of local, state, and federal governments. The high social and economic costs of disasters at all levels are powerful arguments for policies and programs to mitigate losses.

Indeed, few local governments have the technical wherewithal to address major natural and technological hazards and many states lack the necessary technical resources to manage some hazards adequately. The federal government, too, lacks important resources for effective hazard reduction and disaster management. FEMA has an ambitious and laudable list of objectives and can call upon other federal agencies to provide resources for the accomplishment of those objectives. While the federal government generally has the fiscal resources to reduce hazards, respond to disasters, and provide disaster relief to victims, it often lacks the legal authority to act upon its priorities.

Second, there is a genuine need to enlist individuals, communities, private firms, and nonprofit organizations in the emergency management effort. It is not enough to provide training for those who wish it, technical assistance to those who ask, and financial support for those who need it. Community capacity building can take many forms, not all obviously related to emergency management. A community that can survive on its own without power and without direct connection with the rest of the world for at least a few days will be far more resilient than one that cannot. A community that understands its own resources (e.g., its medical system) will be more resilient.

Third, resources are finite and there is a need to set appropriate priorities. The all-hazards model provides a framework for a flexible, generic program, but most communities choose to pitch their emergency management programs toward the kinds of hazards they know and disasters they expect. Therefore a narrower, locale-specific concept of "all hazards" may be the most that can be expected. Indeed, this makes political and economic sense. Effective local and regional hazard analyses should guide policy design, rather than priorities set by officials or agencies far removed from the communities that are to implement them.

Fourth, cooperation is not just an administrative or political issue. Cooperative processes encourage capacity building and consensus building, more effective decision making at all levels, more investment of money and energy, and more community commitment to the success of the policies and programs. There is a social need that is not being met currently. American society and its governance processes have changed over the last several decades. It is no longer the case that agencies can simply show up; tell a community, "We are from the government and we are here to help you"; and take control of the situation. Local officials have legal responsibilities to their constituents, and members of the community increasingly want to participate in decision making. Indeed, public involvement in such decision making is a capacity-building exercise that helps create a more resilient community (see, e.g., King and Stivers 1998).

MAJOR POLICY ISSUES

Emergency management is an intensely political arena. Issues range from how much risk a community is willing to accept and how much money it is willing to spend to reduce that risk to what kinds of programs should be developed to address the long- and short-term effects of hazards and disasters. The first issue a community needs to address is just what hazards exist within its borders and what hazards may spill over from neighboring communities or from more distant sources. Notwithstanding the possibilities for asteroid strikes and other cosmic or worldly disasters, the hazard assessment usually begins with known geophysical risks, such as seismic and volcanic hazards, and meteorological risks, such as evidence of floods and storms. Historical data are combined with observational data. Lifelines, such as transportation and communication systems, are evaluated in terms of vulnerability to disruption or destruction and the potential impact of such disasters. Once the assessment is complete, communities can determine whether the risk is great enough to invest money and effort to reduce the hazards. Responsibility for hazard management is an intergovernmental issue. Responsibility for disaster management is both an intergovernmental issue and an administrative one. How should disaster operations be organized and managed? Who should pay for disaster relief and recovery? Should individuals at risk be required to buy insurance? Should governments force private individuals to reduce their exposure to hazards in order to quality for disaster assistance?

The Issue of Acceptable Risk

There is no such thing as a completely safe environment. While many communities face relatively little danger from earthquakes and other common disasters, with the exception of structural fires, others face all manner of catastrophe. The term "OINC" (pronounced "oink") is used to identify those disasters and hazards that are found "*only in C*alifornia" or seldom found anywhere else in the United States. Certainly California has disasters that are relatively uncommon in the rest of the United States, such as landslides, and hazards that are more widespread than elsewhere, such as earthquakes. However, the increasing incidence of sinkholes in Florida, damage resulting from acid rain in the upper Midwest and New England, drought in the Plains states and the Southwest, and other exotic hazards are forcing many communities and individuals to think about how much risk they are willing to live with.

First, it should be recognized that all communities and individuals live with some risk from natural and technological hazards. Even if there are no risks from windstorms, earthquakes, and other common natural hazards, hazardous materials spills can occur along highways and rail lines, epidemics may develop, aircraft may crash, and so on. Relative to specific hazards, the risk may be at "acceptable" levels, not requiring or necessarily justifying government intervention, or it may be "unacceptable," requiring small to massive investments to mitigate the threat to life and property. The distinction between "acceptable risk" and its corollary is important. In public policy terms, the level of threat posed by a particular hazard should determine its priority vis-à-vis other threats and problems. With finite resources, communities, like individuals, have to choose when and where to invest their money and their energy. The notion of "acceptable risk" is an acknowledgment that it is not possible to eliminate completely all risk from natural and technological hazards. Acceptability is related to the state of knowledge about the hazard (e.g., the likelihood of a major earthquake or hurricane and its probable effects), the credibility of the warning, and perceptions about exposure to the hazard. Those who choose to live in California with its well-known seismic hazards, for example, assume some risk. Some people may not fully understand the risk and, after their first experience with a major earthquake, may pack the car and move to a more stable state, while others may simply adjust to living with the hazard. Similarly, those who choose to live along the Gulf Coast or on barrier islands along the East Coast, assume some risk from hurricanes. It is uncertain, however, just how well people may understand such hazards and the real risk that they pose to life and property. The lack of experience of most people in southern Florida with major hurricanes was a source of great concern among emergency managers and other public officials, until Hurricane Andrew sensitized the public to the hazard and demonstrated the need for better building code enforcement, evacuation planning, and other emergency management programs.

The determination of acceptable risk also raises questions about how much money to spend and how much effort to expend on hazard reduction. Are the risks serious enough to warrant major investments of precious public moneys to reduce the potential property damage and loss of life? It also raises questions about individual responsibility for risk reduction. To what extent should individuals be held responsible for their own actions (or inaction)? Should their neighbors be obliged to assist when tragedy strikes?

The determination of "acceptable" levels also may be controversial because different individuals and different communities may well have different notions of how much risk they are willing to accept. Younger people may be more risk taking or accepting than older people. Those with children may be less inclined to accept risk that may threaten their families (Riad 1997). Property owners may be less willing to ignore environmental hazards than renters and other more transient populations. Business owners and managers, too, may be less inclined to take actions to reduce risk when the actions may result in significant financial losses. Hotel and restaurant managers, for example, are often reluctant to close their businesses and may well underplay the risk to keep customers, until their own employees choose safety over work or their families over their employers (Drabek 1994).

In addition, people with little experience with disasters may be less concerned about the potential for catastrophe. To be sure, choosing to live in a known hazardous area indicates a greater willingness to live with risk. It is a concern for emergency managers and other public officials that people who choose to live in hazardous areas may need assistance more frequently or even more direly. How to define what is acceptable and to adjust public policy accordingly is a methodological problem and a political problem. Risk-taking behaviors by individuals and communities can increase the level of risk for others. As a consequence, some governments are requiring victims of disaster to pay for rescue operations when they have knowingly put themselves at risk. Recent cases have involved skiers and hikers in the

Rocky Mountains who have let themselves get caught in snowstorms despite warnings of bad weather. While there is little debate concerning the need to rescue such individuals, there is increasing debate concerning their responsibility for the cost of the rescue operations and their liability for deaths and injuries to search and rescue personnel. That concern about the risk to rescue and other emergency response personnel, as well as the cost, can also be extended to individuals who choose to live in hazardous areas. For example, when individuals build homes or businesses in woodlands prone to wildfires, should public monies be spent fighting fires and should public employees be put into danger? Developing such areas also increases the likelihood of fire due to human carelessness and electrical malfunctions.

Agencies, too, are increasingly adopting policies to limit the amount of assistance available for people who do not act to reduce risks to themselves and their property. Homes that have been flooded more than once may not be rebuilt.

Organizational Issues

Emergency management has historically suffered from fragmented authority and responsibility. The intergovernmental system is complex and, ironically, the "first responders" to disaster are typically those with the fewest resources. That is not to say, however, that they are the least capable. The major difficulty in relying on local agencies to address complex technical problems is the unevenness of capabilities. To reiterate a point made earlier and critical to an understanding of intergovernmental efforts in many policy areas, some local government agencies have more technical capacity and experience than their state and federal counterparts, some have very little capacity to address even simple problems, and the rest are somewhere in between those two extremes. Practically speaking, this presents a dilemma for policymakers because they cannot always rely on local capacities. It also becomes a source of irritation for local officials who might be treated as "second-class" participants in a disaster operation despite their abilities.

A first consideration in structuring an emergency management agency is whether it should be a "command-and-control–type" organization or a coordinative organization. Given that authority and responsibility are often ambiguous in a disaster operation, the trend is toward more coordinative roles. Emergency managers may see their roles as being primarily to provide mechanisms to coordinate the efforts of emergency response and recovery organizations. Therefore, emergency operations centers provide common communication technologies, decision support (e.g., maps, situation reports, data collection), and a forum for agencies to share information. That is in marked contrast to the image of the emergency manager as the "tactician" or "field general."

However, the most common organizational structure used in emergency operations is the incident command system (ICS), which has been adopted by many fire departments and has been integrated into other emergency systems. In brief, ICS was developed in California in the early 1970s, largely due to the problems that were evident in the response to a series of wildfires in 1971. Conflicts among agencies from a number of jurisdictions prompted Congress to fund a study of the problem of coordinating multiorganizational, intergovernmental disaster operations. The focus was on firefighting operations and the U.S. Forest Service and representatives of state and local fire departments participated in the study. The Fighting Resources of Southern California Organized for Potential Emergencies (FIRESCOPE) Program was developed, and the participants identified the following problems experienced during the fires: lack of a common organization, poor on-scene and interagency communications, inadequate joint planning, lack of valid and timely intelligence, inadequate resource management, and limited prediction capability (Irwin 1989, 135–36).

The criteria identified as important for the new management system were that it should be:

- effective in facilitating operations for single jurisdictions and/or agencies, multiple agencies within one jurisdiction, and multiple jurisdictions and/or multiple agencies;
- adaptable to a broad range of disasters and emergencies;
- adaptable to new technologies;
- adaptable to small and large disasters;
- based on common structures, terminology, and procedures;
- implementable with minimal disruption to existing procedures; and
- simple to learn, use, and maintain (Irwin 1989, 137).

ICS was based on the following management concepts:

- agency autonomy—to assure that the system does not violate the jurisdictional responsibilities of individual agencies;
- Management-by-objectives—to assure that there is a clear set of realistic operational objectives and that they are communicated to all involved;
- unit integrity—to assure that agency or unit personnel are kept to-

gether, so that accurate records can be kept concerning work time and communication will be more effective;
- functional clarity—to assure that tasks are clear.

In keeping with the management theory of the time, the "span of control" (i.e., the number of personnel supervised by a commander, supervisor, or unit leader) was expected to be no more than five to assure ease of communication and coordination. The command component of ICS includes the incident commander and his or her command staff, normally information, liaison, and safety officers. Support is provided by (1) an operations section responsible for implementing directives, tactical decision making, adapting plans to circumstances, and so on; (2) a finance section responsible for record keeping and for managing the financial aspects of the operation; (3) a logistics section responsible for assuring that necessary human and material resources are secured; and (4) a planning section responsible for monitoring resource status and developing strategies and plans to achieve objectives (Irwin, 1989, 142–151). ICS also provides for integrated communications and resource management, and standardizes a number of forms to facilitate communication.

ICS has gained the support of the U.S. Fire Administration and is a component in the training program of the U.S. Fire Academy. It was adapted to provide an on-scene management structure for the National Interagency Incident Command System, and, through use by the U.S. Forest Service in fighting wildfires nationally, it has become the standard control structure in the field. ICS was endorsed by the International Association of Police Chiefs in 1987 and has been adapted to a variety of other disaster types, including the effort to manage the crises and consequences of events involving "weapons of mass destruction."

Most emergencies do not involve more than one jurisdiction and the designation of an incident commander to coordinate the operation is not controversial or complicated. The senior commander on the scene is usually the one in charge. Other senior officers may be present, but the senior "line" officer normally directs the operation. When more agencies and jurisdictions become involved, the "command" or leadership function becomes more complex and a *Unified Command* structure is created. The ICS organization is expanded to include more units under the Unified Command structure, but each unit remains largely autonomous. Coordination of multiorganizational efforts is accomplished by using a unified emergency operations center; joint planning; sharing of information; providing a single source of information for the media; and, to the extent possible, resource sharing. Each of the agencies with jurisdictional responsibilities and authority assigns its own unified commander to the *Unified Command Group*. The optimum size of the group is six to eight. Additional units may be integrated into the operation, but they will not have representation in the command group.

An ICS structure was activated during the response to the bombing of the Murrah Federal Building in Oklahoma City in 1995 (Tamillow 1995; Foley 1995). The Oklahoma City Fire Department established an Incident Command and set up a command post to oversee the rescue operation within minutes after the explosion (see OKC 1996). Within hours of the bombing, FEMA dispatched an incident support team to assess the situation. Ultimately, FEMA ended up coordinating the efforts of eleven urban search and rescue task forces and other federal agencies for thirteen days. As the number of agencies increased, the *Multi-Agency Coordination Center* was opened at the Myriad Convention Center to coordinate agency tasks, provide a satellite communications link with FEMA headquarters in Washington, and provide a joint public information center. Principal responsibility for the Oklahoma City operation was clear. The target was a federal building and a large number of victims were federal employees, some law enforcement officers. The FBI became the lead agency for the law enforcement response, with FEMA coordinating the federal rescue effort and the Oklahoma City Fire Department became the lead agency for the rescue operation. Jurisdictional responsibilities were clearly defined and cooperation was facilitated by the development of the multiagency center.

ICS and the Unified Command System are not without critics. ICS was created utilizing management concepts and theories that are now over 30 years old. Even though elements of those earlier theories, such as Management by Objectives (MBO), can be found in many of the newer management theories, much has changed. For example, management theory today is far less "command and control" oriented. It is based on a more participative, consensus-building approach to decision making. The ICS concepts are largely drawn from the classic Weberian model of bureaucracy in which a clear hierarchy, unity of command, formal communications, divisions of labor, and task specialization were expected. Efficiency was the principal goal. Such structures and processes are commonly found in military-type organizations and in assembly-line factories where tasks are routine and decision making can be centralized. However, in public and nonprofit agency administration, executive control or "unity of command" is often far less clear than in organizations with very hierarchical structures. For example, within some local governments, there is no single chief executive officer. Executive authority is shared in some cases (e.g., in commission forms of government), limited in many more (e.g., weak mayor forms of government), and hard to locate in others. In some county governments, the "head" of the government is a probate judge who has no administrative responsibilities beyond running his or her court. The lack of a single executive officer may result in confusion when there is an emergency or it may encourage a more cooperative and collaborative approach to decision making (Waugh 1994). Strict hierarchies and executive control are even becoming less common in businesses where flexibility and creativity are prized.

According to current management theory, organizations with unstable task environments need to be much more flexible so that they can adapt to circumstances. Disasters, by their very nature, create an unstable work environment for victims and emergency response organizations. As a result, emergency plans are only rarely implemented without changes. To assure flexibility to respond to changing demands, public, private, and nonprofit organizations today tend to be:

- more structurally fluid, developing *ad hoc* structures (e.g., task groups and self-managed work teams) to accomplish specific tasks;
- more organizationally flexible, assigning employees with complementary knowledge, skills, and competencies to teams and task groups;
- less hierarchical or even nonhierarchical, giving work groups greater autonomy and assigning leadership responsibility on the basis of specific technical skills or personality traits rather than rank in the organization; and
- more participative and consensus-based, encouraging open communications, shared decision making, and nondirective leadership.

New information technologies, too, are making it easier to decentralize and, thereby, speed up decision making. Personnel in the field have access to decision support systems via laptop computers with cellular modems and may well have a better grasp of situational needs than officials in the emergency operations center or in the headquarters facility in the capital. Disaster response protocols can be adapted on-site, in other words. While there are inherent problems in a "Lone Ranger" approach to decision making, such as not having a broad strategic perspective, there are also serious problems when operations are directed from afar. Reconciling the needs for both tactical and strategic perspectives is a serious administrative issue, but, on the whole, information technologies are making it possible for those in the field to get a broader perspective than they could a few years ago, so there is less of a trade-off when decision making is decentralized. It is possible to see the forest *and* the trees, in other words.

A second concern with the command-and-control model has to do with communication among the participants and victims. Significant differences in organizational structure and culture complicate communication and make cooperation more difficult. Agencies literally have different technical languages that may prove confusing and dangerous. While joint exercises and the adoption of common terminology (e.g., the all-hazards model terms and concepts) can reduce the confusion, communication problems may arise during a disaster operation. The military's use of acronyms is legendary and it can become a serious problem when dealing with civilian agencies and disaster victims. The language of police work and firefighting are generally more familiar because of their use on television shows and in movies. Nonetheless, communication can be much less precise than it could be with all parties speaking the same language and using the same concepts. Differences in value systems and cultures among units within a single agency, among agencies within a single government, and even among agencies that have the same basic mission can also complicate communication. Joint exercises can help identify those differences, but the underlying assumptions may be more difficult to reconcile.

The "political model" of emergency management takes into account the variability among emergency response agencies in terms of their organizational structures, cultures, and value systems and focuses on providing a forum that encourages open communication, sharing of resources, preserving the autonomy of the agencies, and involving all in strategic and operational decision making as much as possible. For major disasters, in which the number of affected jurisdictions is large and the variety of functional concerns (i.e., medical, environmental, structural) is large, the "political model" provides a mechanism to reconcile the social, political, and economic interests of those involved in the disaster operation and the victims of the disaster, as well as to coordinate the emergency response and recovery efforts.

There are several serious problems with the ICS structure. First, coordination becomes more difficult when a disaster crosses political boundaries and authority becomes more ambiguous. ICS accommodates the expansion of a response to include more emergency response units from a single jurisdiction and even provides for the addition of units from other jurisdictions. However, as events get larger, participation in decision-making processes is limited. Second, coordination is even more difficult when a response involves organizations and individuals who are not government agents. Integrating nongovernmental organizations (NGOs) into the effort when the incident commander or even a unified command group has little or no authority over them is difficult in relatively minor events, such as a small wildfire, and even more problematic in large events. ICS works in managing fire responses precisely because the events are localized and seldom require the involvement of nonfire service organizations. Managing volunteer organizations is very different from managing a disciplined organization with a classic bureaucratic structure (see, e.g., Waugh 1993) and, in large disasters, the participation of volunteer organizations is critical. Consensus building, collegial approaches to decision making may be more appropriate in a multiorganizational effort and critical in a catastrophic disaster.

Emergency management has also suffered from the turf battles among agencies concerned about their own prerogatives. During the 1980s, FEMA officials began focusing on the potential for terrorist violence. The agency sponsored conferences on terrorism and initiated programs to secure likely targets of violent attacks. Jurisdictional conflicts arose when the agency attempted to assume responsibility for antiterrorism measures within nuclear facilities. FEMA had treaded on the turf of the Nuclear Regulatory Commission. Interestingly, security measures adopted for nuclear facilities were sometimes found to interfere with normal plant operations and, in particular, emergency operations because they often impeded the movement of emergency responders within the plants.

Antiterrorism measures adopted during the Atlanta Olympics in 1996 included structures to facilitate cooperation and collaboration. Planning bodies involved representatives from local, state, and federal agencies, for example. The bombing in Centennial Olympic Park was much like other kinds of disasters in terms of the local emergency medical response. However, the use of a bomb automatically gave authority to the FBI and other federal agencies. Legislation clarified legal jurisdiction by giving federal authorities authority over "terrorist" events. Presidential Decision Directive 39 in 1995, for example, makes the FBI the lead agency in dealing with terrorism. Presidential Decision Directive 62 in 1997 deals with "weapons of mass destruction" and initially assigned lead responsibility to the Department of Defense (DOD) with FEMA responsible for "consequence management" and with central roles for the FBI and the Public Health Service. The FBI has now replaced DOD as the lead agency for "crisis management." Under the Stafford Act, FEMA can call upon other federal agencies to exercise their responsibilities under the Federal Response Plan. Notwithstanding the institutionalized mechanisms for cooperation, a multiorganizational response is still a tentative arrangement. Joint exercising, negotiated collaboration, and personal contact among agency representatives, as well as disaster experience, help resolve conflicts. For example, law enforcement officers have interfered with emergency medical responses in Oklahoma City in 1995 and in other disasters because they have been trying to preserve evidence and to seal off crime scenes while responders have been trying to locate and remove victims. Protocols have been developed to reduce the likelihood that law enforcement efforts will endanger victims' lives. But, given that initial disaster responses, such as search and rescue, are most often *ad hoc* efforts by bystanders followed by more systematic efforts by local public safety and emergency management agencies and community disaster assistance groups (e.g., the local American Red Cross organization), evidence will be lost.

Insurance Issues

At the federal and state levels, the costs of disasters encourage greater attention to the need for risk reduction. It is also argued that the availability of state and federal assistance may discourage individual home and business owners from adequately insuring their property. The National Flood Insurance Program, for example, requires that property owners purchase flood insurance if their property is located in a floodplain. It also requires local governments to regulate building within that floodplain. Studies indicate that property owners would not purchase insurance, particularly those in lower risk areas, if not required by the federal government in order to qualify for Federal Housing Administration (FHA) and Veterans Administration (VA) mortgage loans and, in the event of a flood, disaster assistance.

That issue has been central to the debate over requiring earthquake insurance in higher-risk areas. While floodplains are managed under federal law, earthquake zones are not as effectively managed under state and local law. States such as California have stringent building codes and land-use plans to reduce earthquake hazards, but many other states have few regulations regarding land-use and building standards. The billions of dollars paid out in the aftermaths of Hurricane Hugo and Hurricane Andrew, however, are encouraging the insurance industry to examine the problem of inadequate regulation of building. Even when building codes are in place, some local governments lack the resources to enforce them effectively. Following Hurricane Hugo, for example, it was found that some county governments in South Carolina had building codes but no inspectors and others had no building standards at all. Faulty construction was judged responsible for much of the property damage in south Florida during Hurricane Andrew, as well. From the perspective of the insurance companies, the problems are how to encourage communities to adopt appropriate building codes and how to help them enforce the codes effectively. State mandated codes are an alternative, but adjustments would necessarily have to be made to accommodate local hazards. State moneys would also be necessary to assure adequate funding. For local officials the problems are twofold, funding and politics. Effective code enforcement costs money that local governments may not have. Land-use and building regulation are intensely political issues at the local level and are issues that local officials may not be equipped to resolve.

The high costs of recent disasters and the potential for even greater losses are encouraging more attention to ways to both compensate for property losses and to encourage mitigation efforts. The costs of disasters to federal and state governments, in particular, are encouraging the examination of alternatives to massive expenditures for disaster relief and recovery. Thus far, the American public has borne much of the costs. An alternative is to shift some or all of the burden to individual property owners through insurance programs.

But a reliance upon private insurance raises other serious questions. First, can the private insurance industry provide enough coverage to assure that substantial proportions of property losses are covered after a major disaster? With some qualification, the answer to that question is yes; but there may be serious problems in states or regions in which a single disaster or series of disasters can overwhelm the capacities of insurance providers. Insurance companies depend upon the existence of a large pool of customers (the "law of large numbers") who share risk but do not all experience losses at the same time.

As Howard Kunreuther (1998b, 19) points out, large disasters make insurance a less viable recovery option. The Great Fire of London in 1666 burned over three-quarters of the city. The "great fires" of New York City in 1835 and Chicago in 1871 also burned very large portions of those cities. While fire insurance was unheard of in 1666, it was becoming a more familiar institution in the cities of the 1800s. When a building, factory, or wharf burned, insurance helped recoup the losses. However, a very large fire could easily outstrip the financial reserves of a company and force it into bankruptcy. Losses from a disaster the scale of the "great fires" or an 8.0 earthquake or a Force 5 hurricane could easily overwhelm an insurance company, even with today's strict government requirements regarding financial reserves. Until Hurricane Hugo in 1989, for example, the insurance industry had never experienced a disaster costing over $1 billion. Since

Hugo, there have been ten disasters causing losses in excess of $1 billion. Following Hurricane Andrew in 1992, nine insurers in Florida failed (Kunreuther 1998a, 4–5).

In anticipation of catastrophic events, insurers can raise rates high enough to cover the "probable maximum loss," require a deductible so that property owners share the risk, and/or buy reinsurance to cover losses in excess of expectations (Kunreuther 1998b, 24–26). While private insurers theoretically can raise rates high enough to cover almost any losses, the cost may be prohibitive for all but the most affluent property owners, and even they may choose to accept the risk rather than pay for the insurance. High deductibles or limits on coverage may reduce the potential losses to insurers by forcing property owners to share the risk from catastrophic events, but, again, property owners may well choose to accept the risk of property loss and not the high insurance costs.

Even with measures to share the risk with property owners and/or to insure themselves against catastrophic losses, insurers can find themselves overexposed. Indeed, a catastrophe may be so great that it overwhelms the reinsurance companies themselves. In fact, flood losses have historically been so high that it is not economically feasible for private insurers to provide coverage without federal backing. As a result, the federal government has had to step in and offer a subsidy to assure that flood insurance is available to property owners. The National Flood Insurance Program (NFIP) was created in 1968 both to assure the availability of flood insurance and to encourage flood hazard mitigation. Property owners in communities with significant flood hazards are eligible for flood insurance if their communities implement land-use regulations to reduce the likelihood of property losses. The NFI Reform Act of 1994 created a community rating system, giving points for specific mitigation efforts, to determine insurance rates for the community. The act also created the Flood Mitigation Assistance Grant Program to encourage more ambitious hazard reduction efforts (Pasterick 1998).

Thus far, the federal government has not underwritten other kinds of disaster insurance, although some may be covered under NFIP. In California, where the earthquake hazard poses serious risk to large portions of the state, a state company was set up to underwrite earthquake policies. The California Earthquake Authority does not require homeowners to buy insurance, but it assures that it is available. State law requires that sellers disclose to buyers the earthquake hazard to property and, in general, property owners tend to purchase earthquake insurance if the risk is high and the estimate of potential destruction is high (Palm 1998, 56–61). By contrast, the Florida Hurricane Catastrophe Fund, which was created in 1993 after the devastation of Hurricane Andrew, provides a buffer for insurers by providing additional emergency reserves (Lecomte and Gahagan 1998).

Second, will private insurance, with or without government backing, encourage risk taking by property owners? Certainly, if property owners find that they are protected against serious losses, they will feel little pressure to protect themselves. The key may be to assure that property owners face significant economic risk themselves, so that they will consider mitigation measures to be good investments to reduce their own exposure.

Howard Kunreuther concludes that "an insurance system with rates based on risk can serve as the cornerstone of a hazard management program" (1998a, 3). He goes on to advocate a system of monetary incentives to reduce risk, fines for noncompliance, tax credits to encourage mitigation programs, "well-enforced building codes," and effective land-use regulations (1998a, 4).

It may also be problematic that governments typically suffer severe property losses during disasters and that they often are self-insured. Municipal governments seldom have reserve funds to repair or replace public facilities and infrastructure damaged during disasters. Bonds and other forms of borrowing against future revenue are the principal means of raising moneys for such emergencies. In other words, local governments are heavily dependent upon federal disaster assistance themselves.

Third, will property owners buy insurance voluntarily? The common wisdom is that they will not. The experience with flood insurance has indicated that property owners will not buy coverage unless they are forced to do so (Cigler and Burby 1990; Kunreuther 1998a, 12).

To assure that the insurance industry can and does provide disaster coverage, it is important to have better estimates of risk and the vulnerability of property, appropriate and strictly enforced building codes, economic incentives to mitigate hazards, and broad efforts to share risk through insurance pools, reinsurance, and so on (Kunreuther 1998c). There should also be more concerted efforts to define and communicate risk to property owners and lending institutions, so that they can reduce their exposure. Insurance companies will have to reduce their own risk through reinsurance, catastrophe bonds, and other means. The insurance industry has been active in promoting federal legislation to establish a national disaster insurance program to cover earthquake losses in much the same way as NFIP does for flood losses (Roth 1997), to permit insurers to develop tax-deferred reserves to cover future disasters, and to provide tax incentives to encourage property owners to adopt mitigation measures (Herres 1999, 3). The alternatives for insurers include: (1) choosing not to issue new or renew old policies in areas that have very high seismic risk, as some did following the Northridge earthquake; (2) limiting how much exposure they can accept in high risk zones (i.e., a capacity limit); and (3) refusing to insure older property until it has been retrofitted to be more earthquake resistant (although property owners may simply choose another insurer rather than pay for retrofitting) (Roth 1997).

Land-Use Regulation Issues

Land-use regulation is the most effective mitigation tool (Burby 1999). Moving people and property away from hazards, limiting what can be built in hazardous areas, setting standards for construction in hazardous areas, and requiring structural mitigation measures when appropriate to reduce the level of risk in a particular area can greatly reduce the likelihood of property damage and the loss of life. However, strict regulations can be difficult to adopt and enforce. The principal opposition is generally from the building industry and land developers who see land-use regulation as a limitation on what they can do with their property. If uses are limited, the potential value of the property may be lessened. For example, residences along a beach are likely to be far more expensive than residences moved farther back from the beach, which may have sand dunes or seawalls blocking the view of the water. Without the natural barriers against storm surges provided by the dunes or man-made barriers like seawalls, the risk to beachfront property may be very high. Were it only the case that building close to the beach presented a risk to those property owners, the issue might not be as controversial as it is. Communities might simply let property owners assume the risk for their own behavior. However, buildings located in areas prone to storm surges may well float into other structures. Walking to the beach may damage the dunes that protect other properties, as well. The effects of individual behaviors can pose a threat to neighbors and the community as a whole.

One of the ways to encourage land-use planning is to provide economic incentives, such as tax breaks. Another is simply to mandate limits on development. For widespread hazards, such as floodplains, the key is providing insurance at reduced cost to those communities that do reduce flood hazards. The National Flood Insurance Program (NFIP) provides low cost flood insurance to communities that agree to regulate development on their floodplains. The NFIP has a community rating system (CRS) that categorizes communities on a scale from 1 to 10 based upon efforts to reduce the risk to life and property on the floodplains. The rating or class determines the amount of the discount residents receive on their insurance. Discounts range from 5 percent to 45 percent.

The CRS give points for the following actions:

- maintaining elevation certificates for new construction (i.e., raising the structures above the expected flood level) (up to 142 points);
- providing flood insurance rate map information to those who inquire and publicizing the availability of the information (up to 140 points);
- sending hazard, insurance, mitigation, and basic floodplain information to residents (up to 265 points);
- disclosing hazard by real estate agents to prospective property buyers (up to 81 points);
- maintaining flood hazard and insurance references in the public library (up to 30 points);
- providing technical advice to property owners on how to protect themselves and their property;
- developing new data on the hazard and other potentially hazardous areas;
- keeping vacant floodplain land free from development;
- developing better regulatory standards (e.g., smaller lot sizes, protection of critical facilities) (up to 905 points);
- maintaining flood and property data (up to 160 points);
- managing stormwater to protect water quality, reduce erosion, and so on (up to 405 points);
- addressing problem of repetitive losses, for example, properties repeatedly flooded (up to 441 points);
- acquiring and relocating flood-prone buildings (up to 1,600 points);
- retrofitting old buildings to make them more flood resistant (up to 1,400 points);
- maintaining the drainage system (up to 380 points);
- providing a warning system and flood response plan (up to 200 points);
- maintaining levees (up to 900 points); and
- maintaining dams (up to 120 points) (FEMA/NFIP 1996).

To qualify for a discount, communities must provide elevation certificates. If designated as a repetitive loss community, it must also have repetitive loss projects. All other activities are optional (FEMA/NFIP 1996). A community earning 4,500 points is categorized as Class 1, and property owners get a 45 percent discount. A community earning at least 500 points is categorized as Class 9, and property owners get a 5 percent discount. All communities that have not applied to join the NFIP and those that do not earn at least 500 points are Class 10, and property owners do not receive a discount (FEMA/NFIP 1996).

Limiting development in hazardous areas is often an intensely political issue, but removing property from such areas is an even more contentious undertaking. There are properties that are damaged time after time. In some cases, implementing mitigation measures when properties are rebuilt would reduce the likelihood of future losses. In other cases, it is far cheaper for the government to purchase the property and, thereby, preclude development. Replacing residences or businesses in floodplains with golf courses, bike paths, baseball fields, hiking trails, or other land uses would also provide a public good. Buyouts have been used to that effect following recent flooding in the Midwest and elsewhere. There have been increasing challenges to land-use regulation in the courts and some support (i.e., the *Lucas v. South Carolina Coastal Council* [112 S.Ct., at 2886, 1992] case) that would require governments to compensate property owners for the reduced value of their property because of the regulations. When regulations are in place before the property is acquired, the owners cannot easily make the case that the value of their property has been reduced. But, when the regulations are adopted after a disaster, property owners may seek compensation for the projected value of their land. In the Lucas case, Lucas had two lots in an area determined to be subject to beach erosion. The South Carolina Beachfront Management Act passed in 1988 restricted development on the lots. The Supreme Court decided that Lucas should be compensated, and he was paid $1.2 million for the two lots. The *Lucas* case and the *Dolan v. City of Tigard, Oregon* (114 S.Ct., at 2309, 1994) case may mean that regulators will have to pay property owners when the value of their property is significantly affected, thus making regulation extremely expensive, and they may have to prove that the public interest outweighs the private interest.

Social Psychological Issues

While there are major economic issues involved in disaster recovery, the largest concern may be the level of stress experienced by victims and responders. Aside from the physical stress and fatigue of long hours, hard work, and poor living conditions, both the victims and those trying to help them suffer psychological stress. For victims, uncertainty and fear prior to and during disasters, physical injuries and threats during the disasters, and economic and personal losses from the disasters can cause psychological, physical, and material distress. Irreplaceable personal items may be lost, family members may be injured or killed, and so on. The loss of photographs, keepsakes, and other personal belongings can be traumatic, particularly for middle-aged victims. Victims on fixed incomes, without insurance, or simply living from one Social Security check to another may suffer devastating financial losses and be in abject fear for their futures. The stress on families and individuals and on the institutions of the community can impede recovery, and providing counseling services may well prove to be the best way to improve the community's chances for quick recovery.

A major disaster can destroy the economic base of a community. A critical mass of stores and other businesses is necessary to make a central business district economically viable. The loss of even a few of the businesses can be devastating. Those businesses without adequate insurance may not be able to recover, even with loans from the Small Business Administration (SBA), banks, and other sources. Businesses that were undervalued (to reduce property tax liability) may not be able to secure enough loans to replace stock and other property. Perhaps more important, elderly or middle-aged business owners may simply choose to take their insurance payments and retire, rather than invest the time, energy, and money necessary to rebuild.

As well as community stress, emergency responders experience very high levels of stress during disaster responses and the recovery effort. Physical stress results from the long hours and poor working conditions. People simply get tired. Psychological stress results from the nature of the work, which involves handling dead bodies, dealing with injured victims, seeing the effects of disasters on individuals and families, and being frustrated by the lack of resources and/or the fact that little or nothing can be done to help some people. Some responders suffer feelings of inadequacy or even guilt because they cannot help everyone. The empathy of health care workers and emergency responders often causes them to suffer along with the more direct victims of disaster. The personal need of many public safety officers to be in control of situations that are clearly out of their control raises their stress levels. Unfortunately, emergency responders and public safety officers often do not see the need for psychological counseling or choose not to participate. Some do not recognize the symptoms of stress, because they are hidden by other personal, family, or job problems, and do not think that they need assistance. Male emergency workers, in particular, may be reluctant to seek assistance because they think that it may be seen as a sign of weakness. Historically, there has been a stigma attached to psychological counseling, and responders may fear being ridiculed or penalized for seeking such assistance. The organizational cultures of some emergency response agencies do not encourage workers to seek assistance even if they desperately need it.

Long-term stress can cause a wide variety of physical and psychological problems. Disaster workers may experience one or more of the following symptoms: grief, depression, anger, anxiety, tension, emotional distress, hostility, sleep disturbances, substance abuse, obsessive-compulsive behaviors, and feelings of helplessness.

It may not be possible to reduce the level of stress in the job itself. Emergency training can prepare responders for a wide variety of experiences, but trainers can seldom anticipate all eventualities. It is particularly difficult to prepare responders for the handling of fatalities (Gibbs et al. 1996, 31). Training that involves graphic descriptions or pictures of casualties may have the opposite effect from what is intended.

If stress is not reduced, some emergency workers may experience posttraumatic stress disorder (PTSD). Symptoms may include intrusive thoughts, avoidant response, and hyperarousal, occurring weeks, months, and even years after a disaster. PTSD became a major issue following the Vietnam War, and there has been considerable research on the progress and treatment of the condition. At least initially, there was criticism that those claiming to suffer from PTSD were weaklings or whiners. More recently, PTSD has been recognized as a serious result of many kinds of traumatic events. Counseling is commonly provided to students after incidences of school violence, the death of a fellow student, and other traumatic events. The impact of terrorist and other mass casualty violence, such as the bombing of the Murrah Federal Building in Oklahoma City in 1995, is particularly problematic (see, e.g., Benight 1996).

Following major structural failures, such as the Hyatt skywalk collapse in Kansas City in 1984 in which suspended concrete walkways fell on dancers, musicians, and bystanders in the hotel lobby, emergency responders have often developed substance abuse problems, as well as other stress-related health problems. As a consequence, many left their emergency response jobs to find less stressful occupations. Much of the impetus for psychological counseling has been the turnover problem. If a large number of experienced emergency response personnel leave, the effectiveness of response agencies will be affected. In short, stress has become a personnel problem. Because of the very high turnover among personnel in emergency response agencies following the Hyatt skywalk collapse, re-

searchers have been monitoring the turnover rates among emergency response agencies in Oklahoma City since the federal building bombing.

Emergency responders and disaster victims often have their own means
of coping with the stress, such as using humor to release tension and talking
to other emergency workers and/or victims about their experiences. Sharing
the experience helps people to put it into perspective and to understand it
better. However, not all find it easy to share their thoughts on a disaster. To
the extent that social networks facilitate recovery, it may be necessary to
require emergency workers to seek assistance and to adjust evacuation
policies and other emergency response and recovery efforts to emphasize
reuniting families. Efforts can be made to put families into the same shelters,
facilitating communication among family members, returning victims to
their homes as quickly as possible, and finding ways to reassure victims
about their safety and security (Riad et al. 1999).

A formal means of dealing with such stress is through *critical incident stress
debriefings* (CISD). CISD involves formal interventions to encourage emergency workers and victims to talk about their experiences. By talking about
their personal feelings, they may come to understand their own reactions better
and thereby learn to cope with the memories and reduce stress. The process
should speed recovery and reduce the likelihood of physical and/or psychological problems (Anderson and Mattingly 1991, 316).

CISD is generally scheduled 24 to 72 hours after the event. Participants
are encouraged to express their personal reactions to the event and not to
evaluate the emergency response or the disaster itself (Anderson and
Mattingly 1991, 316). CISD generally includes:

- An overview of the debriefing process, emphasizing the confidential-
  ity of contributions and the expected value of participation;
- A review of the facts of the disaster and their effects;
- A time for participant reactions to the events, focusing on feelings and
  emotions;
- A discussion of the symptoms experienced by the participants (i.e.,
  their reactions during and since the event);
- A learning period to let participants know that their reactions are
  normal; and
- A concluding session during which participants can ask questions and
  clarify issues, and counselors can refer those needing additional
  assistance to other programs (Anderson and Mattingly 1991, 316).

Much the same general process typically occurs during community counseling. Individuals, families, and community groups are encouraged to examine their own experiences and are reassured that their reactions are normal. Grief, anger, frustration, and "survivor's guilt" are normal reactions. State and local mental health agencies, private mental health services under contract with government agencies or acting on their own, and church and other community organizations may be involved in the process.

Other Issues

The preceding issues are certainly not all the important concerns in emergency management. Other major issues include:

- Should communities be required to invest in hazard mitigation (perhaps based upon their tax base or some other measure of fiscal resources) as a condition for being eligible for federal and/or state disaster assistance? The National Flood Insurance Program requires such investments in floodplain management, but should the same requirement be extended to all communities for all kinds of disasters? How can communities be encouraged to invest in hazard mitigation without its becoming yet another unfunded mandate that diverts fiscal and other resources away from other essential local services?
- Should more military technologies, such as satellite imaging, be adapted for civilian use in hazard management and disaster operations? To some extent, satellite imaging and other technologies have been used in disaster operations, but should the Department of Defense release more of its data-gathering and analysis technologies to civilian use now that the Cold War is over? The value of information in managing hazards and disasters is undeniable, but does it outweigh the value of information gathered through clandestine surveillance to national defense.
- Should active duty military units be assigned to disaster operations on a regular basis? As the discussion of the Posse Comitatus law in an earlier chapter suggested, military commanders are permitted to use their discretion when a disaster strikes close by and their intervention can prevent or lessen the loss of life and property. However, large-scale military involvement in catastrophic disasters may compromise the Department of Defense's ability to respond to international crises and domestic threats. For example, had a major natural disaster struck just prior to the North Atlantic Treaty Organization (NATO) operation in the Balkans, the military's airlift capabilities

may have been overwhelmed. As it happened, the airlift capabilities were severely taxed simply moving equipment to the Balkans. Emergency shelters, food and water, and medical supplies were needed for refugees, as well. Involvement in a disaster operation, too, may slow deployment in a national security crisis; there are still legal limitations on what military commanders can do in a "civilian" disaster; and there are costs associated with disaster operations and arrangements would have to be made to pay for the use of military personnel, equipment, and other resources (see Schrader 1993).

- Should federal and state governments simply prohibit development in hazardous areas? Effective and strict land-use regulation is one answer. Reducing or eliminating disaster assistance programs, the National Flood Insurance Program, and tax deductions for disaster losses might make it economically infeasible for people to build in hazardous areas (see Burby et al. 1999).

- How can hazard management and disaster response technologies be transferred to Third World nations to reduce the likelihood of catastrophic losses on life and property? The unwillingness and/or inability of Third World governments to reduce hazards affects other nations involved in humanitarian efforts by diverting resources from other economic and social development efforts, and diverts domestic resources from other essential programs, as well as causing human casualties and suffering.

CONCLUSIONS

Managing hazards and dealing with disasters raises a great many policy issues, and this analysis only touches upon the broader issues. There have been longstanding debates over the modernization of the National Air Space system with many policymakers and aviation experts voicing concerns over the frequency of power, radar, and computer failures in the FAA's air traffic control operations. There have been longstanding debates over the storage and destruction of chemical weapons at Anniston Ordnance Depot in Alabama and other sites with many fearful of a lethal leak from the aging stockpile. The list could go on with new issues being added to the debate each time that there is a disaster or someone identifies a new hazard.

Emergency managers are generally very pragmatic in their approaches, but very much constrained by the federal system of government and the nature of American politics. While pragmatic answers are appealing and may well work for a time, there are compelling reasons to work within the existing system and to lobby for change when the system presents serious difficulties. Personal legal liability for failing to follow administrative procedures may be a risk worth taking in some circumstances, but not in all. Political liability (e.g., lost votes or lost confidence in hired officials) may also result from abuses of authority or inattention to legal or accepted procedure. Emergency managers have to weigh those risks and should be familiar enough with the field to have a repertoire of policy choices that may be less risky in legal or political terms. Local government in the United States is a maze of jurisdictions, personalities, and political interests, and one has to be attentive to the relationships. Therefore, understanding the political environment is critical.

DISCUSSION QUESTIONS

1. When a community chooses to ignore (i.e., accept) the risk posed by a natural or technological hazard, why should the federal or state governments provide relief if a disaster occurs?
2. Should governments charge individuals and businesses when they knowingly put themselves in danger and rescue is expensive and/or endangers the lives of emergency response personnel?
3. Should governments prohibit or strictly limit development in hazardous areas?
4. Should governments buy out private property in very hazardous areas to keep it from being developed?
5. How should disaster operations be structured—hierarchically (i.e., using the ICS model) or flexibly (i.e., using the political model)?
6. Why is psychological counseling important for disaster workers and when should it be mandatory?

REFERENCES

Anderson, William A., and Shirley Mattingly. 1991. "Future Directions." In *Emergency Management: Principles and Practice for Local Government,* eds. Thomas E. Drabek and Gerard J. Hoetmer, 311–335. Washington, DC: International City/County Management Association.

Benight, Charles C. 1996. *Coping Self-Efficacy and Psychological Distress Following the Oklahoma City Bombing.* Quick Response Report 87. Boulder: University of Colorado, Natural Hazards Center. http://www.colorado.edu/hazards/qr/ qr87.html.

Burby, Raymond J.; Timothy Beatley; Philip R. Berke; Robert E. Deyle; Steven P. French; David R. Godschalk; Edward J. Kaiser; Jack D. Kartez; Peter J. May; Robert Olshansky; Robert G. Paterson; and Rutherford H. Platt. 1999. "Unleashing the Power of Planning to Create Disaster-Resistant Communities." Paper presented at the National Conference of the American Society for Public Administration, Orlando, FL, April 9–14.

Cigler, Beverly A., and Raymond J. Burby. 1990. "Floods." In *Handbook of Emergency Management,* eds. William L. Waugh, Jr., and Ronald John Hy, 81–105. Westport, CT: Greenwood.

Cowardin, David. 1985. "ICS, IEMS, and NIIMS: The Evolution of Incident Management," *American Fire Journal* (September): 6, 43.

Drabek, Thomas E. 1994. *Disaster Evacuation and the Tourist Industry.* Monograph 57. Boulder: University of Colorado, Institute of Behavioral Science, Program on Environment and Behavior.

Fesler, James W., and Donald F. Kettl. 1991. *The Politics of the Administrative Process.* Chatham, NJ: Chatham House.

Foley, Stephen. 1995. "Incident Management—Successful Utilization at Oklahoma City," *Responder* (July): 36–38.

Herres, Robert T. 1999. "Disaster Protection," *USAA Magazine* (March-April): 3.

Irwin, Robert L. 1989. "The Incident Command System (ICS)." In *Disaster Response: Principles of Preparation and Coordination.* ed. Erik Auf der Heide, 133–163. St. Louis, MO: C.V. Mosby.

Klein, Robert. 1998. "Regulation and Catastrophe Insurance." In *Paying the Price: The Status and Role of Insurance Against Natural Disaster in the United States,* eds. Howard Kunreuther and Richard J. Ross, Jr. 171–208. Washington, DC: Joseph Henry.

Kunreuther, Howard. 1998a. "A Program for Reducing Disaster Losses Through Insurance." In *Paying the Price: The Status and Role of Insurance Against Natural Disaster in the United States,* eds. Howard Kunreuther and Richard J. Ross, Jr., 209–228. Washington, DC: Joseph Henry.

———. 1998b. "Insurability Conditions and the Supply of Coverage." In *Paying the Price: The Status and Role of Insurance Against Natural Disaster in the United States,* eds. Howard Kunreuther and Richard J. Ross, Jr., 17–50. Washington, DC: Joseph Henry.

———. 1998c. "Introduction." In *Paying the Price: The Status and Role of Insurance Against Natural Disaster in the United States,* eds. Howard Kunreuther and Richard J. Ross, Jr., 1–16. Washington, DC: Joseph Henry.

Kunreuther, Howard, and Richard J. Roth, Jr., eds. 1998. *Paying the Price: The Status and Role of Insurance Against Natural Disasters in the United States,* Washington, DC: Joseph Henry.

Lecomte, Eugene, and Karen Gahagan. 1998. "Hurricane Insurance Protection in Florida." In *Paying the Price: The Status and Role of Insurance Against Natural Disaster in the United States,* eds. Howard Kunreuther and Richard J. Ross, Jr., 97–124. Washington, DC: Joseph Henry.

May, Peter J., and Walter Williams. 1986. *Disaster Policy Implementation: Managing Programs Under Shared Governance.* New York: Plenum Press.

Morris, Gary P. 1992. "Incident Command: Past, Present, Future, and Merger." *The Voice/ISFSI* (January): 13–14.

National Academy of Public Administration. 1997. *The Role of the National Guard in Emergency Preparedness and Response.* Washington, DC: NAPA.

———. 1993. *Coping with Catastrophe: Building an Emergency Management System to Meet People's Needs in Natural and Manmade Disasters.* Washington, DC: NAPA, February.

Oklahoma City, The City of. 1996. *Final Report: Alfred P. Murrah Federal Building Bombing, April 19, 1995.* Stillwater, OK: Fire Protection Publications.

Ouchi, William. 1981. *Theory Z: How American Business Can Meet the Japanese Challenge.* Reading, MA: Addison-Wesley.

Palm, Risa. 1998. "Demand for Disaster Insurance: Residential Coverage." In *Paying the Price: The Status and Role of Insurance Against Natural Disaster in the United States,* eds. Howard Kunreuther and Richard J. Ross, Jr., 51–66. Washington, DC: Joseph Henry.

Pasterick, Edward J. 1998. "The National Flood Insurance Program." In *Paying the Price: The Status and Role of Insurance Against Natural Disaster in the United States,* eds. Howard Kunreuther and Richard J. Ross, Jr., 125–154. Washington, DC: Joseph Henry.

Perrow, Charles. 1984. *Normal Accidents: Living with High-Risk Technologies.* New York: Basic Books.

Petak, William J. 1998. "Mitigation and Insurance." In *Paying the Price: The Status and Role of Insurance Against Natural Disaster in the United States,* eds. Howard Kunreuther and Richard J. Ross, Jr., 155–170. Washington, DC: Joseph Henry.

———. 1985. "Emergency Management: A Challenge for Public Administration." *Public Administration Review* 45, Special Issue (January): 3–7.

Riad, Jasmin. 1997. "Hurricane Threat and Evacuation Intentions: An Analysis of Risk Perception, Preparedness, Social Influence, and Resources." Ph.D. Dissertation. Georgia State University.

Riad, Jasmin, William L. Waugh, Jr., and Fran H. Norris. 1999. "The Psychology of Evacuation and Policy Design." In *Handbook of Crisis and Emergency Management,* ed. Ali Farazmand. New York: Marcel Dekker, forthcoming.

Roth, Richard J., Jr. 1998. "Earthquake Insurance Protection in California." In *Paying the Price: The Status and Role of Insurance Against Natural Disaster in the United States,* eds. Howard Kunreuther and Richard J. Ross, Jr., 67–96. Washington, DC: Joseph Henry.

———. 1997. *Earthquake Basics Brief No. 3: Insurance.* Oakland, CA: Earthquake Engineering Research Institute, April.

Schrader, John Y. 1993. *The Army's Role in Domestic Disaster Support: An Assessment of Policy Choices.* Santa Monica, CA: RAND.

Southern Governors Association, *Emergency Management Assistance Compact,* as amended January 31, 1995. Washington, DC: SGA, 1995.

Sylves, Richard T. 1998. *The Political and Policy Basis of Emergency Management.* Emmitsburg, MD: Federal Emergency Management Agency, Emergency Management Institute, Higher Education Project.

———. 1996. "The Politics and Budgeting of Emergency Management." In *Disaster Management in the U.S. and Canada,* eds. Richard T. Sylves and William L. Waugh, Jr., 26–45. Springfield, IL: Charles C. Thomas.

Tamillow, Michael. 1995. "Oklahoma City Bombing Incident," *Special Oklahoma City Issue,* 4–5.

Waugh, William L., Jr. 1994. "Regionalizing Emergency Management: Counties as State and Local Government." *Public Administration Review* (July–August 1994): 253–258.

———. 1993. "Co-ordination or Control: Organizational Design and the Emergency Management Function." *International Journal of Disaster Management and Prevention* 2 (December): 17–31.

————. 1990. "Emergency Management and State and Local Government Capacity." In *Cities and Disaster: North American Studies in Emergency Management,* eds. Richard T. Sylves and William L. Waugh, Jr., 46–68. Springfield, IL: Charles C. Thomas.

————. 1988. "States, Counties, and the Issues of Trust and Capacity." *Publius: The Journal of Federalism* (Winter): 189–198.

Waugh, William L., Jr., and Ronald J. Hy. 1996. "The Hyatt Skywalk Disaster and Other Lessons in the Regulation of Building." In *Disaster Management in the U.S. and Canada,* eds. Richard T. Sylves and William L. Waugh, Jr., 253–269. Springfield, IL: Charles C. Thomas.

————. 1988. "The Policymaking, Administrative, and Fiscal Capacities of County Government." *State and Local Government Review* 20 (Winter): 28–31.

6

THE CHALLENGE
OF EMERGENCY
MANAGEMENT

The threat of catastrophe is following us into the new millennium. Quite apart from the Y2K problem, the probabilities of earthquake storms, volcanic eruptions, megadroughts, bioterrorism, and failures of fragile technology are being more clearly defined and the risks may be greater than experts have expected. In short, the more we know about the nature of hazards and the history of disasters, the more we understand their inevitability. However, on the plus side, we are getting better at mitigating the effects of disaster and, in some few cases, actually preventing them. Technological innovations, organizational reforms, and better-designed policies and programs are preparing us better for uncertain events. The increased focus on mitigation (i.e., proactive rather than reactive programs), is reducing known hazards. The professionalization of the field of emergency management is also expanding capabilities to manage hazards and disasters (Sutphen and Waugh 1998). In many respects, we should be optimistic about the prospects of living with hazards and dealing with disasters.

The impact of technological advances on the practice of emergency management has been profound. Satellite imaging is revealing disasters in the making and guiding disaster mitigation and response efforts. Telecommunications technologies are putting decision support systems into the field so that operational decision making can be done by emergency managers on site, rather than by officials miles away. Disaster data can be loaded into a laptop computer and, via cellular modem, sent to emergency operations centers a few yards away or thousands of miles away. At the same time, updated maps and spatial analyses can be forwarded to disaster workers supervising evacuations, search-and-rescue operations, and other activities. Computer applications perhaps don't seem as miraculous as they did a few years ago, but the speed of innovation is making it difficult for emergency managers to keep abreast of the tools available to them. To give one example, little more than a decade ago, the spatial analysis of disasters was accomplished by superimposing a grid on a standard map—essentially marking it off in squares—so that operations could be oriented toward particular areas. Spatial analysis or geographic information systems (GIS) analysis was used for little else than generating situation maps and locating medical facilities, shelters, and other sites. In fact, during the Hurricane Andrew response in 1992, such maps were the principal product of the GIS effort, not because that was all the analysts could do but because that was the only kind of information that responders seemed to know how to use (see, e.g., Waugh 1995). GIS now can provide sophisticated analyses with layered data on the population and structures in the disaster area, the geophysical characteristics of the region, the changing meteorological conditions, and any number of other variables important to decision makers. Special needs populations, critical facilities, evacuation routes, flood and landslide areas, and almost any other kind of data that can be arrayed on a map can be included. Large databases can be stored and manipulated, exotic data can be integrated into the database, and analyses can be done quickly and accurately to meet the specific needs of decision makers. There are still some limits on the amount of data that can be fed into the system, but those limits are pushed further with every advance in computer technology.

It must also be noted that technological advances are also creating new challenges for emergency managers. Complex systems are fragile and, as Charles Perrow notes, "normal accidents" can occur (1984). Thousands of lives may be lost if a computer system fails and disrupts civil aviation or a mass transit system. Thousands more may be in jeopardy if a power grid collapses and cuts off power to homes, businesses, streetlights, telephone networks, and the countless other technologies on which we depend. While redundancy can be built into such systems, failure is always possible. Fortunately, technological advance may help us build "intelligent cities" that will recognize and respond to emergencies very quickly. Monitoring systems will warn of impending disaster and activate the disaster response mechanisms. Intergovernmental and interorganizational efforts will be co-ordinated. Most important, mitigation programs and disaster preparedness will be integrated into other municipal systems. Some of those technologies are already in place for traffic management, as well as other functions. Cameras are used to monitor traffic flows and traffic can be slowed or speeded up by altering traffic light patterns and/or it can be diverted when accidents and other problems occur (Stanley and Waugh 2000). Automated flood gauges are already being used to issue warnings of rising river waters. Homeowners can now buy wireless gauges that will give warnings of cold temperatures that may damage the plants in their yards.

Organizational reform is having a positive impact on some agencies, but not all. Structural reforms may be increasing program effectiveness, although enthusiasm for reorganizations and "reinvention" efforts is waning as officials realize that budget savings do not mean more efficient or more effective operations. Moreover, emphasizing the cost effectiveness of programs may have a negative effect on other important public values. That may be all the more true for emergency management programs because of the nature of the problems with which agencies deal. Treating all communities the same, while it may sound equitable, does not necessarily provide the same benefit. Some are more capable in terms of having the fiscal and political wherewithal to address their own problems (i.e., hazards) than others and simply do not need as much help.

Also, there has been too little emphasis on capacity building, including human resource development (i.e., training and education of personnel), in the National Performance Review process and the reinvention efforts. Although emergency managers are in a growth field, budgets are not secure and many agencies are so underfunded that they have little capacity to design and implement programs. The professionalization of the field may, in fact, exacerbate problems for smaller agencies because they will not be able to recruit highly qualified personnel nor retain their own experienced personnel. A perennial problem in dealing with local agencies is the very unevenness of capabilities. They cannot always be trusted to address problems and operate programs because some lack the capacity to do so, although neighboring agencies are very capable. Until the capacities of the weak agencies are improved, it will be difficult to have an effective emergency management system.

The transition to all-hazards emergency management approaches with generic programs may also alienate the supporters of disaster-specific programs. For example, while there may be ample political support among voters, technical experts, community activists, and public officials to assure adequate funding for seismic hazard programs in California, there may be much less interest in and support for a generic disaster preparedness program even though it will have utility in earthquakes. The funding of emergency management programs has historically been more disaster-specific (e.g., the National Flood Insurance Program and the National Earthquake Hazard Reduction Program) than generic (Waugh 1999a).

Organizational reform may also make it possible to bring other agencies into the national emergency management system. The antiterrorism effort is involving the Department of Defense, the Department of Justice, and the Public Health Service with the larger emergency management community, but it is still uncertain whether that effort will be integrated into the national emergency management system. By all appearances, the antiterrorism programs are simply being layered over the national system with very little attention to the existing networks of local emergency response agencies, nonprofit organizations, and private firms. Local officials are being trained in 120 cities, but there is little effort to involve officials in the surrounding jurisdictions who have mutual aid agreements and are normally involved in "metropolitan" operations. An "open systems" approach in which nonprofit agencies, private firms, and ad hoc volunteer groups, as well as neighboring governments, who are normally involved in hazard mitigation programs and in disaster response and recovery operations will certainly expand capabilities and may be critically important in very large terrorist events. Similarly, greater collaboration among FEMA, the U.S. Geological Survey, the National Oceanic and Atmospheric Administration, the U.S. Army Corps of Engineers, and other hazard-related agencies would also expand capabilities. There are mechanisms for collaboration (e.g., working groups and liaison arrangements), but they still don't speak the same technical languages and their organizational cultures are so different that effective interaction is often difficult. California's development of the Standardized Emergency Management System, with its common terminology and information system, may be a model to follow. Joint exercising and training also facilitates interaction. Part of the common wisdom in the field is that personal contact, being able to associate a face with a name, improves communication and helps develop the trust that is essential in a collaborative effort. Trust, rather than legal arrangements, may be the key element in assuring effective collaboration in a disaster operation.

Policy design is improving as disaster-specific programs are being replaced by generic all-hazards programs. The focus on mitigation, rather than simply reacting to disasters, is changing the orientation of agencies and programs. The cost of recent disasters and the potential costs of future disasters are strong arguments for a more proactive approach to emergency management. Rather than being peripheral actors in state and local government, emergency managers should be actively involved in land-use planning, the adoption and enforcement of building codes, environmental protection, public health, and even law enforcement. Of course, that also means emergency managers should be professionally educated, broadly trained, and experienced administrators, as well as good politicians. They should be sensitive to the trade-offs inherent in economic development projects and other land-uses, and should help the public make sensible decisions concerning appropriate and sustainable development.

The professionalization of the field is speeding up. The Certified Emergency Manager program is focusing attention on the technical skills, knowledge, and experience needed. Training and educational programs are also broadening the knowledge base. If emergency management develops as other professions have, the current emphasis on technical specialists in disaster-specific areas (e.g., seismic hazards), or functional areas, such as planning, will require the development of career paths that will encourage broader exposure to the field so that personnel can develop the leadership and administrative skills to become agency directors. Just as the U.S. Army provides training through its War College, Command and General Staff College, and other service schools for senior officers to broaden their perspectives, degree programs in public administration will be necessary for emergency managers. Once those emergency managers without college degrees are "grandfathered in," in terms of receiving professional certification based on their experience, the minimum requirements will increase. A graduate degree in public administration, emergency management, or a related field will become the minimum standard in the foreseeable future.

Tom Drabek concludes in *The Professional Emergency Manager* (1987) that the successful emergency managers are those with the requisite interpersonal skills and political acumen to promote their programs and to convince the public and other officials that hazards should be taken seriously and that the community should be prepared to deal with disasters when they occur. As suggested earlier, when emergency management programs become more generic, greater political skill will be required to sell them to voters and to the elected officials who control budgets (Waugh 1999a). Professional credibility and strong interpersonal skills are also necessary to hold together the diverse participants in the emergency management system. Even at the local level, considerable skill is needed to help disciplined emergency response agencies interact effectively with more fluid volunteer groups. And, it is important that citizen groups be involved in disaster operations, both to ensure that they understand the importance of emergency management (and, thus, support policies and programs) and to ensure that they develop survival and recovery skills that will make their communities more resilient.

A NEW EMERGENCY MANAGEMENT FOR THE NEW MILLENNIUM?

Time is running out for public officials to arrive on the scene saying, "We're from the government and we are here to help you" and expect to be met with enthusiastic public support. In severe disasters, assistance is certainly welcome and the people are grateful. But expectations are changing. Now there is more expectation of public participation, more need for consensus building regarding hazard and disaster reduction, and fewer resources to support broadly focused, expensive public programs that may or may not be needed. Citizens expect to be involved in policymaking, treated with respect, and informed about options and results. In many respects, current expectations reflect a less trusting public that is not content simply to delegate responsibility for programs to public officials and wait for services. They understand more about the programs. They are also more educated and understand issues and the policymaking process better than their parents and grandparents. They are more informed because they have access to more information on particular hazards than previous generations had. When a crisis occurs today, a president, governor, or mayor may have little more information on the events than the average citizen watching CNN, WNBC, or another news network. The Internet further expands access to national and international news and can give users direct contact with victims, eyewitnesses, and others knowledgeable about events. The competing media and Internet stories from the United States and its NATO allies and from Serbia during the Kosovo crisis in 1999 is a good example of the flow of information. Not all of that information is correct or truthful, however. International crises generate propaganda. By the same token, a disturbing amount of the information on disasters and how to deal with them is inaccurate or incomplete. In some cases, well-meaning but ill-informed people are posting information on the Internet that may cause problems for those who desperately need accurate information. In other cases, people with biases toward particular approaches, technologies, or results may mislead readers.

According to a growing body of literature in public administration, a revolution is taking place in how people relate to government in the United States. Whether because of the growing distrust of government in general or the increasing intensity of policy debates, the dominant models of citizen participation in government are changing. While it may be too early to suggest that the revolution is won or lost or even that there will be fundamental change in how agencies operate and deal with the public, the effect is being felt broadly in American government. In many respects, the revolution is being caused by the recognition that public administrators cannot continue to presume that their technical expertise is justification for supplanting or simply ignoring the interests and desires of the public at large. Managing public participation in policymaking is becoming more and more difficult and the very effort to limit or strictly structure public input can cause a political furor.

Public administration in the United States, as well as elsewhere, has been based on the assumption that there is a great divide between the government and the governed. Scientists and technicians (i.e., the technocracy) know best how to address problems and to run programs. Technocrats and professional administrators exercise their expertise in the best interests of the public or at least in the interests that the public is assumed to have. One result of this view of citizen participation (or nonparticipation, as it were) in government has been a general feeling of alienation. The government takes money (taxes) and turns it into programs that citizens may or may not like or support. In most cases, there is a general feeling of disconnection between the taxes paid and the services received, although some local governments do identify revenue sources for the services they deliver, and some taxes at all levels are earmarked for particular purposes. Nonetheless, there is a general feeling that the government is not responsive to the interests of the people. This may be particularly problematic in terms of hazard mitigation programs. The public has to agree that the hazard exists, that it should be reduced, and that the buyout program or building code or other mitigation program is an appropriate response.

The "we-them" dichotomy has strained relations between the public and its appointed and elected employees. That dichotomy persists, but there is less inclination to view government as separate from the people it governs, as an elite based on technical expertise and/or socioeconomic standing that manages the affairs of the citizenry with little real public input. The arrogance of technocracy is giving way to a more democratic arrangement. As the title of a recent public administration text states, *The Government Is Us* (King and Stivers 1998). Public participation in policymaking and administration is expanding as "town meetings" and citizen advisory councils provide input on important issues and the process becomes a consensus-building exercise. As a result, the political and economic underpinnings of emergency management are undergoing something of a revolution as agencies "partner" with their nonprofit sector and private sector counterparts, as well as with other public agencies. Rules and regulations are being negotiated, rather than imposed and enforced. While national standard setting is still necessary in some cases, implementation strategies can be flexible.

Project Impact was announced by the Federal Emergency Management Agency at the El Niño Summit in October of 1997. Seven pilot communities were identified and FEMA began the process of "partnering" with the local governments, private firms, and others to develop hazard assessments, capability assessments, hazard management plans, and disaster plans. The list of participating communities has recently been expanded and the project continues to add partners. The partnerships are formal, negotiated arrangements that define organizational and intergovernmental responsibilities and assure sustainability of the effort. They also suggest strong political commitments to a set of values that include environmental protection, sustainable development, and hazard mitigation. The negotiated intergovernmental relationships, the commitment of financial and human resources, and the political commitment appear to be significant departures from past national programs.

In large measure, Project Impact reflects the administrative changes that have occurred in the U.S. federal government over the past several years. In early 1997, FEMA was developing a strategic plan that listed goals and objectives in a traditional input-output manner. The goals were formulated so that the agency could accomplish them on its own, with minimal contributions from other organizations. As the agency was required to develop broader performance goals to satisfy the requirements of the Government Performance and Results Act (GPRA) of 1993, the performance goals in the strategic plan evolved into broad, long-term objectives that require the cooperation and "partnership" of state and local governments, nonprofit organizations, and private firms. The new performance goals are not the traditional input-output measures, they are less output oriented than they are results or impact oriented. To reiterate briefly the goals listed in Chapter 2, FEMA is seeking to reducing the risk of loss of life and injury, the risk of property loss and economic disruption, and human suffering from the impact of disasters and to increase the speed of recovery from disasters, the efficiency with which FEMA delivers its services, and overall customer satisfaction with FEMA services. Although the language of FEMA's plan is still couched in terms of efficiency with benchmarks and references to customers, the overall thrust of the document is on the impact on disaster losses and human suffering, as well as on efficient administration (Waugh 1999a, 1999b).

The relationship between federal and local governments has often been contentious, but it has occasionally been quite close and effective. The term "picket fence federalism" has been used to describe the close administrative and political relationships that developed in the 1970s between the federal agencies that formulated policy and funded programs and the local agencies that implemented and operated the programs. State agencies were often part of the "picket" if they had a substantive role in the programs and/or were responsible for allocating moneys among communities or monitoring local agencies' performance (rather than simply being involved in a "pass through" without a substantive role in deciding where money should be spent or on what). Over time, the relationships became closer as local officials and agencies came to mimic their federal counterparts in agency and office names, job titles, and other structural and cultural features. They shared a common language, largely acronyms in some cases but a complex technical language nonetheless, and a value system. Typical career paths in, say, transportation might involve employment in two or three different levels of government. The federal, state, and local agencies involved in the welfare system, environmental protection, transportation, and emergency management were closely intertwined. The slow transition of state and local emergency management agencies to the FEMA model is illustrative of the process. The trend is for state and local agencies to be called "emergency management agencies" (EMAs) rather than "civil defense" or "disaster preparedness." The EMA officials, too, are increasingly likely to have position titles that mirror their FEMA counterparts. This is a natural part of administration that has been speeded up as state and local EMAs have acquired more visibility and more autonomy. Slowly, the picture of EMAs drawn by Tom Drabek in *The Professional Emergency Manager* (1987) as a mix of professional, part-time, and volunteer offices, sometimes with staff and often without, is changing. The legal liability of local officials for failure to prepare reasonably for disaster and the political liability of elected chief executives at all levels when they have not invested appropriately in emergency management offices and programs are encouraging innovation and reform (Sutphen and Waugh 1998; Waugh 1996).

Living with hazards is getting easier as we understand them more and manage them better. Clearly there are still major obstacles in terms of getting communities to adopt appropriate land-use regulations and building codes, property owners to take responsibility for reducing the risk to their own homes and businesses, and individuals to become more aware of hazards and to develop their own mitigation strategies. Dealing with disasters is also getting easier, although they are occurring more frequently and affecting more people. While many communities are still not adequately prepared to deal with disasters, the framework for an effective system is being implemented. More individual and community responsibility for risk reduction and less reliance upon outside (i.e., state and federal) assistance should be encouraged. But, that also means providing more financial resources and technical assistance to communities to ensure that human and property losses are reduced, human suffering is reduced, and the system operates more effectively and efficiently (to take a page or two from the FEMA strategic plan). It also means more consensus building to assure that all understand and support those goals.

REFERENCES

Adams, Guy B., and Danny L. Balfour. 1998. *Unmasking Administrative Evil.* Thousand Oaks, CA: Sage.

Drabek, Thomas J. 1987. *The Professional Emergency Manager.* Boulder: University of Colorado, Institute of Behavioral Science.

King, Cheryl Simrell; Camilla Stivers, et al. 1998. *The Government Is Us: Public Administration in an Anti-Government Era.* Thousand Oaks, CA: Sage.

Stanley, Ellis M., Sr., and William L. Waugh, Jr. 2000. "Emergency Managers for the New Millennium." In *Handbook of Crisis and Emergency Management,* ed. Ali Farazmand. New York: Marcel Dekker, forthcoming.

Sutphen, Sandra, and William L. Waugh, Jr. 1998. "Organizational Reform and Technological Innovation in Emergency Management." *International Journal of Mass Emergencies and Disasters* 16 (March): 7–12.

Waugh, William L., Jr. 1999a. "The Fiscal Risk in All-Hazards Emergency Management OR the Political Hazards in Rational Policy." *International Journal of Public Administration* 22: 611–636.

———. 1999b. "Assessing Quality in Disaster Management." In *Performance and Quality Measurement in Government: Issues and Experiences,* ed. Ari Halachmi, 65–82. Burke, VA: Chatelaine.

———. 1996. "Emergency Management for the New Millennium." In *Disaster Management in the U.S. and Canada,* eds. Richard T. Sylves and William L. Waugh, Jr., 344–359. Springfield, IL: Charles C. Thomas.

———. 1995. "Geographic Information Systems: The Case of Disaster Management." *Social Science Computer Review* 13 (Winter): 422–431.

SELECTED
BIBLIOGRAPHY

Abernathy, Ann Marie, and Leslie Weiner. 1994. *"FEMA's Changing Role in Disaster Management."* Forum Publications.

Aldrich, Howard. 1979. *Organizations and Environments.* New York: Prentice-Hall.

Alexander, David. 1993. *Natural Disasters.* New York: Chapman and Hall.

American Friends Service Committee. 1969. *In the Wake of Hurricane Camille: An Analysis of the Federal Response.* Philadelphia: AFSC.

American Nuclear Society. 1979. "Special Report: The Ordeal at Three Mile Island." *Nuclear News* (April 6): 1–6.

American Red Cross. 1992. *Community Disaster Education.* Washington, DC: ARC, Disaster Services Division.

———. 1991. *Natural Hazards Risk Profile: Hurricanes, Floods, Tornadoes, Lightning, Earthquakes.* Washington, DC: ARC, Disaster Services Division, March.

American Rivers. 1994. *The Real Choices Report: America's Flood Control Policy Failures.* Washington, DC: American Rivers, June 13.

Anderson, Mary B., and Peter J. Woodrow. 1998. *Rising from the Ashes: Development Strategies in Times of Disaster.* Boulder, CO: Lynne Reinner.

Auf der Heide, Eric. 1989. *Disaster Response: Principles of Preparation and Coordination.* St. Louis, MO: C.V. Mosby.

Ayre, Robert S. 1975. *Earthquake and Tsunami Hazards in the U.S.* Boulder: University of Colorado, Institute of Behavioral Sciences Monograph.

Bates, F.L., et al. 1963. *The Social and Psychological Consequences of a Natural Disaster: A Longitudinal Study of Hurricane Audrey (1957).* Washington, DC: National Academy of Sciences, National Research Council.

Benthall, Jonathan. 1993. *Disasters, Relief, and the Media.* London: I.B. Tauris.

Berke, Philip, and Suzanne Wilhite. 1988. *Local Mitigation Planning Response to Earthquake Hazards: Results of a National Survey.* College Station: Texas A&M University, Hazard Reduction and Recovery Center, May.

Bernard, E.N., ed. 1991. *Tsunami Hazard: A Practical Guide for Tsunami Hazard Reduction.* Dordrecht, The Netherlands: Kluwer Academic.

Bernknopf, Richard L., and David R. Soller. 1994. *Earthquake Hazard Mitigation: Using Science for Safety Decisions.* Reston, VA: U.S. Geological Survey.

Bhowmik, N.G. 1994. *The 1993 Flood on the Mississippi River in Illinois.* Champaign, IL: Illinois State Water Survey.

Birkland, Thomas A. 1997. *After Disaster: Agenda Setting, Public Policy, and Focusing Events.* Washington, DC: Georgetown University Press.

Blaikie, Piers; Terry Cannon; Ian Davis; and Benjamin Wisner. 1994. *At Risk: Natural Hazards, People's Vulnerability, and Disasters.* New York: Routledge.

Bolin, Robert, and Lois Stanford. 1998. "The Northridge Earthquake: Community-Based Approaches to Unmet Recovery Needs." *Disasters* 22 (March): 21–38.

Bourriau, Janine, ed. 1992. *Understanding Catastrophe: Its Impact on Life on Earth.* New York: Cambridge University Press.

Bruner, Stephanie Polsley. 1994. "The Galloway Report: New Floodplain Management or Business as Usual?" *Journal of Soil and Water Conservation* 19 (November): 528–534.

Bryant, E.A. 1991. *Natural Hazards.* New York: Cambridge University Press.

Burby, Raymond J., ed. 1998. *Cooperating with Nature: Confronting Natural Hazards with Land-Use Planning for Sustainable Communities.* Washington, DC: Joseph Henry.

Burby, Raymond J., and Linda C. Dalton. 1994. "Plans Can Matter! The Role of Land Use Plans and State Planning Mandates in Limiting the Development of Hazardous Areas." *Public Administration Review* 54, No. 3 (May/June): 229–238.

Burby, Raymond J., Scott A. Bollens; James M. Holloway; Edward J. Kaiser; David Mullan; and John R. Shaeffer. 1988. *Cities Under Water: A Comparative Evaluation of Ten Cities' Efforts to Manage Floodplain Land Use.* Boulder: University of Colorado, Institute of Behavioral Science, Monograph 47.

Burby, Raymond J.; Beverly A. Cigler; Steven P. French; Edward J. Kaiser; Jack Kartez; Dale Roenigk; Dana Weist; and Dale Whittington. 1991. *Sharing Environmental Risks: How to Control Governments' Losses in Natural Disasters.* Boulder, CO: Westview.

Burkhart, Ford N. 1991. *Media, Emergency Warnings, and Citizen Response.* Boulder, CO: Westview.

Burton, Ian; Robert W. Kates; and Gilbert F. White. 1993. *The Environment as Hazard,* 2d ed. New York: Oxford University Press.

Cassels, Janice. 1993. *The Uncertain Promise of Law; Lessons from Bhopal.* Toronto: University of Toronto Press.

Charles, Michael T., and John Choon Kim, eds. 1988. *Emergency Management: A Casebook.* Springfield, IL: Charles C. Thomas.

Cochrane, H. 1992. "Overview of Economic Research on Earthquake Consequences." In *The Economic Consequences of a Catastrophic Earthquake,* ed. National Research Council, 100–111. Washington, DC: National Academy Press.

Cole, S., and V. Razak. 1992. *Social Accounting for Disaster Preparedness and Planning: An Application to Aruba.* Buffalo, NY: National Center for Earthquake Engineering Research, State University of New York at Buffalo, NCEER Report 93–002.

Comerio, Mary C. 1998. *Disaster Hits Home: New Policy for Urban Housing Recovery.* Berkeley: University of California Press.

Comfort, Louise, ed. 1988. *Managing Disasters: Administrative and Policy Strategies.* Durham, NC: Duke University Press.

Cutter, Susan L., ed. 1994. *Environmental Risks and Hazards.* Englewood Cliffs, NJ: Prentice Hall.

————. 1993. *Living with Risk.* London: Edward Arnold.

Davis, Lee. 1993. *Man-Made Catastrophes: From the Burning of Rome to the Lockerbie Crash.* New York: Facts On File.

Disaster Information Task Force. 1997. *Harnessing Information and Technology for Disaster Management: The Global Disaster Information Network.* Washington, DC: Task Force, November.

Doehring, Fred; Iver W. Duedall; and John M. Williams. 1994. *Florida Hurricanes and Tropical Storms, 1871–1993: An Historical Survey.* Gainesville: University of Florida/Florida Institute of Technology, Sea Grant College Program, June.

Donovan-O'Meara, Donna, and Stephen James O'Meara. 1994. *Volcanoes: Passion and Fury.* Cambridge, MA: Sky Publishing Corp.

Drabek, Thomas E. 1994. *Disaster Evacuation and the Tourist Industry.* Boulder: University of Colorado, Institute of Behavioral Science, Monograph 57.

————. 1990. *Emergency Management: Strategies for Maintaining Organizational Integrity.* New York: Springer-Verlag.

————. 1987. *The Professional Emergency Manager.* Boulder: University of Colorado, Institute of Behavioral Science, Monograph 44.

Drabek, Thomas E., and Gerard Hoetmer, eds. 1991. *Emergency Management: Principles and Practice for Local Government.* Washington, DC: International City Management Association.

Drabek, Thomas E.; Harrett Tansminga; Thomas Kiljanik; and Christopher Adams. 1981. *Managing Multiorganizational Emergency Responses.* Publication 6. Boulder: University of Colorado, Institute of Behavioral Sciences.

Dynes, Russell R. 1990. *Community Emergency Planning: False Assumptions and Inappropriate Analogies.* Preliminary Paper 145. Newark: University of Delaware, Disaster Research Center.

————. 1970. *Organized Behavior in Disaster.* Lexington, MA: Lexington Books.

Federal Emergency Management Agency. 1999. *Federal Response Plan.* Washington, DC: FEMA, April.

————. Emergency Management Institute. 1998a. *Senior Officials' Workshop Manual: Preparedness and Response for Terrorist Incidents.* Emmitsburg, MD: FEMA, September.

————. 1998b. *The Role of Voluntary Agencies in Emergency Management.* Emmitsburg, MD: FEMA, IS-288, August.

————. 1997a. *A Citizen's Guide to Disaster Assistance.* Emmitsburg, MD: FEMA, IS-7, January.

————. 1997b. *Report on Costs and Benefits of Natural Hazard Mitigation.* Washington, DC: FEMA, Mitigation Directorate, March.

————. 1996. *NBC Terrorism Response Focus Group for Local Government: Focus Group Report.* Emmitsburg, MD: FEMA, October 29.

————. 1995. *National Mitigation Strategy: Partnerships for Building Safer Communities.* Washington, DC: FEMA, Mitigation Directorate, December 6.

————. 1994. "Reinventing Disaster Response: Northridge Earthquake, the First Five Weeks." Washington, DC: FEMA, March.

————. 1993a. "National Performance Review Report." Washington, DC: U.S. Government Printing Office, September 7.

————. Office of Inspector General. 1993b. "FEMA's Disaster Management Program: A

Performance Audit After Hurricane Andrew." Washington, DC: FEMA, H-01–93, January.

———, and the National Emergency Management Association. 1997. *State Capability Assessment for Readiness (CAR), Version 1*. Emmitsburg, MD: FEMA, June 6.

Federal Interagency Floodplain Management Task Force. 1995. *A Unified National Program for Floodplain Management 1994*. Washington, DC: Federal Emergency Management Agency, March 6.

———. 1992. *Floodplain Management in the United States: An Assessment, Report Volumes 1 and 2* (FIA-17 and FIA-18). Washington, DC: Task Force.

Finegold, A.F., and J. Solyst. 1994. *Emergency Planning and Community Right to Know Act: A Status of State Actions—1993*. Washington, DC: National Governors' Association.

Fire, Frank L.; Nancy K. Grant; and David H. Hoover. 1990. *SARA Title III: Intent and Implementation of Hazardous Materials Regulations*. New York: Van Nostrand Reinhold.

Fischer, Henry W., IV. 1994. *Response to Disaster: Fact Versus Fiction and Its Perpetuation—The Sociology of Disaster*. Lanham, MD: University Press of America.

Foxell, Joseph W., Jr. 1997. "The Prospect of Nuclear and Biological Terrorism." *Journal of Contingencies and Crisis Management* 5 (June): 98–108.

French, Steven P. 1995. "Damage to Urban Infrastructure and Other Public Property from the 1989 Loma Prieta (California) Earthquake." *Disasters: The Journal of Disaster Studies and Management* 19, 1 (March): 57–67.

Friesema, H. Paul, ed. 1979. *Aftermath: Communities After Natural Disasters*. Beverly Hills, CA: Sage.

Geipel, Robert (translated by Philip Wagner). 1982. *Disaster and Reconstruction: The Friuli, Italy, Earthquakes of 1976*. Boston: Allen and Unwin.

Gigliotti, Richard, and Ronald Jason. 1991. *Emergency Planning for Maximum Protection*. Boston: Butterworth-Heinemann.

Gillespie, D.G.; R.A. Colignon; M.M. Banerjee; S.A. Murty; and M. Rogge. 1993. *Partnerships for Community Preparedness*. Boulder: University of Colorado, Natural Hazards Research and Applications Information Center.

Gillespie, D.G., and C.L. Streeter. 1987. "Conceptualizing and Measuring Disaster Preparedness." *International Journal of Mass Emergencies and Disasters* 5 (August): 155–176.

Gist, Richard, and Lubin N. Barnard, eds. 1989. *Psychological Aspects of Disasters*. New York: John Wiley.

Gleser, Goldine C.; Bonnie L. Green; and Caroline Winget, eds. 1981. *Prolonged Psychosocial Effects of Disaster: A Study of Buffalo Creek*. New York: Academic Press.

Godschalk, David R., and Timothy Beatley. 1989. *Catastrophic Coastal Storms: Hazard Mitigation and Development Management*. Durham, NC: Duke University Press.

Godschalk, David R.; Timothy Beatley; Philip Berke; David J. Brower; and Edward J. Kaiser. 1999. *Natural Hazard Mitigation: Recasting Disaster Policy and Planning*. Washington, DC: Island Press.

Grant, Nancy K., and David H. Hoover. 1994. *Fire Service Administration*. Quincy, MA: National Fire Protection Association.

Grigsby, Gordon. 1977. *Tornado Watch*. Columbus: Ohio State University Press.

Hamm, Mark S. 1997. *Apocalypse in Oklahoma: Waco and Ruby Ridge Revenged*. Boston: Northeastern University Press.

Herken, Gregg. 1987. *Counsels of War,* expanded ed. New York: Oxford University Press.

Hodgkinson, Peter E., and Michael Stewart. 1998. *Coping with Catastrophe: A Handbook of Post-Disaster Psychosocial Aftercare.* London: Routledge.

Hoetmer, Gerald J. 1983. "Emergency Management." *Baseline Data Reports* 15 (August): 13. Washington, DC: International City Management Association (ICMA).

Hutchinson, Sally A. 1983. *Survival Practices of Rescue Workers: Hidden Dimensions of Watchful Readiness.* Washington, DC: University Press of America.

Insurance Institute for Property Loss Reduction and Insurance Research Council. 1995. *Coastal Exposure and Community Protection: Hurricane Andrew's Legacy.* Boston, MA: Insurance Institute for Property Loss Reduction (IIPLR) and Insurance Research Council (IRC), April.

Interagency Floodplain Management Review Committee. 1994a. *Science for Floodplain Management into the 21st Century.* Washington, DC: U.S. Government Printing Office.

———. 1994b. *Sharing the Challenge: Floodplain Management into the 21st Century* (Galloway Report). Washington, DC: U.S. Government Printing Office.

Interagency Hazard Mitigation Team. 1989. *Interagency Hazard Mitigation Team Report: Hurricane Hugo.* Washington, DC: Federal Emergency Management Agency, FEMA 843–DR-SC, October.

International Association of Fire Chiefs. 1994. "Observations and Comments on the Southern California Fire Storms." Fairfax, VA: IAFC.

Kunreuther, Howard, and Richard J. Roth, Sr., eds. 1998. *Paying the Price: The Status and Role of Insurance Against Natural Disasters in the United States.* Washington, DC: Joseph Henry.

Kurzman, Dan. 1987. *A Killing Wind: Inside Union Carbide and the Bhopal Catastrophe.* New York: McGraw-Hill.

Kuszaj, James M. 1997. The EPACRA *Compliance Manual: Interpreting and Implementing the Emergency Planning and Community Right-to-Know Act of 1986.* Chicago: Section of Natural Resources, Energy, and Environmental Law, American Bar Association.

Leaning, Jennifer, and Langley Keyes, eds. 1984. *The Counterfeit Ark: Crisis Relocation for Nuclear War.* Cambridge, MA: Ballinger.

Levin, Pamela. 1996. *Property Insurance Issues in Catastrophic Losses.* Chicago: Tort and Insurance Practice Section, American Bar Association.

Levy, Louis J., and Llewellyn M. Toulmin. 1993. *Improving Disaster Planning and Response Efforts: Lessons from Hurricanes Andrew and Iniki.* Reston, VA: Booz-Allen and Hamilton, August.

Lindell, Michael K.; D.J. Whitney; C.J. Futch; and C.S. Clause. 1995. *Organizational Characteristics of Effective LEPCs.* East Lansing: Michigan State University, Department of Psychology.

———. 1994. "Are Local Emergency Planning Committees Effective in Developing Community Disaster Preparedness?" *International Journal of Mass Emergencies and Disasters* 12 (August): 159–182.

Lindell, Michael K., and M.J. Meier. 1994. "Effectiveness of Community Planning for Toxic Chemical Emergencies." *Journal of the American Planning Association* 60: 222–234.

McLoughlin, David. 1985. "A Framework for Integrated Emergency Management." *Public Administration Review* 45 (Special Issue): 165–172.

Majumdar, Shyamal K., et al., eds. 1992. *Natural and Technological Disasters: Causes, Effects and Preventive Measures*. Easton, PA: Pennsylvania Academy of Science.

Mason, Owen K.; William J. Neal; and Orrin H. Pilkey. 1997. *Living with the Coast of Alaska*. Durham, NC: Duke University Press.

May, Peter J. 1997. "State Regulatory Roles: Choices in the Regulation of Building Safety." *State and Local Government Review* 29 (Spring): 70–80.

———. 1993. "Mandate Design and Implementation: Enhancing Implementation Efforts and Shaping Regulatory Styles." *Journal of Policy Analysis and Management* 12 (Fall): 634–663.

———. 1991. "Addressing Public Risks: Federal Earthquake Policy Design." *Journal of Policy Analysis and Management* 10, 2 (Spring): 263–285.

———. 1985. *Recovering from Catastrophes: Federal Disaster Relief Policy and Politics*. Westport, CT: Greenwood.

May, Peter J., and Raymond J. Burby. 1996. "Coercive Versus Cooperative Policies: Comparing Intergovernmental Mandate Performance." *Journal of Policy Analysis and Management* 15 (Winter): 171–201.

May, Peter J., and Walter Williams. 1986. *Disaster Policy Implementation: Managing Programs Under Shared Governance*. New York: Plenum.

Medvedev, Zhores A. (translated by George Saunders). 1979. *Nuclear Disaster in the Urals*. New York: Norton.

Meehan, Richard L. 1984. *The Atom and the Fault: Experts, Earthquakes, and Nuclear Power*. Cambridge, MA: MIT Press.

Mileti, Dennis S., ed. 1999. *Disasters by Design: A Reassessment of Natural Hazards in the United States*. Washington, DC: Joseph Henry.

Mileti, Dennis S.; Thomas E. Drabek; and J. Eugene Haas. 1975. *Human Systems in Extreme Environments: A Sociological Perspective*. Boulder, CO: Institute of Behavioral Science Monograph, University of Colorado.

Mittler, Elliott. 1993. *The Public Policy Response to Hurricane Hugo in South Carolina*. Boulder: University of Colorado, Natural Hazards Research and Applications Information Center, Working Paper 84, April.

———. 1991. *Building Code Enforcement Following Hurricane Hugo in South Carolina*. Boulder: University of Colorado, Natural Hazards Research and Applications Information Center, Quick Response Research Report 44, 1991.

Moore, Jamie W., and Dorothy P. Moore. 1989. *The Army Corps of Engineers and the Evolution of Federal Flood Plain Management Policy*. Boulder: University of Colorado, Institute of Behavioral Science.

Munasinghe, Mohan, and Caroline Clarke, eds. 1995. *Disaster Prevention for Sustainable Development: Economic and Policy Issues*. A report from the Yokohama World Conference on Natural Disaster Reduction, May 23–27, 1994. Washington, DC: The World Bank/International Decade for Natural Disaster Reduction.

Myers, Mary Fran. 1993. "Bridging the Gap Between Research and Practice: The Natural Hazards Research and Applications Information Center." *International Journal of Mass Emergencies and Disasters* 11 (March): 41–54.

National Academy of Public Administration. 1993. *Coping with Catastrophe: Building an Emergency Management System to Meet People's Needs in Natural and Manmade Disaster*. Washington, DC: NAPA.

National Governors' Association. 1980. *Emergency Mitigation: Strategies for Disaster*

Prevention and Reduction. Washington, DC: NGA.

National Research Council. 1994. *Facing the Challenge: U.S. National Report to the IDNDR World Conference on Natural Disaster Reduction, Yokohama, Japan, May 23–27, 1994.* Washington, DC: National Academy Press.

National Seismic Policy Conference. 1984. *Conference Proceedings for Meeting of 1–3 November 1983, Seattle, Washington.* Olympia, WA: Department of Emergency Services, March.

Nigro, Lloyd G., and William L. Waugh, Jr. 1998. "Workplace Violence Policies and Programs in Cities and Counties." In *Municipal Yearbook 1998,* ed., 3–8. Washington, DC: International City/County Management Association.

————. 1996. "Violence in the American Workplace: Challenges for the Public Employer." *Public Administration Review* 56 (July/August): 326–333.

Noji, Eric K., ed. 1997. *The Public Health Consequences of Disaster.* New York: Oxford University Press.

Oklahoma City, City of. 1996. *Final Report: Alfred P. Murrah Federal Building Bombing, April 19, 1995.* Stillwater, OK: Fire Protection Publications.

Palm, Risa I. 1995. *Earthquake Insurance: A Longitudinal Study of California Homeowners.* Boulder, CO: Westview.

————. 1990. *Natural Hazards: An Integrative Framework for Research and Planning.* Baltimore, MD: Johns Hopkins University Press.

Partridge, William R. 1994. "Disaster Declaration Decisions: Staff Support by FEMA." Memorandum: Inspection Report I-02–93 for Richard Krimm, Associate Director of the Response and Recovery Directorate, May 17. Washington, DC: Federal Emergency Management Agency.

Peacock, Walter Gillis; Betty Hearn Morrow; and Hugh Gladwin, eds. 1997. *Hurricane Andrew: Ethnicity, Gender, and the Sociology of Disasters.* London: Routledge.

Penick, James, Jr. 1976, 1981. *The New Madrid Earthquakes of 1811–1812.* Columbia: University of Missouri Press.

Perrow, Charles. 1984. *Normal Accidents.* New York: Basic Books.

Perry, Ronald W., and Alvin H. Mushkatel. 1984. *Disaster Management: Warning, Response and Community Relocation.* Westport, CT: Quorum Books, Greenwood.

Petak, William J., and Arthur A. Atkisson, 1982. *Natural Hazard Risk Assessment and Public Policy: Anticipating the Unexpected.* New York: Springer-Verlag.

Philippi, N.S. 1994. *Revisiting Flood Control: An Examination of Federal Flood Control Policy in Light of the 1993 Flood Event on the Upper Mississippi River.* Chicago, IL: Wetlands Research, Inc.

Phillips, Steven. 1994. *The Soil Conservation Service Responds to the 1993 Midwest Floods.* Washington, DC: Soil Conservation Service.

Platt, Rutherford H., ed. 1999. *Disasters and Democracy: The Politics of Extreme National Events.* Washington, DC: Island Press.

Porfiriev, Boris N. 1998. *Disaster Policy and Economics in Russia.* Commack, NY: Nova Science Publications.

Quarantelli, E.L. 1988a. "Disaster Crisis Management: A Summary of Research Findings." *Journal of Management Studies* 25, 4 (July): 373–385.

————. 1988. "Local Emergency Management Agencies: Research Findings on Their Progress and Problems in the Last Two Decades." Preliminary Paper 126. Newark, DE: University of Delaware, Disaster Research Center.

————. 1984. *Organizational Behavior in Disasters and Implications for Disaster Planning.* Emmitsburg, Md.: Federal Emergency Management Agency, National Emergency Training Center, Monograph Series.

Reich, Michael R. 1991. *Toxic Politics: Responding to Chemical Disasters.* Ithaca, NY: Cornell University Press.

Research Institute of America. 1997. *Tax Relief for Victims of Casualties and Disasters.* New York: RIA.

Riad, Jasmin. 1997. "Hurricane Threat and Evacuation Intentions: An Analysis of Risk Perception, Preparedness, Social Influence, and Resources." Ph.D. Dissertation. Georgia State University, Atlanta, Georgia.

Riad, Jasmin; William L. Waugh; and Fran H. Norris. 1999. "The Psychology of Evacuation and Policy Design." In *Handbook of Crisis and Emergency Management,* ed. Ali Farazmand. New York: Marcel Dekker. Forthcoming

Rosenthal, Uriel, and Paul 't Hart. 1998. *Flood Response and Crisis Management in Western Europe: A Comparative Analysis.* New York: Springer.

Rosenthal, Uriel, and Michael T. Charles. 1992. *Crisis Management: International Perspectives.* Springfield, IL: Charles C. Thomas.

Rosenthal, Uriel; Michael T. Charles; and Paul 't Hart. 1990. *Coping with Crises: The Management of Disasters, Riots, and Terrorism.* Springfield, IL: Charles C. Thomas.

Rossi, Peter; James D. Wright; and Eleanor Weber-Burdin. 1982. *Natural Hazards and Public Choice: The State and Local Politics of Hazard Mitigation.* New York: Academic Press.

Rossi, Peter, et al. 1983. *Victims of the Environment: Loss from Natural Hazards in the U.S., 1970–1980.* New York: Plenum.

Scanlon, Joseph. 1994. "The Role of EOCs in Emergency Management: A Comparison of American and Canadian Experience." *International Journal of Mass Emergencies and Disasters* 12, 1 (March): 51–75.

Schneider, Saundra K. 1995. *Flirting with Disaster: Public Management in Crisis Situations.* Armonk, NY: M.E. Sharpe.

————. 1994. "FEMA, Federalism, Hugo, and 'Frisco." *Publius: The Journal of Federalism* 20 (Summer): 97–115.

Slovic, Paul; Howard Kunreuther; and Gilbert F. White, 1974. "Decision Processes, Rationality, and Adjustment to Natural Hazards." In *Natural Hazards: Local, National, Global,* ed. Gilbert F. White, 187–205. New York: Oxford University Press.

Smith, Keith. 1992. *Environmental Hazards: Assessing Risk and Reducing Disaster.* New York: Routledge.

Smithsonian Institute. 1994. *Nature on the Rampage.* Washington, DC: Smithsonian.

Sorenson, John H. 1990. "Society and Emergency Preparedness." In *Nothing to Fear: Risks and Hazards in American Society,* ed. Andrew Kirby, 241–260. Tucson: University of Arizona Press.

Stallings, Robert A. 1995. *Promoting Risk: Constructing the Earthquake Threat.* Hawthorne, NY: Aldine de Gruyter.

Stanley, Ellis M., Sr., and William L. Waugh, Jr. 2000. "Emergency Managers for the New Millennium." In *Handbook of Crisis and Emergency Management,* ed. Ali Farazmand. New York: Marcel Dekker.

Stern, Gerald H. 1976. *The Buffalo Creek Disaster.* New York: Random House.

Sutphen, Sandra, and William L. Waugh, Jr. 1998. "Organizational Reform and Techno-logical Innovation in Emergency Management." *International Journal of Mass Emergencies and Disasters* 16 (March): 7–12.

Svenson, Arthur G. 1984. *Earthquakes, Earth Scientists, and Seismic Safety Planning in California.* Lanham, MD: University Press of America.

Sylves, Richard T. 1998a. *The Politics of Disaster: An Instructors Guide.* Emmitsburg, MD: Federal Emergency Management Agency, Higher Education Project.

———. 1998b. "How the Exxon Valdez Disaster Changed America's Oil Spill Emergency Management." *International Journal of Mass Emergencies and Disasters* 16 (March): 13–43.

———. 1994. "Ferment at FEMA: Reforming Emergency Management." *Public Administration Review* 54 (May–June): 303–307.

———. 1991. "Adopting Integrated Emergency Management in the U.S.A.: Political and Organizational Challenges." *International Journal of Mass Emergencies and Disasters* 9, 3 (November): 413–425.

Sylves, Richard T., and William L. Waugh, Jr., eds. 1996. *Disaster Management in the U.S. and Canada,* 2d ed. Springfield, IL: Charles C. Thomas.

———. 1990. *Cities and Disaster: North American Studies in Emergency Management.* Springfield, IL: Charles C. Thomas.

Tobin, Graham A., and Burrell E. Montz. 1997. *Natural Hazards: Explanation and Integration.* New York: Guilford.

Toft, Brian, and Simon Reynolds. 1994. *Learning from Disasters: A Management Approach.* Boston, MA: Butterworth-Heinemann.

Turner, Barry A. 1997. *Man-Made Disasters.* Oxford, UK: Butterworth-Heinemann.

United Nations Department of Humanitarian Affairs. 1993. *Strategic Aspects of Geological and Seismic Disaster Management and Disaster Scenario Planning.* New York: UN.

U.S. Comptroller General, U.S. General Accounting Office. 1998. *Combating Terrorism: Observations on the Nunn-Lugar-Domenici Domestic Preparedness Program.* Statement of Richard Davis, Director, National Security Analysis, National Security and International Affairs Division. Washington, DC: GAO, GAO/T-NSIAD-99–16, October 2.

———. 1994a. "Federal Disaster Insurance: Goals Are Good, but Insurance Programs Would Expose the Federal Government to Large Potential Losses." Statement for the record by Thomas J. McCool, Associate Director, General Government Division. Washington, DC: GAO, GAO/T-GGD-94–153, May 26.

———. 1994b. *Flood Insurance: Financial Resources May Not Be Sufficient to Meet Future Expected Losses.* Washington, DC: GAO, GAO/RCED-94–80, March.

———. 1993a. *Disaster Management: Improving the Nation's Response to Catastrophic Disasters.* Washington, DC: U.S. Government Printing Office, GAO-T-RCED-93–20, July.

———. 1993b. *Statement of Charles A. Bowsher: Disaster Management: Recent Disasters Demonstrate the Need to Improve the Nation's Response Strategy.* Washington, DC: GAO, GAO/T-RCED-93–20, April 29.

U.S. Congress, Bipartisan Task Force on Funding Disaster Relief. 1995. *Federal Disaster Assistance* (John Glenn, Chair, and Christopher S. Bond, Co-Chair), 104th Congress, 1st Session, Document 104–4. Washington, DC: U.S. Government Printing Office, March 15.

————. House of Representatives, Committee on Government Operations. 1978. *Reorganization Plan No. 3 of 1978, Message from the President of the United States,* 95th Congress, 2d Session, 1978, House Document 95–356.

————. Senate, Committee on Governmental Affairs, Hearing. 1993. "Rebuilding FEMA: Preparing for the Next Disaster," 103d Congress, 1st Session, Senate Hearing 103–257, May 18.

U.S. Department of Energy, Office of Safeguards and Security, *Anti-Government Terrorism and Related Activities in the U.S., 1992–96.* Washington, DC: DOE, January 1997.

U.S. National Oceanic and Atmospheric Administration. 1994. *Natural Disaster Survey Report: The Great Flood of 1993.* Washington, DC: U.S. Department of Commerce, NOAA.

————. 1993. *Natural Disaster Survey Report: Hurricane Andrew: South Florida and Louisiana, August 23–26, 1992.* Washington, DC: U.S. Department of Commerce, NOAA, November.

Ursano, Robert J.; Brian G. McCaughey; and Carol S. Fullerton, eds. 1994. *Individual and Community Response to Trauma and Disaster: The Structure of Human Chaos.* Cambridge, UK: Cambridge University Press.

Verluise, Pierre (translated by Levon Chorbajian). 1995. *Armenia in Crisis: The 1988 Earthquake.* Detroit: Wayne State University Press.

Volcano: The Eruption of Mount St. Helens. 1980. Longview, WA: Longview Publishing.

Wamsley, Gary L.; Aaron D. Schroeder; and Larry M. Lane. 1996. "To Politicize Is Not to Control: The Pathologies of Control in Federal Emergency Management." *American Review of Public Administration* 26 (September): 263–285.

Waugh, William L., Jr. 2000. *Terrorism and Weapons of Mass Destruction: From Crisis to Consequence Management.* New York: Marcel Dekker. Forthcoming.

————. 1999a. "Assessing Quality in Emergency Management." In *Performance and Quality Measurement in Government: Issues and Experiences,* ed. Ari Halachmi, 65–82. Burke, VA: Chatelaine.

————. 1999b. "The Fiscal Risk of All-Hazards Emergency Management OR the Political Hazard in Rational Policy." *International Journal of Public Administration.* 22: 611–636.

————. 1999c. *Public Administration and Emergency Management: An Instructors Guide.* Emmitsburg, MD: Federal Emergency Management Agency, Emergency Management Institute).

————. 1998. "Emergency Management." In *International Encyclopedia of Public Policy and Administration,* 2, ed. Jay M. Shafritz, 747–752. Boulder, CO: Westview.

————. 1994. "Regionalizing Emergency Management: Counties as State and Local Government." *Public Administration Review* 54 (May–June): 253–258.

————. 1993. "Co-ordination or Control: Organizational Design and the Emergency Management Function," *International Journal of Disaster Prevention and Management* 2 (December): 17–31.

————. 1990. *Terrorism and Emergency Management: Policy and Administration.* New York: Marcel Dekker.

Waugh, William L., Jr., and Ronald J. Hy, eds. 1990. *Handbook of Emergency Management: Policies and Programs for Dealing with Major Hazards and Disasters.* Westport, CT: Greenwood.

Weaver, John D. 1995. *Disasters: Mental Health Interventions.* Sarasota, FL: Professional Resources.

Wenger, Dennis; E.L. Quarantelli; and Russell R. Dynes. 1990. "Is the Incident Command System a Plan for All Seasons?" *Hazard Monthly* (March).

Western, Karl A. 1982. *Epidemiological Surveillance After Natural Disaster.* Washington, DC: Pan American Health Organization.

White, Gilbert F., ed. 1974. *Natural Hazards: Local, National, Global.* New York: Oxford University Press.

Wright, James D., ed. 1979. *After the Clean-Up: Long Range Effects of Natural Disasters.* Beverly Hills, CA: Sage.

Wright, James D., and Peter H. Rossi. 1981. "The Politics of Natural Disaster: State and Local Elites." In *Social Science and Natural Hazards,* eds. James D. Wright and Peter H. Rossi, 45–67. Cambridge, MA: Abt Books.

Zelinsky, Wilbur, and Leszek A. Kosinski. 1991. *The Emergency Evacuation of Cities: A Cross-National Historical and Geographical Study.* Savage, MD: Rowman and Littlefield.

Zucherman, Edward. 1984. *The Day After World War III: The U.S. Government's Plans for Surviving a Nuclear War.* New York: Viking Press.

Emergency Management Information Sources

American Academy of Veterinary Disaster Medicine
3910 Morehouse Road
West Lafayette, IN 47909
Email: seh@vet.purdue.edu

American Association of Avalanche Professionals
P.O. Drawer 2757
Truckee, CA 96160
(916) 587–3653
Email: 7141351@mcimail.com

American Association of Wind Engineers
Department of Civil Engineering and Geological Sciences
University of Notre Dame
Notre Dame, IN 46556–0767
(219) 631–6648 or 631–7385
Email: kareem@navier.ce.nd.edu

American College of Emergency Physicians,
Section on Disaster Medicine
P.O. Box 619911
Dallas, TX 75261–9911
(800) 798–1822
Email: rmurray@acep.org
WWW:http://www.acep.org

American Engineers for Disaster Relief
P.O. Box 684
Princeton Junction, NJ 08550–0684
(609) 730–0510
Email: jccpc@msm.com

American Institute of Architects
1735 New York Avenue, N.W.
Washington, DC 20006
(202) 626–7383
Email: 47334@t-mail.telescom.com

American Meteorological Society
45 Beacon Street
Boston, MA 02108
(617) 227–2425
Email: hallgren@ametsoc.org
WWW: http://www.ametsoc.org/AMS

American Planning Association
122 South Michigan Avenue, Suite 1600
Chicago, IL 60603
(312) 431–9985
Email: research@planning.org
WWW: http://www.planning.org

American Psychological Association
Disaster Response Network, APA Practice Directorate
750 First Street, N.E.
Washington, DC 20002
(202) 336–5898
Email: jlp.apa@email.apa.org
WWW: http://www.apa.org

American Public Works Association,
Council on Emergency Management
1301 Pennsylvania Avenue, N.W., Suite 501
Washington, DC 20004–1710
(202) 393–2792
Email: Kern.Wilson@mail.pubworks.org
WWW:http://www.pubworks.org

American Red Cross, Disaster Services
National Headquarters
Disaster Services Department
8111 Gatehouse Road, Second Floor
Falls Church, VA 22042
(703) 206–7460
Email: infor@usa.redcross.org
WWW: http://www.redcross.org

American Society for Public Administration
Section on Emergency and Crisis Management
c/o Frances E. Winslow, Director of Emergency Services
City of San Jose
855 North San Pedro Street, Room 404
San Jose, CA 95110–0718
(408) 277–4595; FAX: (408) 277–3345
WWW: http://www.aspanet.org

American Society of Civil Engineers
1801 Alexander Bell Drive
Reston, VA 20191
(703) 295–6085
Email: mperalta@asce.org
WWW: http://www.asce.org

American Water Resources Association
950 Herndon Parkway, Suite 300
Herndon, VA 20170–5531
(703) 904–1225
Email: awrahq@aol.com
WWW: http://www.uwin.siu.edu/awra

Applied Technology Council
555 Twin Dolphin Drive, Suite 550
Redwood City, CA 94065
(415) 595–1542
Email: crojahn@atcouncil.org
WWW: http://www.atcouncil.org

Argonne National Laboratory,
Emergency Systems Group
DIS Division, Building 900
Argonne National Laboratory
Argonne, IL 60439
(630) 252–5626
Email:bertramk@smtplink.dis.anl.gov

Association of Bay Area Governments
P.O. Box 2050
Oakland, CA 94604–2050
(510) 464–7900
Email: shaky@abag.ca.gov
WWW: http://www.abag.ca.gov

Association of Contingency Planners
National Headquarters
421 North Rodeo Drive, Suite 15–565
Beverly Hills, CA 92010
(800) 445–4223
Email: mlc2resq@ix.netcom.com

Association of Engineering Geologists
323 Boston Post Road, Suite 2D
Sudbury, MA 01776
(508)443–4639
Email: aegh@aol.com
WWW: http://www.geoweb.tamu.edu/aeg/

Association of State Dam Safety Officials
450 Old East Vine, Second Floor
Lexington, KY 40507
(606) 257–5140
Email: 72130.2130@compuserve.com
WWW: http://ourword.compuserve.com/homepages/ASDSO/

Association of State Floodplain Managers
4233 West Beltline Highway
Madison, WI 53711
(608) 274–0123
Email asfpm@execpc.com

Association of State Wetlands Managers
P.O. Box 269
Berne, NY 12023–9746
(518) 872–1804
Email: aswmi@aol.com
WWW: http:members.aol.com/ASWMI/homepage.html

Building Seismic Safety Council
1201 L Street, N.W., Suite 400
Washington, DC 20005
(202) 289–7800
Email: jsmith@nibs.org
WWW: http://www.nibs.org/bssc1.htm

Business and Industry Council for Emergency Planning & Preparedness
P.O. Box 1020
Northridge, CA 91328
(213) 386–4524

Business Emergency Preparedness Council
c/o Emergency Management Agency
125 North Main, Room 2B49
Memphis, TN 38103
(901) 528–2780

California Seismic Safety Commission
1900 K Street, Suite 100
Sacramento, CA 95814
(916) 322–4917
WWW: http://earthview.sdsu.edu/SSC/index.html

California Specialized Training Institute
California Office of Emergency Services
P.O. Box 8123
San Luis Obispo, CA 93403–8123
(805) 549–3535

Cascadia Region Earthquake Work Group
University of Washington Seismology Laboratory
Pacific Northwest Seismic Network
Box 251650
Seattle, WA 98195–1650
WWW: http://www.geophys.washington.edu/CREW/index.html

Center for Excellence in Disaster Management
    & Humanitarian Assistance
1 Jarrett White Road (MCPA-DM)
Tripler AMC, Hawaii 96859–5000
(808) 433–7035; FAX: (808) 433–1757
WWW: http://coe.tamc.amedd.army.mil

Center for the Study of Emergency Management
1241 Johnson Avenue, Department 160
San Luis Obispo, CA 93401
(805) 782–6787
Email: wbalda@simeon.org
WWW: http://www.simeon.org/msm.html

Central United States Earthquake Consortium
2630 East Holmes Road
Memphis, TN 38118–8001
(901) 544–0544
Email: cusec@ceri.memphis.edu
WWW: http://gandalf.ceri.memphis.edu/CUSEC/index.html

Disaster Emergency Response Association International
P.O. Box 37324
Milwaukee, WI 53237–0324
(970) 532–3362
Email: disasters@delphi.com
WWW: http://www.disasters.org/dera.html

Earthquake Engineering Research Institute
499 14th Street, Suite 320
Oakland, CA 94612–1934
(510) 451–5411
Email: skt@eeri.org
WWW: http://www.eeri.org

Insurance Information Institute
110 William Street
New York, NY 10038
(212) 669–9200
Email: IIIConsumer@aol.com
WWW: http://www.iii.org

Insurance Institute for Property Loss Reduction
73 Tremont Street, Suite 510
Boston, MA 02108–3910
(617) 722–0200; FAX: (617) 722–0202

Insurance Research Council
211 South Wheaton Avenue, Suite 410
Wheaton, IL 60187
(630) 871–0255; FAX: (630) 871–0260
Email: insrescoun@aol.com

International Association of Emergency Managers
111 Park Place, Falls Church, VA 22046–4513
(703) 538–1795; FAX: (703) 241–5603
WWW: www.iaem.com

International Association of Fire Chiefs
4025 Fair Ridge Drive
Fairfax, VA 22033–2868
(703) 273–0911; FAX: (703) 273–9363
Email: iems@connectinc.com
WWW: http://www.ichiefs.org

International Association of Wildland Fire
P.O. Box 328
Fairfield, WA 99012
(509) 283–2397; FAX: (509) 283–2264
Email: greelee@cet.com
WWW: http://www.neotecinc.com/wildfire

International City/County Management Association
777 North Capitol Street, N.E., Suite 500
Washington, DC 20002–4201
(202) 962–3531; FAX: (202) 962–3500
Email: dgeis@icma.org
WWW: http://www.icma.org

International Critical Incident Stress Foundation
4785 Dorsey Hall Drive, Suite 102
Ellicott City, MD 21042
(410) 730–4311; FAX: (410) 730–4313
Email: icisf@erols.com
WWW: http://www.erols.com/icisf/Intro.html
Debriefing Team Coordination Center (410) 313–2473

National Association of Flood and Stormwater Management Agencies
1225 Eye Street, N.W., Suite 300
Washington, DC 20005
(202) 682–3761; FAX: (202) 842–0621

National Center for Atmospheric Research,
Environmental and Societal Impacts Group
P.O. Box 3000
Boulder, CO 80307
(303) 497–8117; FAX: (303) 497–8125
Email: Kathleen@ucar.edu
WWW: http://www.dir.ucar.edu/esig/

National Center for Earthquake Engineering Research
SUNY at Buffalo
Red Jacket Quadrangle
Box 610025
Buffalo, NY 14261–0025
(716) 645–3391; FAX: (716) 645–3399
Information Service: c/o Science and Engineering Library
304 Capen Hall
Buffalo, NY 14260–2200
(716) 645–3377; FAX: (716) 645–3379
Email: nernceer@ubvms.cc.buffalo.edu
WWW: http://nceer.eng.buffalo.edu

National Center for Post-Traumatic Stress Disorder
VA Medical Center
White River Junction, VT 05009
(802) 296–5132; FAX: (802) 296–5135
Email: matthew.friedman@dartmouth.edu

National Conference of States on Building Codes and Standards
505 Huntmar Park Drive, Suite 210
Herndon, VA 20170
(703) 437–0100; FAX: (703) 481–3596

National Emergency Management Association
P.O. Box 11910
Lexington, KY 40578–1910
(606) 244–8000; FAX: (606) 244–8239
Email: thembree@csg.com
WWW: http://www.nemaweb.org

National Fire Protection Association
One Batterymarch Park
Box 9101
Quincy, MA 02269
(617) 984–7270; FAX: (617) 770–0700
Email: public_affairs@mfpa.org
WWW: http://www.nfpa.org

National Governors Association,
Natural Resources Group
444 North Capitol Street
Washington, DC 20001
(202) 624–5389; FAX: (202) 624–5313

National Institute for Urban Search and Rescue
P.O. Box 91648
Santa Barbara, CA 93190–1648
(800) 767–0093; FAX: (805) 569–3270
Email: 3090usar@ucsduxa.ucsb.edu
WWW: http://emergencyservices.com/niusr

National Lightning Safety Institute
891 North Hoover Avenue
Louisville, CO 80027
(303) 666–8817; FAX: (303) 666–8786
Email: rich@lightningsafety.com
WWW: http://lightningsafety.com

New England States Emergency Consortium
607 North Avenue, Suite 16
Wakefield, MA 01880
(617)224–9876; FAX: (617) 224–4350
Email: nesec@serve.com
WWW: http://www.serve.com/NESEC

Oak Ridge National Laboratory/
Disaster Management & Mitigation Group
Energy Division, Building 4500 North, MS 6206
P.O. Box 2008
Oak Ridge, TN 37831–6206
(423) 576–2716; FAX: (423) 574–5938
Email: jhs@ornl.gov
WWW: http://stargate.ornl.gov/StarGate/MBBG/dmmg.html

Public Risk Management Association
1815 North Fort Myer Drive, Suite 1020,
Arlington, VA 22209.
(703) 528–7701; FAX: (703) 528–7966
Information Services: (703) 528–7718
Email: primahq@aol.com

Seismological Society of America
201 Plaza Professional Building
El Cerrito, CA 94530–4003
(510) 525–5474; FAX: (510) 525–7204
Email: info@seismosoc.org
WWW: http://www.seismosoc.org

Society for Risk Analysis
1313 Dolley Madison Boulevard, Suite 402
McLean, VA 22101
(703) 790–1745; FAX: (703) 790–2672
Email: sraburkmgt@aol.com

State and Local Emergency Management Data Users Group
c/o SDS, Inc.
684 Country Club Drive
Lake Ozark, MO 65049
(573) 365–7373; FAX: (575) 365–2163 or 356–2581
Email: mmcneill@mail.advertisnet.com
WWW: http://www.salemdug.dis.anl.gov

The Tornado Project
P.O. Box 302
St. Johnsbury, VT 03819
Email: tornproj@plainfield.bypass.com
WWW: http://www.tornadoproject.com/

Urban and Regional Information Systems Association
900 Second Street, N.W., Suite 304
Washington, DC 20002
(202) 842–1685; FAX: 842–1850
Email: members@urisa.org
WWW: http//www.urisa.org

Volunteers in Technical Assistance
Disaster Information Center
1600 Wilson Boulevard, Suite 500
Arlington, VA 22209
(703) 276–1800; FAX: (703) 243–1865
Email: muffley@vita.org
WWW: http://www.vita.org

Western States Seismic Policy Council
121 Second Street, 4th Floor
San Francisco, CA 94105
(415) 974–6435; FAX: (415) 974–1747
Email: wsspc@wsspc.org
WWW: http://wsspc.org

SELECTED RESEARCH INSTITUTIONS

Florida International University
International Hurricane Center
University Park Campus
Miami, FL 33199
(305) 348–1607; FAX: (305) 348–1605
Email: hurrican@fiu.edu
WWW: http://fiu.edu/hurrican/

George Washington University
Institute for Crisis and Disaster Management, Research, and Education
Virginia Campus
20101 Academic Way, Room 220
Ashburn, VA 22011
(202) 994–7153
Email: harrald@seas.gwu.edu

Monterey Institute of International Studies
Center for Nonproliferation Studies
425 Van Buren Street
Monterey, CA 93940
(831) 647–4154; FAX: (831) 647–4154
cns@miis.edu
WWW: http://cns.miis.edu/research/cbw (National Domestic
    Preparedness Program)

University of Colorado
Natural Hazards Research and Applications Information Center
Campus Box 482
Boulder, CO 80309–0482
(303) 492–6818; FAX: (303) 492–2151
Email: hazctr@colorado.edu
WWW: http://www.colorado.edu/hazards

University of Delaware
Disaster Research Center
Newark, DE 19716
(302) 831–6618; FAX: (302) 831–2091
Email: joanne.nigg@nvs.udel.edu or tierney@udel.edu
WWW: http://www.udel.edu/DRC/homepage.htm

University of North Texas
Emergency Administration and Planning Institute
School of Community Service
P.O. Box 13438, NT Station
Denton, TX 76203
(817) 565–3292; FAX: (817) 369–8771
Email: Neal@scs.unt.edu
WWW: http://www.ias.unt.edu:9510

University of South Carolina
Hazards Research Laboratory
Department of Geography
Columbia, SC 29208
(803)777–1699; FAX: (803) 777–4972
Email: uschrl@ecotopia.geog.sc.edu
WWW: http://www.cla.sc.edu/geog/hrl/home.html

Texas A&M University
Hazard Reduction and Recovery Center
College of Architecture
College Station, TX 77843–3137
(409) 845–7813; FAX: (409) 845–5121
Email: hrrc@archone.tamu.edu
WWW: http://archone.tamu.edu/centers/hrrc.html

University of Wisconsin-Madison
Disaster Management Center
Department of Engineering
Professional Development
432 North Lake Street
Madison, WI 53706
(608) 263–7757; FAX: (608) 263–3160
dmc@engr.wisc.edu
WWW: http://epdwww.engr.wisc.edu/dmc

Note: Information on educational institutions with emergency management courses and programs is available via the FEMA website www.fema.gov through the Higher Education Project.

SELECTED U.S. GOVERNMENT AGENCIES

Federal Emergency Management Agency
500 C Street, S.W.
Washington, DC 20472
Email: eipa@fema.gov
WWW: http://www.fema.gov

Federal Insurance Administration
    (202) 646–2781; FAX: (202) 646–3445
Information Technology Services Directorate
    (202) 646–3006; FAX: (202) 646–4622
Mitigation Directorate
    (202) 646–4622; FAX: (202) 646–3231
Office of Emergency Information and Public Affairs
    (202) 646–4600; FAX: (202) 646–4086
Office of Policy and Assessment
    (202) 646–3011; FAX: (202) 646–4215
Operations Support Directorate
    (202) 646–2965; FAX: (202) 646–3155
Preparedness, Training and Exercises Directorate
    (202) 646–3487; FAX: (202) 646–4557
Response and Recovery Directorate
    (202) 646–3692; FAX: (202) 646–4060

Learning Resource Center
  (800) 638–1821
National Emergency Training Center
  16825 South Seton Avenue
  Emmitsburg, MD 21727
  (301) 447–1000.
National Fire Academy
  (301) 447–1117
Publications: FEMA Distribution Facility
  8231 Stayton Drive
  Jessup, MD 20794
  (800) 480–2520; FAX:(301) 497–6378

Regional Offices:

Region I (CT, MA, ME, NH, RI, VT)
  Room 442, J.W. McCormack Post Office and Courthouse Building
  Boston, MA 02109–4595
  (617) 223–9540; FAX: (617) 223–9519
Region II (NJ, NY, PR, VI)
  26 Federal Plaza, Room 1337
  New York, NY 10278–0002
  (212) 225–7209; FAX: (212) 225–7281
Region III (DC, DE, MD, PA, VA, WV)
  Liberty Square Building, Second Floor
  105 South Seventh Street
  Philadelphia, PA 19106–3316
  (215) 931–5608; FAX: (215) 931–5621
Region IV (AL, FL, GA, KY, MS, MC, NC, SC, TN)
  3003 Chamblee-Tucker Road, Atlanta, GA 30341
  (770) 220–5200; FAX: (770) 220–5230
Region V (IL, IN, MI, MN, OH, WI)
  175 West Jackson Boulevard, Fourth Floor
  Chicago, IL 60604–2698
  (312) 408–5503; FAX: (312) 408–5234
Region VI (AR, LA, NM, OK, TX)
  Federal Regional Center, Room 206
  800 North Loop 288
  Denton, TX 76201–3698
  (817) 898–5104; FAX: (817) 898–5325

Region VII (IA, KS, MO, NE)
    2323 Grand Boulevard, Suite 900
    Kansas City, MO 64108–2670
    (816) 283–7061; FAX: (816) 283–7582
Region VIII (CO, MT, ND, SD, UT, WY)
    Denver Federal Center, Building 710
    Box 25267
    Denver, CO 80225–0267
    (303) 235–4812; FAX: (303) 235–4976
Region IX (AS, AZ, CA, GU, HI, NV, CM, TT)
    Presidio of San Francisco, Building 105
    San Francisco, CA 94129–1250
    (415) 923–7100; FAX: (415) 923–7112
Region X (AK, ID, OR, WA)
    Federal Regional Center
    130–228th Street, S.W.
    Bothell, WA 98021–9796
    (206) 487–4604; FAX: (206) 487–4622

Centers for Disease Control and Prevention (DHHS)
WWW: http://www.cdc.gov

National Oceanic and Atmospheric Administration
WWW: http://www.noaa.gov

National Weather Service
WWW: http://www.nws.noaa.gov

Tropical Predication Center, National Hurricane Center
WWW: http://www.nhc.noaa.gov

Environmental Protection Agency
WWW: http://www.epa.gov

Small Business Administration, Disaster Assistance Division
WWW: http://www.sbaonline.sba.gov/disaster/

Tennessee Valley Authority
WWW: http://www.tva.gov

U.S. Agency for International Development
WWW: http://www.info.usaid.gov

U.S. Office for Foreign Disaster Assistance
WWW: http://www.ofda.gov

U.S. Geological Survey
WWW: http://www.usgs.gov

Emergency Information Infrastructure Partnership - EIIP Virtual Forum
WWW: http://www.emforum.org

United Nations - Disaster and Humanitarian Organizations
WWW: http://www.un.org

Reliefweb (Directory of Humanitarian Organizations)
WWW: http://www.reliefweb.int

World Food Programme (Relief and Development Sites)
WWW: http://wfp.org/links

CARE
WWW: http://www.care.org

Disaster Relief (Worldwide Disaster Aid and Information Via
    the Internet)
WWW: http://www.disasterrelief.org

Most of the sources can be found through the Natural Hazards Information
and Applications Center, University of Colorado, website. The Hazards
Center's listing of information sources is updated annually and available in
the *Natural Hazards Observer*. Other sources may be found be going to a
public agency's website and finding its list of public and private sector
"partners" or its list of "links."

INDEX

William L. Waugh, Jr. teaches public administration at Georgia State University. His publications include *Disaster Management in the U.S. and Canada* (1996), *State and Local Tax Policies* (1995), *Cities and Disaster* (1990), *Handbook of Emergency Management* (1990), *Terrorism and Emergency Management* (1990), and *International Terrorism* (1982). He is a past chair of the American Society for Public Administration's Section on Emergency and Crisis Management and has been a consultant to U.S. and international agencies, nonprofit organizations, and the media on managing disasters and terrorist events.